December

John

Thank you for

your interest!

W. Adam Clatsoff

"Capt Tuh"

The One Cent Solution

A Health Care Plan to Free Americans

W. Adam Clatsoff, CLU, ChFC, RHU, CFP

Noble House

Baltimore, Maryland

The One Cent Solution: A Health Care Plan to Free Americans

Library of Congress
Cataloging in Publication Data
ISBN 1-56167-132-0

Published by

Noble House

8019 Belair Rd., Ste. 10
Baltimore, Maryland 21236

Manufactured in the United States of America

CONTENTS

PREFACE

February 4, 1993
Hillary Rodham Clinton
First Lady
The White House
1600 Pennsylvania Avenue, NW
Washington, D.C. 20500

As you are presently engaged as the chairperson of an appointed task force on health care reform, I wanted to introduce to you an idea that embraces the most positive aspects of other proposed solutions and also conforms to the President's philosophy on economic reform. This letter is intended to give you a brief overview of my plan, called EqualCare USA, with complete program documentation to follow in four to six weeks.

My plan would create a public health system, providing basic health benefits for everyone, by expanding the current Medicare system to all Americans. This program would end the current accessing of coverage through employment, and remove, once and for all, this weight from around business' neck, allowing them to use these dollars in a more productive way. The costs for public health care would be paid through a premium assessment on all income, including salary, interest, dividends, municipal bonds and similar revenue generating vehicles, with no cap. (An even better way to pay for it is in Chapter 11. While writing this book, it occurred to me that America would be best served by a payment method that did not punish the productive, could not be politicized, and one which would assess all of us fairly.)

The present Medicare system, Parts A and B, is a strong basic benefits plan, similar (and, in some cases, better) to the idea of basic coverage for all that is the common theme in all of the current proposals being considered. Here, the premium responsibility would rest with each individual, assessed on their ability to pay, and the federal government would be the premium collector. No cap means the wealthy would help to subsidize the poor, unlike our present system which allows high income earners to pay virtually the same as the middle income wage earner.

Each American with a Social Security number will be issued an EqualCare USA card, which they would present to a physician or a hospital upon need for services. Through an electronic processing system, the provider's office can immediately access the current claims history of the patient, including current deductible and coinsurance status to determine what amount needs to be collected from the patient and what amount to file with EqualCare USA. This electronic system would eliminate the usual paperwork processing and speed up the reimbursement to the provider.

Additional savings would result from simplification of the fee for service variations that currently exist in the Medicare system. There are as many as 233 geographical regions at present, fluctuating charges for physician services and coding complications that have created a paper nightmare for most providers and increased costs needlessly. My system would have one charge per procedure. That's it. Whether you provided the service in Missoula, Montana or Great Neck, New York, the fee would be exactly the same. The doctor in Missoula would make more per procedure than in the current system, but the Great Neck practitioner has a wider population base and, most likely, more potential procedures to perform. This would also encourage physicians to locate in rural areas, a current problem in our present health care system.

Physicians and hospitals would have the choice of participating in EqualCare USA or practicing privately on their own. There would be powerful incentives to be in the new system, including the already mentioned electronic processing and simplified fee structure. The majority of Americans holding the EqualCare USA card would be seeking an EqualCare USA provider. In addition, those participating in EqualCare USA would be covered under a new National Malpractice Program designed to keep provider costs down, pay equitable settlement costs for bad results and eliminate the long arduous legal process which hurts both claimant and physician at present.

EqualCare USA cardholders could also participate in an HMO just as some senior citizens do currently with Medicare. While this limits doctor and hospital choice, there are many who prefer this type of health care delivery and we want to encourage its use.

There will be many Americans who will want to have more coverage than the current Medicare system has, and, like senior citizens today, they would have the ability to purchase an EqualCare USA Supplement through a private health insurance company. In 1992, the Medicare supplements being sold were standardized nationwide, and this has made it easier for purchasers of the plan to understand and compare it to other programs.

Physicians who do not wish to be in the EqualCare USA system, for whatever reason, are certainly welcome to practice on their own and take patients on a pay as you go basis. It would be required that they post in a visible place that they are not in the EqualCare USA system. They would also be required to post their fees as a multiple of the fee allowed under EqualCare USA, such as 2 X EQ or 3 X EQ, so that potential patients would know what their cost will be and compare physicians accordingly.

This brief summary is only intended to give you an orientation to this health care delivery system. From where I sit, it is the only proposal you have which can be put into operation within 12 months since the Medicare system is already in place. The modifications and expansion of it can be effected more rapidly than creating an entire new system as would be the case with national health insurance, pay or play, or managed competition.

EqualCare USA would have effects on a number of other current programs. COBRA, Workers' Compensation (medical portion), and Medicaid would be eliminated, easing the bottom line for both business and state, both of whom are struggling with health care costs. Veterans hospitals would no longer be necessary; all would be in the EqualCare USA system. Group health insurance would become extinct with businesses out of the health care providing loop.

Americans would be excited about such a plan. While it may represent more cost and less benefits to some, the great majority would now enjoy coverage without fear, the real problem with our present system. People fear job lock because they might lose health insurance. People fear the policy they have won't pay off when they need it the most. People fear the loss of coverage because their employer can no longer afford increasing health insurance premiums.

Businesses would be excited about such a plan. That business is even considered to be the provider of health coverage is a historical accident, brought on by wage controls during the 1940's. Lifting this burden will give them the opportunity to compete better globally, hire the people they need without worrying about the cost of insurance and the ability of their new hire to qualify for benefits. Economic rejuvenation with these dollars is inevitable, both in reducing the cost of goods sold (if you believe Chrysler, health care represents $1100 per car) and in increased hiring. Consumers will see their money go much further under the EqualCare USA scenario and it might be this spending which can continue to bolster the economy.

Providers would be excited about such a plan. Simplified claims procedures, malpractice reform, reduced initial cost containment procedures which currently drives up costs would all be attractive to both hospital and physician. It is my suggestion that a new medical school scholarship program could be established to attract minorities and the less wealthier in exchange for agreed to service under EqualCare USA in an area needing more provider help.

This is truly equal health care. Everyone has the same benefits; everyone is assessed the same percentage to pay for it with contributions varying by income. Once prices are fixed, it genuinely empowers the consumer to handle one's own health care in the way they desire.

None of the other alternatives offer either the simplicity or the rapid establishment that EqualCare USA does. It gives equal access for all, not tied to either employment (pay or play) or ability to pay (private health insurance). It utilizes the extraordinary resources of our current system where advanced technology and efficient efforts mean quality care without a waiting line (Canada's system). It doesn't offer complexity and additional layers of bureaucracy (managed competition) that threaten to make the system even less effective than in its current state. Above all, it's a truly unique American system, and one that will be the envy of the rest of the world.

The media has offered that spending 13% of our gross national product on health care is wrong. To me, this is the wrong way to look at it. The health care system employs one out of every eight workers. Doesn't that correlate with GNP expenditures? Let's try to encourage technology and make the U.S. system one that people from all over the world come to for the best in quality care. Pharmaceutical companies should be encouraged to develop new and better drugs and retain their current status as a leader in exports, helping to keep our foreign trade deficit from worsening.

EqualCare USA keeps everyone in the system. All have roles, from hospitals and doctors to insurance companies and agents, with government as the manager of the health care funds. I will have a complete description of EqualCare USA ready, as I said, in four to six weeks.

However, I wanted you to have this information as you are in the early stages of your task force work and considering any number of proposals.

They won't work! EqualCare USA will! I would be glad to meet with you and/or your committee to advise you further on the specifics of this program. Together, we can create a health care system all Americans will be proud to have.

Best regards,

W. Adam Clatsoff, CLU, ChFC, RHU, CFP

EQUALCARE USA PPO PLAN

Benefits	EqualCare USA Pays	You Pay
Hospitalization (including semiprivate room and board, general nursing and misc. hospital services and supplies		
First 60 days	All but $696	$696
61st - 90th day	All but $174/day	$174/day
91st -150th day	All but $348/day	$348/day
151+	-0-	100%
Medical Expenses (including physician services, inpatient and outpatient medical and surgical supplies, physical and speech therapy, diagnostic tests, maternity, prescription drugs, durable medical equipment, outpatient hospital treatment	80%, after $100 deductible	$100, then 20% of costs
Short-term Recuperative Nursing Care		
First 100 days	100%	-0-
101 +	-0-	100%

Long Term Care
First 100 days (use Recuperative care above)
101+ (use Public/Private Sponsored Benefit Plan)

EqualCare USA HMO Plan

Benefits	EqualCare USA Pays	You Pay
Primary Care Physician Office Visits	100%	-0-
Participating Specialist Office Visits	100%	-0-
Periodic Health Evaluations	100%	-0-
X-ray, Laboratory, and other diagnostic services	100%	-0-
Health education	100%	-0-
Professional counseling, nutrition and medical social services	100%	-0-
Semi-private hospital room and board	100%	-0-
Surgeon and physician's inpatient services	100%	-0-
Anesthesia services	100%	-0-
Inpatient drugs and medications	100%	-0-
Intensive care unit, operating and recovery room	100%	-0-
Radiation, inhalation, physical and rehabilitative therapy	100%	-0-
Emergency room service	100%	-0-
Prescription drugs	100%	-0-
Mental health care		
outpatient visits	100%	-0-
first 190 inpatient days	100%	-0-
191+ inpatient days	-0-	100%

EqualCare USA HMO Plan

Benefits	EqualCare USA Pays	You Pay
All Maternity costs	100%	-0-
Outpatient surgical, radiation, physical and rehabilitative services	100%	-0-
Short-term Recuperative Nursing Care		
first 100 days of any type of long term care services	100%	-0-
101+ days of long term care	-0-	100%
Long term care		
days 0 - 100 (see Recuperative care)		
days 101+ Utilize the Public/Private Sponsored Benefit Plan		
Rental of Durable Medical Equipment	100%	-0-

INTRODUCTION

THIS WON'T REQUIRE A COLLEGE DEGREE

Now, like Hillary Rodham Clinton, you've had a chance to read the short version of my health care proposal for the future. This book will expand on the concept of EqualCare USA and illustrate how everyone, from providers to consumers, fits into this system.

Before doing that, I want to discuss the evolution of the current health care system and uncover the scenarios and trends that have placed us in a difficult situation with one of our most precious needs. Each contributor to the system will be viewed as to recent events and their roles carefully explained to enable a better understanding of where we are today and why the major solutions being considered to improve health care do not change or reverse the ever worsening concerns that have emerged. I hope you'll agree when you've finished reading that EqualCare USA can and will bring health care to its next evolution.

I do not use the word "reform". One of the suggested definitions for this term, in Webster's Dictionary, is to "abandon or give up evil ways". Our health care system does need change, but to characterize it as evil is emphatically wrong. We must never forget that Americans have the best health care technology in the world today and what we want to accomplish is not to tear it down and start over, but to both ensure that all of our population has access to and is willing to share equitably in the cost of, the best medicine anywhere.

There are health care problems in this country. Before examining the specifics of what may be wrong, I want you to know about some of my basic principles that you will read over and over again throughout this text. These concepts are different than what you've been reading about health care, making it more important that you have knowledge of these issues before reading further.

Number One: Why does government, the media and various consumer groups cry foul when health care services increase as a percentage of our Gross Domestic Product (GDP) or our Gross National Product (GNP)? If any other industry in the country increased as a percentage of these measurements, we'd be celebrating in the streets. Any other business that has the success the American health care system has had, both socially and economically, would be the toast of the world. Yet, because health care spending is now 13% of GNP, our reaction, prompted by acamedicians, politicians and the media, has been one of deep concern. What we have been encouraged to believe by the doomsayers is that the price of health care is the cost. But price doesn't reflect what our return is. Americans play harder and live more healthy, fulfilling lives than anyone in the world. American workers are the most productive in the world. Health care job formations picked up the slack during the 1980's as manufacturing plants downsized.

The fact is health care provides jobs. Nearly 1 in 8 of all Americans are employed in some way by our health care industry. Doesn't that correlate with a 13% GNP? According to the March 8, 1993 edition of USA Today, health care has been creating 20,000 jobs a month. The 1991 Statistical Abstract indicates that among the 12 fastest growing jobs were four in the health field: medical assistants, home health aides, radiology technicians and medical secretaries. A 1992 Standard & Poor's report shows that U.S. medical equipment manufacturers account for nearly 48% of the global medical products market, while U.S. drug companies are responsible for over 40% of the major pharmaceuticals marketed throughout the world. This is great news, isn't it?

Yet many of the media, politicians and academics would have us believe that we are pouring 13% of our GNP down a black hole. The idea that every dollar spent on health care is a dollar that can't be spent to educate a young child or produce an automobile doesn't make sense to me. What should we educate an American child to do? Become a lawyer? Or worse, become another politician? What better thing to educate our children to do then to serve as medical healers? Should the future of America be in cars? Should the future of America be to sue people? Or should the future of America be to produce the medical practitioners of the world? What will America's role be for mankind in the next 50 years?

We industrialized America. Why should we slow down or stop industrialization in other countries? As they do industrialize, they will next focus on what our goals have become: to live longer and healthier lives. Why shouldn't we provide this medical technology for them? Isn't that a more noble role than to provide them with cars, weapons, films or CD's? Building more cars or educating more lawyers won't cure the diseases that exist in our world. What if, 100 years from now, every American was a health care specialist, traveling the globe, healing people? Is this such a bad vision for America?

Currently, we talk about exporting cars and rock and roll tapes. How long can that go on? Wouldn't it make more sense to export life-extending drugs? To export medical practitioners? What's wrong with investing in medical technology and educating our children to work in medicine, an industry with a future? I'm not sure building cars has an endless future. Extending life always will.

Wouldn't a more worthy vision for our future be to provide food and health care for the rest of the world? During the last fifty years, socialized health care has destroyed the health care delivery system of the world. Now, because of our private enterprise system, we have a major jump start in health care and the rest of the world needs it. Why not take advantage of it? As other nations continue to industrialize and produce all the cars, VCRS and designer jeans they need, their attention, like ours, will be focused on combating the discomfort of pain and disease. We can be there with our health care industry. That's the future of America. Instead of viewing the money spent on health care as dollars down the drain, why not see it as an investment in our children's' (and the children of the world's) tomorrow?

We are told the problem is the $900 billion spending that accounts for the 13% GNP figure. But what is actually in this figure? Analysts say $100 billion of it comes from life-style-related illnesses. We jog, drive cars, play tennis, eat, drink and smoke. We're Americans. We're where and what the rest of the world want to be and become. Is that the health care industry's fault? Countless millions of this $900 billion are spent not by Americans, but by foreign visitors. Should we care if Quebec Premier Robert Bourassa has experimental cancer treatment in Bethesda, Maryland? Or if former Canadian Prime Minister Brian Mulroney's mother has heart bypass surgery in Florida? Or if anyone else comes to the United States for the best treatment available anywhere? Our technology is the best. That's why many world leaders come here for health care. Socialized medicine may be fine for their citizens, but the rich and powerful of these other countries want the health care every American now enjoys. President Clinton has also talked about refocusing our energies on new technology. What better use of technology than for fighting disease?

Americans themselves voluntarily spend billions each year for orthodontics, hair transplants, liposuctions, plastic surgery; all elective surgeries, all part of that $900 billion dollar number. Are we saying, by criticizing that spending figure, that we should cease these procedures? We are the wealthiest country in the world. If we want to spend our money on health care, why not?

We have more elderly people in this country than most countries have people. The elderly consume the greater amount of health care costs as they age. Our population is going to get older very quickly over the next two decades, further indication that the $900 billion dollar number will continue to increase. If, as a result, the health care industry continues to provide new jobs to handle the increase in demand for services, what's wrong with that?

Why should our hospitals look like our public schools or our prisons? If hospitals charge more for a better environment and patients are willing to pay it, shouldn't they have it? Why should we spend the last few days of our lives in Spartan surroundings? Why not spend money on health care? What better resource to spend our money on? A VCR? A cruise? A new Lexus?

Health care technology is expensive. Thirty years ago if you had a heart attack, the physician tried a few things, you passed away and your family was billed $1,200 for the effort. Today, you'd get heart bypass surgery, live another 20 years in comfort, and receive a bill for $30,000. Are we now putting a price on extending life? Is that what these discussions on high costs of health care are really about?

Health care could be the industry of the 1990's and on into the next decade. If we spend 90% of our GNP on health care and it employs 9 of 10 Americans, what's the beef? What more noble way to make a living is there?

Number Two: Employers have had the responsibility, for several decades of providing health insurance. This was an industrial-based concept that came about in the 1940's when wage controls were in effect. Since the boss couldn't give the employees a raise, health benefits were furnished instead. It has evolved into a major dependence on employment to obtain coverage for health care and caused problems like "job lock", hiring freezes, wage freezes, higher prices, business failures and an increasingly larger uninsured population.

Our industrial-based system is rapidly yielding to a new, service-oriented economy. Fortune magazine, in its February 8, 1993 issue, discussed the concept of the "modular corporation", where the new, successful breed of business keeps only a few core tasks in-house and "outsources" the other activities to outside specialists. These specialists aren't employees, per se, nor are they located in the central office. What they can do is perform tasks at a much lower overall cost. Business doesn't have to provide benefits, thus reducing unit costs. USA Today, March 3, 1993, called these specialists the "contingent workforce" and noted that this kind of worker now represents 25% of the total U.S. workforce and will grow, by conservative estimates, to 33% by decade's end.

This is the future. The traditional employer-employee contract is fading and any health care system that mandates employer-based health care coverage is destined to fail. There will be too many uninsureds; too many outsourced workers who won't be included in the health care program the employer provides.

There is a mistaken impression in this country that, if we make business pay for health care, we, as consumers, won't have to pay for it ourselves. If you retain no other concept from this book, don't forget this one: business does not, has not, now or ever, paid for health insurance. First, corporations take a $60 billion dollar per year tax break for buying health insurance. Second, the actual net outlay for this coverage is moved in any combination of three ways in a business. It might go forward into higher prices for goods, which we all buy and thus indirectly pay for health costs; it could be moved backward, resulting in lower or no income increases for employees or no additional hirings; or it could be moved upward, resulting in a lower or no dividend distribution to its shareholders. So, who really pays? We do, as taxpayers, consumers, employees and shareholders.

This makes you wonder. Does IBM really pay for health insurance for their employees or do we pay for it when we buy a computer? Chrysler estimates that it adds an extra $1,100 per car to pay their employee's health care costs.

We would all pay in an employer-mandated system. There is also a lack of control for employees when the employer pays for health insurance and we come to rely on it. Ask the employees of Eastern or Pan Am about losing their benefits when a company files for bankruptcy. One day you have coverage, the next day it's gone. As an employee, one of the rights you have is to make the best possible deal for yourself with your boss. You should be able to go in and negotiate your own value. Your health, or health care costs, should never be part of the discussion.

Another problem with employer-mandated coverage is that you give your proxy to the boss to select the best health insurance plan for you. When the boss chooses a health plan, you can be reasonably certain that choice is going to be based, in large part, on what's best for him or her. The boss chooses the Mercedes-Benz plan on his budget when, if the decision were yours, you would have opted for the basic Chevrolet plan because it more closely fit your budget. But you are now stuck with the boss' choice. If the boss pays for the employee portion of the plan, and you don't have dependents, you likely won't care. If you do have to pay for any of your costs or your dependents' premium, you will pay the price of the higher premium plan, even if it exceeds your budget, or go without coverage. This often results in non-coverage of dependents, adding even more uninsureds to the system.

Taking business off the hook for buying health care coverage would free up their capital to invest in lower prices, higher wages and more hiring. There are many who don't want this to happen; who believe that American business should pay its "fair share". There would seem to be an underlying resentment that American business is allowed to make any money at all. Why shouldn't General Motors make money? Who should, if not them? Toyota? Volvo? BMW? Did I miss a memo somewhere?

Number Three: In much of the media, political and academic discussions about health care over the last thirty years, the idea that health care is a human right has evolved into a given. I'm not sure why this is happening and I don't believe our forefathers envisoned health care as one of our Constitutional inalienable rights, but this is now becoming their conventional wisdom.

Why health care? Why not food? Why not housing? Why don't we say everyone should be entitled to clean teeth? Instead we say everyone should have identical health care. We have said education is a right and created a public education system. But we don't say everyone should have an identical education. Thankfully, we still allow parents to send their children to private schools. Have you ever noticed how disproportionately those that have private school educations are represented in the ranks of the productive?

Why health care? Certainly food is a more urgent need than health care. Some of us will need very little health care over our lifetimes, but we all need to eat every day. Why not food as a human right? If so, should everyone eat the same food? Many of us did that once in our lives. Remember the pre-paid meal plans in college?

How about housing? Should everyone be entitled to exactly the same house? Would that work? Would it be possible?

Health care has become expensive, so now many believe it should be an entitlement. They claim we should all have health care and government should give it to us. They tell us it's only fair and that the poor are entitled to health care. But the poor in this country already do have health care. When they need medical care, they go to a community hospital and receive better treatment than they could get anywhere else in the world, without having to pay for it. In America, we all have essential health care, but some do have easier access than others. Yet many politicians, media and academics tell us that this is a poor vs. rich struggle, that one of the biggest fears Americans have is that we will suddenly become ill, incur substantial health care bills, and lose everything we own. But what are they really saying? The poor have access to free health care and the rich can afford to pay for it themselves, if necessary. Isn't the fear of losing everything a middle class concern? If so, what we are asking for is social legislation to protect the assets of the middle class. These Americans are the ones truly at risk here. So why not say this, rather than turning discussions of health care into a crusade for the poor? The poor have access and no real assets to protect; the rich can afford to pay for health care, leaving the middle class as the ones with assets in potential peril.

While I don't think everyone should have exactly the same house or food in this country, I do believe everyone should have easy access to affordable health care. That is exactly what my EqualCare USA system is all about. I wouldn't want to live in a country where I'm so rich I can have everything I want, while someone else is so poor he has to watch his child die. That being said, none of the proposed health care plans are truly fair and regardless of which plan we select, it will favor one American over another. EqualCare USA will ensure that everyone gets a basic plan of essential health care; a worthy goal for a great country.

Number Four: Health care is not an infinite resource. The prevailing academic, political and media mindset is that everyone should have unrestricted access to the highest quality medical care in the world, free of charge. This is the creed of the single-payer system enthusiasts.

The people who tell us this are often the same folks who have advised us air is not an infinite resource and our ozone layer is disappearing; that water is not an infinite resource and that we must conserve or die; that even the spotted owl is not an infinite resource and risks extinction if we continue to log our forests. All of these, they claim, now must be rationed or protected. Loggers can no longer work in areas where spotted owls live. If we go to a gas station and want air or water, we're often directed to machines that charge us twenty-five cents.

Yet, in meeting after meeting, I have heard these same people stand up and say how reprehensible it is that every American cannot have the best of health care at any time for no charge at all. They passionately claim that everyone should be able to get all the health care they want, when they want, and not have to pay.

Well, do I have news for them! Health care is a finite and valuable resource. It costs money; in some cases, substantial amounts, to provide the technology and services Americans want when we're sick. There is not an endless supply of it. It has a high value and we must all pay for it.

It is rationed in every country in the world. In the United States, we ration based on our ability to pay. In most countries, it is rationed by political edict. For example, in Great Britain, few, if any, people over the age of 55 are eligible for kidney dialysis. In Canada, EKGs and CAT-Scans must be scheduled weeks in advance due to the demand and the lack of machinery to meet that demand. There are more EKG machines in Seattle, Washington than there are in all of Canada. North of the border, contrary to popular belief, rationing is also done based on wealth, as the rich often avoid their system and come here for health care as evidenced by the recent headlines for well-connected leaders, celebrities, and politically powerful who come to this country for the best health care treatment available anywhere in the world.

Any finite and valuable resource has to be rationed. If we agree that affordability is a poor way to ration, what other methods can we devise? What parameters should we use? Age? That's usually the first criteria for a nationalized health care system because the elderly utilize health care the most. Do the retirees who are campaigning for national health insurance realize this? If not age, what else? Gender? Political affiliation? Sexual preference? What? We uncomplicated rationing in America by doing it on the basis of our ability and willingness to pay. Where do we go from here?

Should we cap services? Canada has six open heart surgery clinics for their entire 30 million population. North Dakota has six for 640,000 people. Capping will make it harder to get services if the technology is not available. End result: a wait. Is that an answer? An American standing in a line at the bank has about a 15 minute toleration point; what would it be for kidney surgery? For brain surgery?

Will we end up with a questionnaire given to us by our health care providers that asks certain questions to see if we qualify for medical benefits that day. Can you picture this? One person comes in and, on the basis of answers to a few questions, the provider determines this individual to be a rich male smoker, Caucasian, 45, of Muslim belief, and a Democrat. Does he get treated? It's a Democratic administration now, so maybe he gets it. The next person is poor, female, overweight, a Native American, 36 and a Republican.

Does she get it? The next person is a female, with alcohol problems, black, Jewish, 55, and a Perot supporter. Does she get it?

How should we ration?

Today we do it on the basis of ability and willingness to pay. If health care were rationed another way, those that wanted to pay for it could still get the best treatment. If America caps resources and makes everyone wait for complex procedures, than those that want to pay will go somewhere else for treatment. Mexico, perhaps? Why? Shouldn't we provide the health care here and keep the money and the jobs in this country?

I believe that everyone should have access to a reasonable and adequate level of health care. But if someone really wants to pay more for special services, why shouldn't they? Why shouldn't a 90 year old get a cataract operation if he wants to better his vision in his last years, and pays for it? Why shouldn't an 85 year old get a new knee if desired, enabling a more comfortable life for the last few years?

In America, we have learned that the fairest way is to ration everything on the ability and willingness to pay: food, clothing, housing, a private school education. What makes health care different as long as everyone has easy access to essential care? This is the goal of EqualCare USA. Rationing will be part of any system that utilizes finite resources.

Here's an example: A Newsweek reporter who came down with a rare hepatitis C virus and was faced with a prognosis of degenerating health and inevitable death had an option of extending his life for a longer time by virtue of a rare liver transplant. Expensive, yes. It gave him 3 1/2 more years; years he would not have had without the transplant. A system of rationing that capped this type of treatment would certainly make this procedure off limits in view of its costs. But how do you truly measure cost in this situation? As columnist Joan Beck points out, "who dares to put a price on 3 1/2 years of life, going to a son's wedding, seeing two grandchildren, writing a book, helping dozens of patients and families, pushing for organ donations, coming to terms with life and death and God?" While it might be unreasonable to expect American taxpayers to provide this sort of treatment, who dares to deny him the right to use his own resources to obtain it. Who dares, indeed.

Number Five: Unless we change our present health care system, small business, the backbone of this country, will continue to suffer, eroding any further economic progress we might accomplish. One of the reasons that our present economic recovery has been sluggish is that financially strapped small businesses aren't creating jobs as they did in the 1980's. Fortune 500 companies stopped growing more than a decade ago, actually cutting 3.5 million jobs during the 1980's. Small business, by contrast, created more than 20 million jobs. An August 10, 1992 news story in the Wall Street Journal noted that one reason fewer jobs are now being created is that the financial environment is unfriendly to small business. A credit crunch plus rising health insurance costs has severely curtailed the natural ability of this critical sector of our economy.

In fact, most Americans without health insurance work for small business. These businesses cannot easily pass along the premium in the goods and services they sell. High health premiums force many difficult choices; in hiring, in salaries, in obtaining insurance coverage at all. Even Senator Ted Kennedy says, "Small businesses are victimized the most. They pay twenty to thirty-five percent more than large firms for identical coverage."

It's even worse than that. Small business is the victim today of the cost-shifting within the medical system we have. Medicare and Medicaid have discounted their reimbursements to providers for services rendered. Big businesses have also negotiated managed care arrangements with providers to deliver health services on a reduced fee basis. This leaves small business. Since they are the only ones who aren't likely to get a discount, they make up for the shortfall. This is cost-shifting and, unfortunately, small business is the cost-bearer.

Small business formations are the lifeblood of any free society. Any health care proposal and, for that matter, any legislative proposal that comes to us from our Washington bureaucracy, should encourage and support the formation and success of small business. Historically, the way up for all disadvantaged people has been to operate their own business. Capitalism has done more good for more people than any other economic system in history. All of the other health care proposals are either socialist (where government owns and controls the enterprise) or fascist (where government lets you own the enterprise, but they control it). We must build a health care system that we the people control, not the bureaucracy. We must build a health care system that we all pay for. We must, once and for all, free small business of the health care cost anchor. Destroy small business and, quite simply, we will destroy this country. We must not let this happen! Removing the health insurance burden from all businesses would have its maximum positive impact on small business. It is small business who would feel the brunt of the "pay or play" or "managed competition" health care proposals the government is currently considering.

Small business is this country. Ford, IBM, Apple Computers all started out as a small business person's dream only to grow into the mega-corporations they are today. Our small business keeps our country vibrant, growing and free. While many of our media, politicians and academics rewrite history, the rest of us should always remember this.

Number Six: The question of health care for everyone should be answered with the idea in mind that, as a social program, it should be a true safety net. That is, in theory, the objective behind any social program. This is not what, in reality, people have come to expect.

Everyone should have equal access to affordable and essential health care. All compassionate people agree on this premise. But there must be some internal limits on this essential care. Overutilization can only be slowed if we have some responsibility for some costs. The more a social program gives, the less it becomes a safety net; instead it tends to function more as a hammock or a trampoline.

What we have currently in health care does not resemble a safety net. For some, it's a very comfortable hammock (the wealthy elderly on Medicare); for others, it's a trampoline (the Congressman or woman who doesn't have to pay for the best health care available); still, sadly, for a few, it's a net with gaping holes (the uninsured middle-income earner). This situation can be changed. What America needs now are some bleeding heart capitalists.

We must get back to the true definition of a safety net. That definition eludes individuals like one I know who buys a new Corvette every three or four months, lives in a $600,000 home, who just refurnished his bedroom, but complains about the high cost of health care. The definition isn't grasped by the 70 year old retiree who lives in a nice, paid-up condo in Palm Aire, plays golf every day and insists that Medicare should cover prescription drugs and long term care. Millionaires collect Social Security benefits while another woman that wants to work to supplement her Social Security income to help pay bills cannot, because if she does, she'll have her Social Security benefits reduced.

If you slip, the safety net should be there to catch you, but not prop you up for the rest of your life. Many have lost sight of that in our country. They believe that if they have political power, they have the right to use this power to make someone else pay for something they want, but don't want to pay for.

Number Seven: My final credo is that we have become a nation that rewards whiners. Whiners want what someone else has, without cost.

There's an "anybody pays but me" philosophy entrenched in the health care debate that will make it virtually impossible to get this issue resolved.

Even AARP, in its news magazine, published an article about the dilemma of health care, noting that "Americans make it clear in poll after poll that they want major health care change - but they don't want to pay for it".

Our desire to have someone else pay for our health care results in what can only be described as "bizarre behavior". Time magazine, in a June 18, 1990 news story entitled "A Nation of Hypochondriacs" noted that "we fail to learn that pain is the body's way of informing us that we are doing something wrong, not necessarily that something is wrong. We don't understand that pain may be telling us that we are eating too much of the wrong things; or that we are smoking too much or drinking too much; or that there is too much emotional congestion in our lives. ... We get the message of pain all wrong. Instead of addressing ourselves to the cause, we become pushovers for pills, driving the pain underground and inviting it to return with increased authority." We want health care immediately and you can't hold down costs with that kind of demand. Still, we are upset when we are handed the bill and we look around for someone to pay it for us.

We direct our anger at smokers and drinkers and rally in support of sin taxes. Let them pay. When asked how health care change can be supported, we say, let business pay, let the rich pay for it, reduce administrative costs, reduce tobacco subsidies; in short, anybody but me.

The system has, in part, caused this. Americans have been largely insulated from the real costs of health care. Many health insurance plans have been blank checks; get your treatment, make a small co-payment or pay nothing. A blank check will always drive costs up. Who wouldn't spend it? If costs are truly the biggest complaint about our health care system, we could change that overnight by outlawing all third party payments. Make everyone responsible for their own medical expenses. How close would we be to spending $900 billion in that type of payment system? It's too easy now because someone else generally pays our bill. This makes it more difficult to attempt change and ask for financial help from the American public to accomplish this change. What we get are polls that indicate a willingness to contribute a little to solve the problem, but not enough to be realistic about adequate funding.

We have it far easier in this country than many of our academics, media and politicians would have us believe. In 1988, America's poor commanded more purchasing power than the middle class did in 1955. America's poor today consume more, on average, for food, housing and automobiles than the average Japanese citizen. Adults qualifying for Medicaid receive more money for medical care than the average Japanese spends. Over age 65 Americans have more discretionary income than any other group of people in the world. But the whiners still want more, more, more.

We complain about gridlock in Washington. But gridlock has gripped all of America. We want the health care problem solved, but someone else to pay for it. And our appetite for health care services grows more insatiable by the minute. Something has to give here, folks, or the consequences will be frighteningly high for all of us.

Keep these concepts in mind as you read ahead and I believe you'll see all the pieces of the puzzle fall into place with EqualCare USA, the only proposal I personally feel can realistically address the aforementioned problems while not endangering that precious resource we call health care. We can and must work together! Divided, we fail!

Chapter One

The Real Health Care Crisis in America

I know of a local restaurant where the manager, who earns $31,000 annually, has his health insurance paid for 100% by this eatery's owners. They take a 100% tax deduction for this executive benefit. In that same restaurant is a waitress, who earns about $10,000 per year, who must purchase her own medical insurance with after-tax dollars. In addition, her tips are estimated for the purpose of deducting FICA taxes, which are used to help pay for free health coverage for senior citizens, many of whom collect more in Social Security benefits than she does in income. She doesn't make enough money to pay the extra cost for dependent medical coverage for her own child, yet her salary is reduced to provide health care for strangers.

Hello? What's wrong with this picture? The answer, of course, is everything.

This disparity in access to health insurance coverage is the real health care crisis in this country. There's a lot of smoke and mirrors about GNP, rationing by wealth, health care as a fundamental right, physician salaries, Canada's system, and on and on and on. But the real truth is right here in this example. It's not health care that's broke. It's the financing of health care that has gone awry. When someone is able to obtain health care coverage at no cost to him and a tax deduction for his company and another person in close proximity can't afford to buy coverage for her child, we have a situation that is out of control. This is the part of the system we must fix.

It's not just about holding down the research and development that makes us the leaders in the world in health care technology. It's not just about whether or not a Medicare-covered individual should have heart bypass surgery at 87 years old. It's not just about getting physicians to make house calls again.

It's access for all to essential care, pure and simple. The financing of health care has, for a number of complex reasons, swerved from the path of reality. It hasn't happened overnight, and there are many, many culprits in its turn off the avenue of common sense, starting with Medicare in 1965. The first part of our book will discuss all of the players in the health care system and attempt to show their roles in bringing it to its potential breaking point.

All Americans should be able to obtain essential health care for themselves and their dependents, while contributing equally to its costs. I don't mean equal with regard to dollar outlay. I do mean equal with regard to economic status. There is no equality in today's health care financing and this must be fixed as a central part of any health care solution, or it will not work.

Let me tell you about another situation:

A three person landscaping business who had purchased group health insurance for its employees and dependents was told in 1982 that the insurance company who had sold them the coverage was discontinuing any acceptance of new health insurance plans. The insurance agent who had sold the group health plan to this firm advised that this likely meant a drastic rise in renewal premium costs since the insurance carrier would not be writing any new premium to help offset claims from the groups already written.

The landscape business owner was concerned by this suddenly unknown future budget expense and accordingly sought to find new coverage somewhere else. Through his agent's efforts, he was able to obtain coverage from a new insurance company. He was told that this was a "Cadillac" plan with guaranteed benefits up to $1,000,000 and limited out-of-pocket expenses and lower premiums.

Everything went smoothly until 1987. At that time, the business owner received a notice from this new carrier that advised of the new renewal premium for his policy and told him that the old benefit structures of this "Cadillac" plan were not in keeping with recent health trends and that costs had become prohibitive, a fact that was reflected in a high premium increase.

Within the same letter was an offer to review a new series of health policies that were designed to meet policyholder needs while utilizing cost containment features that would hold costs down to a more reasonable level. A new proposal was enclosed that showed one of these new plans that most closely resembled the current "Cadillac" plan with its corresponding premium. The insurance agent advised the business owner to take the new plan, advice that the owner took. The owner wanted to be sure that the company was not in trouble since he'd already had a carrier that voluntarily left the health insurance business back in 1982. His two other employees and their dependents counted on him to act with prudence when selecting health insurance since it had become important as part of their overall employment benefits.

In that same year, the insurance agent was advised that this company would, in fact, not be seeking any additional new group health insurance business, but would continue to service existing business. Neither the agent nor the insurance company informed the business owner of this decision. He was repeatedly assured by his agent that he had an excellent health policy that was essentially the same plan as he had bought from the company in 1982. Accordingly, and in good faith, the owner continued to pay the premiums as they changed each year.

In 1989, an employee's 13 year old son was diagnosed with a brain tumor, which was handled with a number of operations and treatments, including the removal of his pituitary gland. This caused a non-production of certain hormones necessary to carry on normal bodily functions for which he was treated with regular injections and other drugs.

One of these hormones regulated the production of insulin from his pancreas. Unable to be controlled, an abnormally high rate of insulin is produced, causing the boy to have an insatiable appetite. This appetite demands food and his parents do all they can to control the amount of food the boy gets. Unable to get what his body says it needs, he experiences tremendous rages which have caused the family to put bars on the windows of his room and locks on his door. As it is, the 13 year old now weighs over 200 pounds on an under five feet frame. Additionally, his vision has deteriorated to a point where he is virtually blind. The costs of his treatment run around $80,000 per year. The health insurance policy this small business owns is critical to this family, to say the least.

In 1991, a new renewal premium notice was sent to the business owner, who was now paying $3,117 per month for coverage for his three person group. The new premium called for an increase to $11,899 per month, a nearly 400% increase over what he had been paying. The rate increases had been, for the previous years since the policy switch in 1987, 75%, 70%, and 55%. These seem high as it is, but nothing had prepared the owner for that 400% hit.

The owner was in the worst kind of predicament. He couldn't afford that kind of premium for the health coverage. How many three person small businesses could pay over $142,000 for health insurance per year? He couldn't switch to another insurance company because the 13 year old boy, battling a brain tumor, would be unable to obtain coverage due to his pre-existing condition. He couldn't drop the coverage he had because that meant no assistance for his employee with his son's immense medical bills. What kind of choices are these for a small business owner to make? Regardless of which direction he takes, he and his employees would suffer severe financial consequences. The business or the employee would soon be forced into a bankruptcy situation.

The premium increase was necessitated, according to the insurance company, by the claims in the pool of risks to which this firm belonged. At the time of the 400% rate increase, his business was the only one in the pool, which had eroded with no new business and much of the old business leaving due to the 70 and 75% premium increases of the years before. Claims for his firm, in the year before the premium increased to $142,000+, were $119,000. In effect, this business was now paying its own claim, administrative and commission expenses.

Had the business owner been told in 1987 that this company was leaving the health insurance field, he would certainly have looked for a new carrier, much as he did in 1982 under similar circumstances. Now he was left with a decision no employer, individual or family should have to face.

Everything that is wrong with the current financing of health care can be seen in this example. Insurance companies who engage in a practice I call sick-sorting, where they separate healthy risks from unhealthy ones and try to drive the unhealthy ones away, have contributed to the financing breakdown. Insurance agents who collect commissions, but who don't properly provide full disclosure to their clients about the coverage they have and the insurance company or third party administrator behind the plan, contributed to this type of intolerable situation. Job lock, whereby an employee cannot leave a firm out of fear that they will not be able to obtain health insurance coverage elsewhere due to an ongoing medical problem, has created unbearable employment conditions for people and, in this case, would prevent the owner's employee from ever leaving the business, since his employment furnishes health insurance which he and his family desperately need for their son.

Ralph Nader has been quoted as saying that health care is a privilege of the wealthy. Well, he's wrong. Today, health care is more a privilege of the healthy, who don't need it. This must change.

On my advice, this business owner sued the insurance company and agent over the premium increase. He was given an arrangement until the suit was settled where he paid the prior premium of $3,117 per month (instead of $11,899), and eventually reached a settlement to provide the balance of the maximum policy benefit on behalf of the 13 year old boy and his medical expenses.

Fear has permeated the health care financing arrangements we have today. Many who own insurance policies are afraid these plans won't pay off when they truly need it. Employers and employees dread the anniversary date of their health insurance policy since renewal notices containing next year's premium notice could bring news of a 400% premium increase. There is fear the insurance company itself may experience financial problems due to costs they can't control either, leaving the employer/employee/individual/family with only a piece of paper denoting benefits that can't be collected because the company no longer exists.

These are a few of the reasons for the breakdown in the financing of health care. We will discuss insurance company and agent practices in an upcoming chapter. Let's look further at the problem of job-lock.

When financing of health care is largely left up to the employer, difficulties result. The March 1, 1993 edition of USA Today cited the story of a California woman injured in an automobile accident in 1976, leaving her with severe arthritis in her hip, making her a future candidate for a hip replacement. She worked at a large university and was covered under their health insurance program. As long as she stayed in a large employer environment (and she has worked for other large employers since), she was covered as larger firms usually don't require that employees answer any medical questions to obtain health coverage.

She was unable to pursue small business offers or self-employment because of the unlikelihood of obtaining health insurance. Smaller firms or sole proprietors are often asked detailed medical questions which would likely deprive her of benefits or, at best, give her coverage with a special exclusion that required her to pay for any expenses relating to her hip. She found this out when she tried to go to work for an eight-person office in 1990. Eventually, she was able to buy her own insurance on an individual basis through a state plan that would cover her without regard to the job she was in. She finally had her hip replacement surgery under this plan. While she is free to look at any size firm now for work since her insurance is no longer tied to her employment, she presently finds herself in the probable position of not being able to leave California since another state may not have this type of individual program. She has progressed from job lock to state lock.

It's not only the health of the employee that can chain a person to one's employment. As illustrated earlier, the health of one's dependent may keep an employee from being able to change jobs, too. The end result can have consequences for the entire economy when individuals are unable to move naturally throughout our system. We live in a tremendously mobile society where people change jobs, residences, and spouses and families at a rapid rate. The current financing of health care does nothing to ensure continuation of health benefits with regard for this type of movement. This has to change.

There is another reason why the financing of health care is impaired and causing the real crisis we all face. The expectation level we have combined with our monstrous appetite for health care has completely changed the nature of health insurance. We no longer want health insurance. We want health care. We want to be able to buy an insurance policy that will pay every time we see a doctor, need a prescription, have surgery, with little or no out-of-pocket costs other than the premium payment.

Insurance has always been intended to be a safety net; to pay for the catastrophic event that you can't possibly prepare for and not the everyday items you can place in your weekly or monthly budget. We expect more than insurance from our health policies today. We want to be able to obtain any health care at any price and have it reimbursed. This is no longer insurance. This is simply the payment of health care for us, an arrangement that's impossible to properly price under an insurance contract.

How did this tide of expectation rise? Again, the financing methods used to pay for health care are the major contributors. We have a system which says, on the one hand, that an employer can buy whatever health insurance program they want, at whatever price, and then obtain a 100% tax deduction for it. On the other hand, the claim payments to the employees, when made, are done on a completely tax-free basis. No incentive exists to take a more common-sense approach to financing this resource. Employers select plans as rich as possible based on what they can afford and employees use the plan to a greater or lesser degree in accordance with the extensiveness of the benefits. The more the plan pays for, the more it is used, leading not only to over-utilization, but the expectation that everything will be covered.

Why should an employer get a tax deduction for buying employee health insurance? You only get a partial deduction for yourself if you're a sole proprietor or a partnership buying coverage. An individual receives no deduction. Large employers, with no limit on the amount of their deduction, usually provide the best plans money can buy and their employees are used to it. The recent trend towards cost containment has caused a hue and cry from the employee ranks as they are forced to shoulder some of the burden for health costs. It's much more difficult to share once you've had it all to yourself for a time.

At my own place of business, we offered the choice of a high deductible plan that provided excellent coverage while requiring the individual to share in the cost responsibility up front or a HMO program that required little or no financial responsibility for the individual when medical services were rendered but limited the choice of providers. While there was some grumbling over the restriction as to which doctor or hospital could be used, everyone without exception chose the HMO plan. I realized then that consumers today no longer want health insurance, they want health care, paid for by someone else.

We must stop using health insurance to simply pay the bills. Insurance is intended to assist one in high expense situations that people cannot afford. It's the $50,000 claim, not the $50 one that insurance is adept at covering. Apparently, we no longer see it that way and, as a result, insurance has ceased to work in any affordable manner.

This attitude must change. There shouldn't be a tax-deduction for the employer to buy health insurance. The employer should not even be involved in it. We are each individually responsible for our medical situations and should handle them as we want and see fit. There is no other way in which the health care system can work.

Expectation levels have long run high amongst providers as well. The reimbursement levels they want from an insurance company often exceed reasonableness. The blame for that can likely be placed squarely on Medicare's shoulders. Prior to the introduction of Medicare, prices for medical services were rational, physicians drove black Buicks and came to your house. Private insurance functioned as just that - insurance. After Medicare, reimbursements for care administered to senior citizens were virtually a blank check. As the government built in provider overhead into all reimbursements, hospitals were built and charged to Medicare. The under age 65 individual had to compete for the provider's attention. That provider knew Medicare was going to pay, making those patients a priority.

This socialization of only a part of the system ensured that the financing of health care would eventually cease to work. When one payer in the field will pay any amount of reimbursement required for services, the pressure is on the other payers to perform similarly or get shut out. The cost controls for Medicare that were put into place over the last decade in the form of Diagnostic Related Groupings (DRG) for hospitals and the new Resource Based Relative Value Scale (RBRVS) for doctors are necessary, but they come too late to bail out the present system.

Health care reimbursements today are as splintered as could be. Medicare reimburses at one level, Medicaid at another, HMOs (Health

Maintenance Organizations) at still another, PPOs (Preferred Provider Organizations) at a fourth level, and traditional indemnity insurance plans at still another. Some programs reimburse less than the provider actually incurs in cost, so another payer is charged more to make up for the shortfall. In short, a nightmare of a system that no longer works.

This is the point we have reached in the delivery of health care in this country and how we pay for it. It has taken years to make this ascent but we are now on the ledge and there's no place to go. The real crisis is in getting everyone equal access to benefits without fear and in the financing of that coverage.

It can be done. It won't be easy and our own expectations will have to change. But, remove the fear that one will go bankrupt because of the high costs of an illness or injury; remove the fear that your health is tied to your employment; remove the fear that your child will not be able to get essential health care; remove the fear that benefits will suddenly no longer be there when you need them the most; remove all of that and you will have a health care system that works for everyone, not just for a few, not just for a given doctor, or hospital, or senior citizen, or insurance agent or insurance company or government employee. A system that will still provide us the very latest in medical technology, the very latest in research, the very latest in drug therapy, the very best of the health care to which we have become accustomed.

This is the system we can construct for this country if we are all prepared to share equally in the costs and benefits of it. It can be a system that will be the envy of the rest of the world and a source of pride for all of us. Divided, we will fail.

CHAPTER TWO

PERCEPTION VERSUS REALITY

To actually solve the real health care crisis in this country, it is critical that we identify the correct, specific problems inherent in our health system to enable us to fix what is really broken. It is vitally important that you understand where the actual trouble spots are because most Americans today have misplaced their outrage towards the system. What we are being told is often wrong and what are truly the obstacles we must overcome are often quite different.

Much of our perception of the events going on around us in our lives is shaped and focused by the media. Major news events today are often reduced to sound bites of thirty to sixty seconds. This places an enormous responsibility of deciding what part of any one story is told to us on a very few. Very often what we hear in those quick visual and/or verbal flashes becomes our own thought process on the subject.

The media has certainly written and talked about health care and helped mold American reaction to the system. What they say, how they say it and in what context they say it in becomes crucial to our ultimate judgement of an issue. Before reviewing the record on health care, let's focus on a disturbing trend that has begun to surface in the reporting of news in this country.

Audis. Global warming. The economy. Somalia. General Motors. Waco.

What do all of these subjects have in common? They each demonstrate the incredible power the media has and often misuses in this country. Americans thirst for information. But what happens when that information they receive is severely flawed?

Audis. Back in 1986, the news media reported in large numbers that the Audi automobile had a major problem with its accelerator pedal and was a danger on the road. This, despite the fact that Audi had been in Car and

Driver magazine's top 10 best rated for five straight years. The highly watched news show, "60 Minutes" did a news special showing a car lurching out of control. Lawsuits were the order of the day for Audi.

As the suits were heard, Audi was a continual winner in overturning the allegations. In 1989, further U.S. studies combined with tests run in Canada and Japan found that apparently drivers were simply hitting the accelerator when they meant to hit the brake. Further investigation revealed that an auto expert had set up the Audi in advance for "60 Minutes" to careen out of control at the appropriate time. Does this sound familiar to you?

In April of 1975, Newsweek magazine reported "The central fact is that ... the earth's climate seems to be cooling down. Meteorologists are almost unanimous in the view that the trend will reduce agricultural productivity." In June, 1992, this same magazine advised, "The atmosphere may be reaching the limit of its capacity to absorb emitted carbon dioxide without falling into a disastrous greenhouse effect." Let's see. In 1975, global cooling was the problem. In 1992, it's global warming. So, which one is it? How will we know?

Throughout the 1992 election year, we were inundated with the news about how poorly the economy was doing, how America was in a severe decline, the worst since the Great Depression. Yet GDP was growing, unemployment was level at around 7%, the stock market moved to an all time record high and, globally, our economic growth was better than most of our capitalist competitors. Industrial production was down in Japan, unemployment up to nearly 12% in Canada and 9.5% for all of Europe.

Where were these stories? We didn't hear bad news about other countries' economies any more than we hear bad news about other countries' national health care programs. We elected a President on the basis of an economy that was perceived to be in a complete shambles. The news is leaking out that the economy is doing better as 325,000 new jobs were created in February and the outlook continues to be positive.

Last year when American troops landed in Somalia to begin Operation Restore Hope, news crews were there before them, lighting up the beaches with strobe lights, waiting for the troops as they landed. It was D-Day directed by Groucho Marx.

Sadly, this could have resulted in casualties for both the soldiers and members of the press corps. What sort of individual would make a decision that could have placed a number of young Americans in real danger? Is it the same person who decides which sound bites air during a given news show?

The Audi "incident" several years ago can certainly be compared to the 1993 rigging of a General Motors truck to ignite on impact to emphasize the "danger" they represent. When does news stop becoming news? When does fact give way to fiction? How does the average American citizen tell the difference or should we take the reporting we get at face value and not worry about whether what we've just seen is real or contrived?

Finally, information comes to us from Waco, Texas in March, 1993 that it is conceivable (to the point of designating a task force) to investigate whether reporters tipped off a religious cult group about a proposed raid by Federal law enforcement officials that resulted in the deaths of four Federal agents. The hope here is that it isn't true, but it clearly serves to remind us of the position of power the media have and its potential danger when it moves from reporting the news to creating it.

The media's influence on how we perceive what is wrong with our health care system can have disastrous consequences for us if we get it wrong. If we focus on areas where a problem is perceived rather than where it is real, we will fail in our attempt to solve our health care problems. That failure will have far-reaching ramifications for all of us.

Much of the information we are receiving through media channels is based on statistical data that is exactly right and absolutely wrong at the same time. This type of presentation fashions our view of the crisis and yet, like the economy of 1992, we may well end up focused on the wrong issue.

The clearest example is the damning of the health care system by citing what we spend, $900 billion dollars, and to correlate that with " what we get", which is measured only in terms of infant mortality and life expectancy. The message is, over and over again, that we spend more than anyone else in the world, and therefore we should have the best infant mortality and life expectancy rates.

These statistics are exactly correct; $900 billion dollars is spent in our health care system and, according to the third edition of the New Book of World Rankings, we are 33rd in the world in life expectancy and 20th in infant mortality. The implication is that the quality of health care in this country is poor; that we spend more for less.

The numbers are right, but, in the context shown, absolutely wrong. Life expectancy and infant mortality are statistics more influenced by social problems than with the type of health care we deliver.

Infant mortality. Japan is first in the world in infant mortality and hailed by the media as such. However, Japan doesn't count babies that die in the first three days after birth. Japan is also a largely homogenous society without the mix of people or the Third World immigration that the United

States invites inside its borders. On our part, we do everything possible to try and keep a baby alive, many of whom are born prematurely, without much chance of succeeding. But, because some infants do survive, and, with a perceived moral obligation to pursue the best possible medical course, we make the effort. An effort that costs because it takes an exorbitant amount of money for neonatal intensive care. The question that should have been asked, especially by the media, is can American medicine be blamed for high infant mortality?

The truth is that infant mortality is primarily caused by premature babies. The baby is born before lungs are fully developed, creating an oxygen deprivation that can cause a multitude of problems. That babies can actually be saved under those circumstances is a credit to the technology of this health care system, not a debit. The cause of premature babies stems from a variety of reasons. Alcohol and drug abuse can account for a damaged fetus and premature birth. They invariably cause low birth weight, which medicine then reacts to following the birth. The best physician in the world cannot necessarily change the health habits of pregnant women. The willingness to avoid smoking, drinking and drug use must come from the individual herself.

The older age at which women are having children increases the possibility of a high risk pregnancy. Combined with the previous life-style habits, it can result in significant problems for the unborn child.

Finally, lack of prenatal care can also cause problems for the newborn. Yet there are clinics all over the country that offer free prenatal treatment for anyone seeking it. Can our medical professions be faulted if this care is not sought? Do we have an education problem here instead of a medical one?

We certainly have a social one, and that is essentially what infant mortality and life expectancy represent: the social measurement of the country. We allow people to come to our country from third world countries where infant mortality is off the charts. Do you expect me to believe that this would have a positive effect on our rates? Yet, what is the alternative? Close our borders? We are the greatest melting pot in the world, a fact that has long been a source of national pride. But you can't have the mix we do and not have some effect on our vital statistics.

Should we refrain from trying to keep these babies alive? Is that our other option? We spend the majority of our health care dollars in the first fourteen days of life and the last fourteen days. Do we turn off the faucet? We clearly can't have it both ways.

Comparing our infant mortality rates with the rest of the world makes no sense since America is a blend of fifty different states with diverse populations, cities and problems. The countries that lead the world, Japan, Iceland, Finland, Sweden, Switzerland, are plainly different societies than ours. Single out some states that may be more aptly compared and you have a different story. Vermont would be tied with Switzerland in fifth place, ahead of Canada (10th), France (11th), West Germany (13th), Spain (15th) and Great Britain (17th). Hawaii would be seventh in the world, Minnesota ninth, Massachusetts tied with Canada for tenth, Kansas and Utah tied with France in the eleventh position. These states, with the possible exception of Massachusetts, are much less varied in their population base and have fewer large metropolitan areas than some of our other states. The District of Columbia has a 23.2 rate for infant mortality (deaths per 1,000 infants) as our highest state rate versus Vermont, lowest at 6.8.

We are also told by the media how much better infant mortality is in Canada, who spends less overall on health care than we do. Yet racial minorities, which have high infant mortality rates in this country, have the same problems in Canada. Two such minorities, the Crees and the Inuits of northern Quebec, have infant mortality rates three and four times greater, respectively, than Canada as a whole. These statistics are not on the evening news shows.

Finally, columnist Thomas Sowell noted, in an article published in March of 1993: "Much media hype followed a report a couple of years ago which showed that (1) blacks received less prenatal care than whites and (2) blacks had higher infant mortality rates than whites. Everyone seemed to jump to the conclusion that this showed the need for more prenatal care and demonstrated the effects of neglect, racism and the rest of the familiar litany of indictment against "society". But the very same report showed that Mexican Americans received even less prenatal care than blacks, and yet had infant mortality rates slightly lower than that of whites. Other racial or ethnic minorities, such as people of Filipino or Chinese ancestry, also had lower infant mortality rates than whites. But none of this made the six o'clock news."

Higher infant mortality then, by definition, will severely impact life expectancy. If you have a higher infant mortality, those infant deaths are averaged in to obtain a life expectancy number. Our average life expectancy is 75.22 (33rd) as compared to Switzerland (1st) at 77.92, or Japan (4th at 77.71), or Sweden (6th at 77.16) or Canada (8th at 77.03).

While higher infant mortality brings our number down, so does the societal problems already noted with earlier vital statistics. Violence, for example, gives us a homicide rate that is four times Canada and ten times that of West Germany (26th at 75.65) and Britain (trailing the U.S. at 75.01). At any given time, there are about 177,000 spinal cord injuries, 45,000 of which result from assault and which costs an average of $600,000 to treat over that individual's lifetime.

In 1984, handguns killed 48 people in Japan, 8 in Great Britain, 34 in Switzerland, 52 in Canada, 58 in Israel, 21 in Sweden, 42 in West Germany and 10,728 in the United States. The combined population of these seven nations is approximately the same as the United States, meaning the rate of handgun deaths per million people is 1.1 for these seven countries as opposed to ours which is 44 per million. This type of violence that permeates our society has a significant effect on medical costs.

Nor is violence the only societal problem driving up spending on health care. Over $10 billion was spent on AIDS patients last year with a projection calling for more than $15 billion is forecasted for 1995. The United States is treating four times the number of AIDS patients than is Canada, based on population. In addition, there are an estimated 18.5 million people in the U.S. that abuse alcohol, often resulting in liver treatments, among the more expensive medical procedures.

Motor vehicles killed 47,093 people in this country in 1988 and was the leading cause of death of Americans under age 35. We have larger, faster and more superhighways in this country than anywhere in the world. Automobile accidents are the leading cause of epilepsy, quadriplegia, paraplegia, facial and head injuries and one of the leading causes of blindness, all conditions that result in a substantial cost to administer treatment.

Violence, AIDS, substance abuse, automobiles.

These are all part of America, all debits on the life expectancy calculation. Should we be more concerned with this statistic? Or is it that $900 billion number that we are upset about? What's the alternative? Let premature babies die? Refuse admission to AIDS patients? Don't treat the teenager just pulled out of a crushed Mustang?

We are told that we spend more and get less and these are the numbers they use to prove it. My eyes tell me a different story. I've done a lot of travelling around the world and certain images stand out. I don't see the number of joggers and cyclers in any other country to the extent that I see them here. Americans work hard, despite our societal difficulties, at being a healthy country. I don't see nearly as many elderly people anywhere else than I see here. The life expectancy numbers don't say that, but 12% of our population is over age 65.

With infant mortality and teenage automobile deaths lowering the overall life expectancy number, what happens if we look at remaining life expectancy once we get to age 55 or 65 versus some of these other countries. After all, we seem to do everything we can to prolong life medically at our older ages. Further, what would happen if we isolate white male and female data from the overall numbers since our minority populations have a lower life span, further affecting the overall life expectancy numbers?

At age 55, a white female in the U.S. has a remaining life expectancy, according to the 3rd Edition of the New Book of World Rankings, (publ. in 1991), of 26.8 years, trailing Japan at 28.8, France, 28.25, Netherlands, 27.56, Canada, 27.5, and Sweden at 27.3, while moving ahead of Spain, 26.54, West Germany, 26.04, and Belgium, 25.17, and continuing ahead of Great Britain, 25.54.

Inasmuch as these are all countries with national health insurance, the wide disparity in these numbers would suggest that having this type of social program seems to have little or no common effect as to life expectancy results.

For a white male, age 55, life expectancy is 22.2 years, placing us behind Japan at 24.07, Sweden at 22.69 and France at 22.37. We are tied with Canada and Spain (both at 22.2), and ahead of Netherlands, 21.95, West Germany, 21.05, Great Britain, 20.89 and Belgium, 20.02.

At age 65, white female life expectancy is 18.7 years, behind Japan, 19.95, France, 19.61, Canada, 19.2, and the Netherlands, 19.04, tied with Sweden (18.7 also), and ahead of Spain, 17.83, West Germany, 17.62, Great Britain, 17.47, and Belgium, 16.9. Again, these are better results than when viewing overall life expectancy statistics.

The numbers for a white male, age 65, are, for the U.S., 14.9 years, trailing only Japan, 16.32 and France, 15.24, tied with Sweden (14.9), and ahead of Canada, 14.89, Spain, 14.77, Netherlands, 14.36, West Germany, 13.78, Great Britain, 13.62 and Belgium, 12.95, showing male life expectancy to be better when viewed at older ages. Now that we've introduced MacDonald's, Kentucky Fried Chicken and Pizza Hut to Japan, their numbers may come back to us. Comparing the United States to Japan for infant mortality and life expectancy makes little sense anyway with two societies that couldn't be farther apart in characteristics and life-style.

We need to lay this issue to rest. Infant mortality and life expectancy are not medical numbers in a pure sense. We could improve our costs rapidly by spending far less trying to keep babies and the elderly alive. Not much publicity has been made about improvements in both numbers in this country over the last decade, but U.S. infant mortality is at its lowest rate ever (now 9.8) and life expectancy continues to rise, both attributable more to medical technology than any improvement in crime rates, auto accidents, alcohol and substance abuse and AIDS cases. Despite our societal problems, we improve medically each year, but we have to spend to accomplish that. This is the avenue we've chosen to travel rather than to draw a line at treatment. We go to any expense to keep someone alive in this country.

Between the years 1960 and 1979, the four leading chronic killers among people aged 45-65, were reduced drastically. The mortality rate for hypertension decreased by 73%, cerebrovascular disease by 48%, heart disease by 29%, and diabetes by 27%, for an average reduction of 32% overall. Why don't we talk about these numbers instead of comparing us to nations that we have absolutely nothing in common with? Why do they consistently present forceful arguments about life expectancy and infant mortality with no chance for they type of rebuttal I've outlined above? Does the media have their own agenda on the health care issue?

Another statistic that is repeated over and over again as a benchmark for our declining health care system is the number of uninsured Americans. 37 million, 35 million, 41 million, 31 million. We hear different numbers from each of these studies. In a sound bite, this is the only number served up for our consumption. What does this number represent? How was it calculated? Which study is correct? Which number is more accurate? Is this the entire fault of the health care system?

The implication in this number, which served as an election rally cry for the Democrats in 1992, is that there are upwards of thirty-something million people completely uncovered by health insurance. These studies made their estimates at one point in time in a given year. From that standpoint, the number, at the time the survey was done, is exactly right. But it is absolutely wrong to assume that this is a chronic problem for all of these individuals.

Alan Reynolds, Director of Economic Research at the Hudson Institute in Indianapolis, Indiana, tells us that a more realistic picture comes from the 1990 Census Bureau, who, rather than looking at a snapshot in time, did a 28 month study from 1986-88. Since there are millions of people who change jobs, move, get married, go back to school, widow, go on welfare, go off welfare, the period of time they go without health insurance is relatively brief. Therefore, to more accurately gauge the chronic uninsured, those without coverage for a long period of time, a longer time frame provides a more concise calculation.

The study's results showed that 4% of our population, or fewer than 10 million people, lacked coverage for the entire period. Less than 10 million. Not 37. Not 35. Not 41. Less than 10 million. Where was this story? Examining the numbers more reveals that, of this group, 50% of them were under age 25, many of whom could conceivably have been covered as dependents under their parents' plan, but, for some reason were not. Some of these individuals are right out of high school or college, not concerned about paying for health insurance at that time, due to their age and health. Did you think much about health insurance when you were 22 years old?

Another study, done by the Urban Institute, turned up similar findings, with an added fact that the highest percentage of short-term uninsureds were those with family incomes greater than $36,000. As an insurance agent, I've encountered people who probably fit this scenario. This is the individual who must decide between the car payment on the BMW or health insurance. Guess which one they select not to pay? The uninsured also inevitably includes a number of self-employed people who simply choose to self-insure.

As long as health insurance coverage is not a compulsory event, there will be uninsured people in this country. But those without coverage for an extended period of time, the chronically uninsured, are one-third less than the numbers we've been told.

We all know how easy it is to manipulate statistics and numbers presented without full explanation are misleading and deceitful at best. Here, the two greatest theories about the decline of the American health care system, vital statistics and the uninsured, have been presented to the American people as negative statistics without the full story. Why does no story about the uninsured indicate that, while these people may lack health insurance, they do not lack health care? A community hospital must treat every patient without considering their insurance status.

A story on "60 Minutes" in 1993 showed two hikers in Tennessee, one of whom was seriously injured and, because he was uninsured, his companion gave the hospital his own medical insurance card. Now the two are in jail for health care fraud and numerous people who were interviewed for the show bemoaned this "deplorable health care situation". Glossed over completely were the comments by hospital personnel who said they would have treated the injured hiker with or without an insurance card. The media apparently doesn't feel that this point is important. They tend to find the most articulate speakers to make the points they wish to stress, while featuring either little coverage, no coverage or someone who comes across poorly, to describe the opposing viewpoint.

EqualCare USA will bring everyone into the system, make it obligatory for all Americans to participate in it and share equitably in the costs. This won't necessarily change vital statistics. Only society can do that. But it will remove the uninsured discussion once and for all, a discussion that has been shaped to misrepresent the quality of our medical delivery.

Beyond the statistics, we see common headlines, such as "Sickly, wheezing U.S. health care system urgently needs radical surgery" and cries for national health insurance (such as the one to the north of us in Canada) are commonplace. As an average reader, what would be your conclusion about the U.S. health care system if you consistently read or watched these types of news stories? Would you feel satisfied with it? Conversely, we are told that Canadians love their health care system (I will discuss that in another chapter). If you had a free choice of doctors, didn't know how much it was costing you since it comes out of taxes, and were consistently told how much better a system it is than the United States, wouldn't you also feel good about it? On the other hand, if you were not able to necessarily choose the physician you wanted to see, saw how much health insurance was costing you in your paycheck every time you were paid, and were regularly browbeaten with infant mortality and life expectancy statistics, how good would you feel about your system? Perception, at times, means everything, even if it isn't grounded in reality.

Media reporting of health care conferences, meetings and seminars is equally slanted. I attended a meeting in West Palm Beach in 1992 and sat through a session sponsored by one of our Congressmen that was ostensibly held to discuss the American health care system. It quickly became apparent that it was more aimed at promoting a single payor program. You were cheered if you bashed the health care system and jeered if you were a physician or an insurance agent or represented an insurer or provider. Still, at the end of the meeting, when asked to vote for a preference between a single payor system, a pay or play plan, or for simply improving on the system already in place, the vote was split roughly in thirds, with no solution emerging as a favorite; a vote that has been consistent in most of these types of meetings.

However, The Palm Beach Post, in an article that appeared reporting on the seminar, led off their story with the following two paragraphs:

" 'There is no health care system in the United States of America' the speaker said. 'For years, we've made accommodations to those who bled the system dry.'

"The crowd at a recent health care conference responded to

criticisms by Paul Olgren, a Minnesota state representative, with the loudest applause of the morning --and the loudest silence. While those who considered themselves victims of the system cheered, those Rep. Olgren had just called bloodsuckers silently fumed.''

Nowhere in the article is the result of the final vote when it was all said and done, of 33%-single payer, 33%-pay or play and 33%-incremental reform. The article inference is that the crowd wanted to scrap the current health care system. The final vote tells us a different result and, for whatever motive, is left out of the story. This is unbiased, objective reporting, we are told, yet this would appear to show the media as being more liberal than the general public.

Much is made of the high administrative costs in the present system. An article in Business & Health magazine, in November, 1992, urged the government to adopt a single payor system and abandon free market attempts to fix the system, citing private insurance overhead of 14 cents out of every premium dollar. Do we really want to hand this system over to the bureaucrats? Will that action save us any money?

Do we really and truly believe this? Should we use the public education system, a government run program, as an example?

In 1970, the Federal budget for education was $12 billion. In 1990, it was $50 billion. 40 cents on every dollar is said to be spent on administration. Public school enrollment, despite the increase in spending, has actually dropped since 1970, as did SAT scores in math (-13) and verbal (-36). We spend 67% more than West Germany and 68% more than Japan for elementary and secondary schooling. Where is the media for this story?

In 1960, we spent 6% of GNP on education and 6% on health care. Today, we still spend about 6% on education, while we spend twice as much on health care. Would anyone want to debate with me that medicine is at least twice as good as it was in 1960 versus education being even as good as it was thirty years ago?

Where is the media for a major news story about the millions of dollars in Social Security disability payments that are made to alcoholics and drug addicts who claim they are unable to work due to their addiction? FICA payments made by people who work hard and try to survive goes towards benefit payments for those who disable themselves through substance abuse. Isn't this a major news story? Where's the outrage here? Instead we get more infant mortality and life expectancy statistics.

News shows and reports on our health care system are dominated with people that want to bash the system. Anyone speaking for it, as noted, rarely has the chance to talk. On a February, 1992 "Nightline" show on ABC, a program entitled "Emergency! Health Care In America!" ran in a prime time slot and, for nearly two hours featured "victims" of the system. During a commercial break, a self-employed businessman asked if he might be allowed to speak when the show resumed. He was and he said, "I'm self employed. I'm one of the uninsured, and I don't want universal health care. If you want to see an example in action, look at any V.A. hospital. That's universal health care - government provided and universally hated."

In his book about what he terms, "America's Cruel, Bureaucratic and Horrendously Expensive Health Care System", and in which he proposes a single payor system loosely based on Canada's plan, author Neil Rolde says, "The ultimate comment on the firestorm raging over health care in the U.S. may well have been provided in July, 1991 by William Benefield of Amarillo, Texas. Outside the Veterans Hospital in that Panhandle city, Benefield, a veteran, set himself afire and died to protest cuts in veterans' benefits." The author singles this event out as the ultimate comment on the shortcomings of the free-market system. Mr. Rolde has apparently forgotten that the free market system has nothing to do with veterans benefits and hospitals, although the machine controlling his proposed single payor system certainly would.

Preventive care is a new area of emphasis for those reporting the news to us about our health care system. The message we are getting is that we could lower our $839 billion dollar health care costs by concentrating more on interventive medicine rather than reactionary delivery. The money spent having diagnostic tests, and seeing our doctors sooner, would save us big dollars in the long run.

However worthy it might be to promote and pay for routine tests in an effort for early detection of illness or disease, it will not save us any money. Most analysts say it will add upwards of $3 billion dollars to the tab. This is not to say wellness tests are not important, but to pretend we'd save money is wrong. It would cost more to give every woman age 40 and over a regular mammogram than it would to treat every breast cancer patient. Early detection is a valid objective, but to believe we should do it in the name of cost-cutting is not accurate.

Interestingly, Canada and Sweden have released studies which show that a mammogram is not helpful in early detection for women under the age of 55. U.S. researchers have not been able to substantiate this data. Since both Canada and Sweden have both admitted to having financially burdened national health care systems, do we accept these studies as purely objective material? Or could we suspect an ulterior motive in discouraging mammograms from a cost standpoint? Are these studies releasing statistics that are exactly right and absolutely wrong?

We don't often see stories about the health care industry itself to the extent we see items about victims of the health care system we have. The media have long thought of themselves as champions of the underdog, so they continually bring us news about the plight of our fellow Americans who have fallen through the cracks in the system. Easier to do that perhaps than to show us an economic perspective? In Florida Trend magazine, one can find that in 1991, while other sectors of the economy were shrinking or stagnating, the health care field added 18,800 jobs, growing by 4.4%. Earlier in our book, we discussed the recent news that indicated health care was creating 20,000 jobs per month for Americans. As the population continues to age, wouldn't it seem likely that the demand for health care services will increase and more and more jobs created? By private enterprise? Isn't this good news? We're spending an amount of GNP on health care that corresponds to the number of people in the country that work in health care. This is a great news story, but one not being told to us today.

The end result of the media coverage of the health care system is an outraged public pointing fingers at everyone involved, holding particular anger towards physician's salaries and charges. The truth is, according to a recent article in Forbes magazine, that the hourly rate a primary care physician earns is $46.00. A small company CEO makes $50.00 per hour, on the average. Where is the contempt for them? A corporate attorney makes $61.00 per hour. Why aren't the press upset over this? Can either of these individuals save our lives?

Our derision is misplaced. How can we be upset with physicians when rock and roll and film stars can earn $60 million dollars and more from record and movie contracts? Why should we pay news anchors more than $3 million dollars per year to tell us our health care system is in shambles? Why aren't we out somewhere protesting that? Do we really want films and CDs to be our legacy to the world? Or would a life-saving liver transplant process be something better for which to be remembered?

The opinions held by the people of this country would seem to indicate a dilemma in selecting which way we should proceed in improving our health care system. This, despite the constant barrage from the press about the unworthiness of the accomplishments made in health care over the past couple of decades. This, to me, means hope. Hope that as a reader you have an open mind about our future health care direction. It can mean the difference between the success or failure of our next move. Divided, we fail.

CHAPTER THREE

THE INSURANCE INDUSTRY'S CONTRIBUTIONS

Having separated some of the myths from realities, we can now focus on the center of the current health care crisis, that of a breakdown in the financing of this necessity. It is here where concentration on solving the problem must begin if we are to move health care to its next evolution.

The health insurance product is in an unenviable position right now. Many people are unable to obtain coverage because of their health. Others have seen rate increases multiply to the extent of complete unaffordability. Still more live in fear that the policy they are paying a substantial amount of money for will let them down when they need it the most.

It wasn't always this way with health insurance. The tradition of health insurance made health care available and affordable for many Americans. It worked well as a safety net against a catastrophic illness or injury whose financial result could never have been paid without it. But one major event turned the tide for insurers, sending them down a path destined for failure, and ensuring the near-complete breakdown for this financing mechanism to cover health care costs.

Many insurers further compounded the problem with some questionable practices, such as cherry-picking, sick-sorting, post-claims underwriting; terms that will be clearly defined in this chapter. Now called "the death spiral" by such experts as Florida's Insurance Commissioner Tom Gallagher, these underwriting practices have positioned the industry in an ethical Rubik's Cube. Instead of making the best of a difficult situation, many chose to try and take the easy way out, making a bad situation even worse. Make no mistake about it. Many of the stories that have surfaced about astronomical rate increases, abrupt cancellations, claim denials and job lock all point the finger in one direction; and the insurance industry can no longer dodge this bullet.

The event that changed health insurance forever was the creation of Medicare. Medicare poured billions of dollars into the health care system, initially lifted provider expectations on reimbursements and eventually the charges as well. This started to weave an insulation around us as regards the true costs of health care. Medicare, in short, encouraged a blank check system; one which the government and the insurance industry supported until the money finally ran out. What followed were cutbacks by the government in the form of increasing deductibles and a ceiling on provider prices, and changes in insurance industry practices which continued to insulate healthy people from the true cost of care at the expense of unhealthy ones.

Consumer expectations rose during this period of advancing medical technology. Being protected from the cost of insurance through employer-paid arrangements, employees demanded the best care for them or for a family member when an illness or injury occurred. There was no incentive to keep costs down since the patient's portion of the bill was relatively minor. As health care providers continued to raise rates and probe the upper limits of what insurers and the government were willing to pay, most of us remained oblivious to the ultimate reality; one day the financing bubble would burst.

You will recall from an earlier discussion that initial provider charges to Medicare allowed them to build in their overhead costs, leading to government subsidizing the building of facilities. These increased prices were passed to insurers, too, who soon began to scramble when policies not priced for this type of billing system were paying more than the premium revenue being generated. The industry adjusted and revamped their plans and prices to meet these new provider expectations.

But the battle was not only to anticipate provider costs. It was also to conform to consumer expectations, many of whom over-utilized the coverage since there was no incentive not to do so. When there is very little out-of-pocket responsibility, health insurance inevitably becomes health care, where it's used to pay the $50.00 tab instead of only the $5000.00 one. Using insurance to pay for virtually all of one's health care bills created an additional crisis for insurance carriers as they struggled to break even on their health business. Higher provider charges; higher consumer anticipations on using insurance to pay the basic health care bills; together they were a dangerous combination that took the word "profit" out of company board-rooms.

Profit is often looked upon as evil when used in conjunction with a health insurance carrier. But health insurance is a business, like any other, that seeks to make a reasonable profit. When profit moves to profiteering, the criticism is justified. However, the thought that insurance companies should not be in it to make a profit is grossly unfair. None of us start a business with the intention of losing money. It's the desire to earn a profit that makes business efficient. Government has no such motive, leading to eventual failure of their programs. What insurers did was try to avoid the losses, leading them into territory that has created a backlash of censure for which there may be no recovery.

The practices engaged in to survive in the health insurance business after the introduction of Medicare are not defensible. As an industry, we should have blown the whistle and kicked the practitioners of these repellent methods out of the game. We didn't, and our failure may well have dictated our future on the sidelines of the health care business.

What were these practices? Were they necessary? Could they have been avoided? There are two major categories to examine. One involves the pre-underwriting position of selecting only the best risks, which I call "cherry-picking". The other is performed after attracting a large volume of business, in an effort to keep it profitable, a practice I call "sick-sorting".

Cherry-picking is the process of choosing risks that won't make claims. The entire theory behind insurance is the law of large numbers. The larger the pool of risks, the more likely you will have a group of individuals where there will be enough healthy folks to subsidize the ones in poor health. Separating the healthy ones breaks down the concept of insurance.

How does an insurance company cherry-pick? One primary way is to lower rates for younger people, who will likely be more healthy because of their age. Another way is to not offer benefits such as maternity.

Let's say one insurance company is marketing health insurance to everyone, not asking medical questions, charging one rate for all applicants, offering a reasonable benefits package that includes maternity. All individuals written by this company stay in the same risk pool, thereby ensuring that future rate increases will be kept as low as possible since all are sharing equally in the risk. This is how health insurance can work.

Enter insurance company #2. This company wants to try and avoid taking any unhealthy risks, so they alter their product offering accordingly. They age-band the rates, charging a 25 year old a low rate, a 35 year old a higher rate, a 45 year old still higher, and so forth. They exclude maternity. They ask a couple of general medical questions.

What individuals will they attract? Younger people will be interested since age-banding gives them a lower price than the first company, who has one rate for everybody. The "one-rate" concept is a community-rating approach, designed to have younger people subsidize the older ones, and healthier helping out the sick in the interests of keeping the costs within reason for all. Carrier #2, however, has just picked up the younger ones who might feel a little resentful about paying a higher rate than their age would dictate so they can help out someone thirty years older.

What risks would carrier #2 discourage from coming to their plan? Families. Husbands and wives who may be considering children at some point will likely not switch to a company that isn't offering some kind of reimbursement for maternity costs. Unhealthy people. Having to answer a question or two about medical history would prevent someone with a major affliction, such as cancer, diabetes, or heart problems, from applying for coverage with carrier #2.

The end result? Carrier #2 has a head start on a more than profitable book of business. Carrier #1 is using a theory of insurance that has just gone sour as the younger, healthy individuals left their risk-spread pool, leaving in more people who will likely file claims, destroying the price structure of the plans. Carrier #1 will have to raise rates, perhaps drastically in the future, making it difficult for some people, even though they may be sick and need the coverage, to stay on the plan. The primary purpose of covering people and paying claims has begun to erode.

That's cherry-picking. It's done in a variety of ways from age to zip codes to health questions to streamlining benefits. Whatever the method, the aim is clear: to take only healthy risks, a practice of claims avoidance that was allowed to happen for years. The losers were older individuals, people in poor health and insurance companies that tried to maintain the traditional insurance practice of accepting everyone and effectively spreading the risk.

As long as there were companies that offered low premium plans for the type of easy to insure risks they wanted, consumers continued to look for the "best deal" in town for health insurance. "Best deal" became a euphemism for lowest price. Insurance agents played along and made a good living by "cheap-changing" a group every year. When it came time for renewal, out went the agent looking for the lower price for his or her client. Insurance companies saw business bounce on and off the books on a regular basis, making it difficult to manage with large fluctuations in premium revenues and claim losses. As long as the demand was for low prices, and insurers were willing to engage in this method of predatory pricing, the doomed practice continued.

Everyone should know by now that if something looks too good to be true, it probably is. The art of finding the lowest cost eventually hurt the people that had to use the policy to pay claims. A number of practices were engaged in to minimize the number of claims that had to be paid. Logic should tell you that low-priced medical coverage is not designed to do what the consumer had, by now, come to expect. That is, to pay for health care bills, small and large, whenever we went to see a doctor.

Okay. You've bought one of the low-cost, super plans your agent told you about. Maybe this agent found you an association plan where you were able to secure this low cost by joining an independent organization which we'll call the Competitive Hospitalization Employers Association Plan (CHEAP). You pay a low premium plus a small monthly fee to belong to the association. The plan appears to have a reasonable set of benefits, a high lifetime maximum of $1,000,000 and the agent was still paid a good commission to write you through this program; in short, all of the normal costs that would be attributed to a policy priced more accurately higher. So how can this association plan charge so little?

Easy. The CHEAP plan does most of its underwriting at claim time, more often than not, delaying a legitimate claim indefinitely or not paying it in full or at all, by taking advantage of your lack of knowledge concerning provider fees. What the provider charged and what the plan covered were often widely disparate.

Here's an example: A 1990 claim benefit summary shows a bill from a physician's office of $11,600. The next line says, "Paid at Plan Coinsurance 100%", which equaled $6,037.50. The line underneath that states, "Amount exceeds Usual and Customary Charges", totalling the balance of $5,562.50. So, you had a 100% of usual and customary charges covered. You simply didn't ask what table the insurer was using to determine what amount usual and customary represented. In this case, it was 100% of 52% of the bill.

The practice of post-claims underwriting is to delay asking for medical records until after the individual has filed a claim, and often leaves the insured without coverage when they truly need it. An example of the letter you receive from an insurer who is denying a claim, based on this practice, would be worded as follows:

"Coverage was issued based upon the answers provided on the application.

"Medical information we have received with your claim indicates that you had a medical condition before applying for the coverage which was not shown on the application. We have enclosed a copy of your application. Please refer to questions 2b and 2c which read as follows:

"2. Has any person proposed for insurance:

b. Ever had or sought advice or treatment for any disease or disorders of the heart, lungs, gastro-intestinal tract, kidneys, back or nervous system, or high blood pressure, diabetes, cancer, tumor or mental disorder?

c. Consulted or been attended by any doctor within the last five years?

"You will note that the answer to question 2b was in the negative. The answer to question 2c was in the positive and the only response was physical in January of 1981 and bronchitis and virus, date of onset and date of recovery, March, 1981.

"Information we now have on file does show that you were seen by Dr. Barr in January and April of 1979, February of 1980 and March, April of 1981 for bronchitis and spasmatic bronchitis. Also, the hospital records show that Dr. Barr has treated you for chronic bronchitis and beginning pulmonary emphysema. The records also indicate a history of asthma as a youngster.

"These omissions may have been an oversight or the information may have seemed unimportant, however, this medical information made you ineligible for this coverage as applied for.

"Rather than terminating all coverage, we wish to extend the following alternative by issuing an exclusion rider retro-actively to the effective date, August 1, 1981. If this is acceptable, please sign the enclosed rider and return the original in the enclosed envelope. If this option is accepted, then 50% of your expense incurred as a result of your confinement of 10/24/82 to 10/30/82 would be payable. The other 50%, or those charges incurred as a result of treatment for your lung disorder would not be payable.

"Should you not find this action acceptable, you may choose to have all coverage for yourself terminated as of the effective date and premium refunded. If this option is accepted, then no claims would be payable."

The end result of buying into a plan with a low premium is to end up with a decision to have half of a 7 day hospital stay paid and no coverage for anything relating to bronchitis or to end up with the entire bill and hope the premiums refunded will be enough to pay a large part of it, a circumstance not likely since the policy is in its first two years and premium payments hadn't been made for long. This option also leaves you now without insurance and, with a recent hospitalization, in the nearly impossible position of having to find coverage elsewhere.

Based on what? That the insurer, even though given information about the relevant physician and condition on the original application, chose to wait until there was a claim to obtain the insured's medical records. This is a company looking to avoid claims. If a policy is priced low initially, it doesn't make economic sense for the company to try and obtain all the medical records on each individual to determine acceptance. Rather than operate on a preventive mode to screen people out up front that present health risks the insurer doesn't care to assume, they further denigrate the insurance process by waiting until you have a claim and react accordingly, paying for medical records on only the cases they must to try and ascertain if there is a semi-legitimate reason to turn down this claim. This method of avoiding claims is far worse than turning someone down for coverage since now the insured has actually incurred costs for which the providers will sensibly expect payment. If the company bails out, who is left holding the bills?

Another practice of claims avoidance and the attempt to separate healthy from unhealthy risks is called sick-sorting. Would you buy health insurance that was designed to take your premium while you were predictably healthy and then, when you needed it most, the insurance company was able to either cancel you or raise your rate to outrageous levels? Of course you wouldn't. Yet this is exactly what many carriers do today and it is, in my mind, unacceptable.

In the beginning of this book, I cited a case where a 3 person landscaping business was eventually sorted out of a larger pool until they had become the only ones in it and the only insurance left was a dollar-trade with the company. This is sick-sorting at its worst.

What companies do is, through the attractiveness of low rates and (apparently) strong benefits, write a substantial amount of cases resulting in a large amount of premium revenue. The policies are priced in the first year to provide a margin to pay expenses, including agent commission, and very little in the way of claims. There usually is not a significant number of claims filed in the first year anyway (and post-claims underwriting can hold down any high claims) so the company survives with little difficulty. Now comes the time to renew the policies written, the anniversary date of the plan. Let the games begin.

One method is to "retire" the first policy form by offering a new, improved, low-cost version to those risks still considered safe and healthy by the insurer. The alternative is to accept the old policy version with a rate increase, usually moderate for the individuals the company has placed in their healthiest pool. If you're the insured, you probably go for the low cost, new version. And why not? It's less expensive; that's usually the barometer by which one measures health insurance. So you take it. You also start a new pre-existing condition period where post-claims underwriting can be done again. You may also be under a new usual and customary table which wasn't as good as the prior version. But, since these factors aren't obvious to anyone, the new plan is selected.

The ones that aren't healthy don't get the offer of the new improved plan, simply a high rate increase on the existing plan. Since they're not in good health and obtaining other coverage elsewhere might be difficult, they are forced to stay and pay the higher rate. Worse yet, the majority of healthy risks have fled to another pool because of the low rate attraction. You are now left in a pool that only includes the unhealthy ones that decided to bite the bullet and pay the higher premium rate. What will next year's rate increase look like if you are in a pool of only potentially high users of the policy benefits? Even more dramatic rate increases await, similar to the 400% jump that the 3 person landscaping group was told they must pay. Essentially, it looks like this:

	PLAN A, SOLD IN 1993		PLAN B, OFFERED AT RENEWAL TIME, 1994
	1000 people enrolled		--
Renewal:			
	50 people in questionable health remain	>>>	950 healthy risks plus 1000 new risks are written

In an instant, you went from a pool of 1000 to a pool of 50 risks if you're not healthy. The company will try and minimize those claims through exorbitant rate increases people can't pay and/or sharply reducing benefits in a targeted attempt to drive the unhealthy risks off.

Another way to sick-sort is by re-entry underwriting. A company takes a look at you or your group on a regular basis to assess the size of risk they can expect. You answer more medical questions, your specific claims experience is reviewed as well as that of the pool you're in and rates are determined accordingly. Healthy, low-claims groups are priced to encourage them to stay. Poorer risks are given high rate increases without the benefit of healthier risks in their pool to keep the costs reasonable. The entire principles behind insurance have been abandoned.

How can you as an individual seeking coverage avoid being taken down this unrewarding path? Ask for and read the policy before you buy it is the best advice. Look for whether you would be issued a policy or a certificate. A policy is a contract directly with the insurance company. A certificate is a copy of someone else's contract, which puts you in a poor bargaining position with a company that is not directly responsible for your claims. Instead, you go through a third party who has the contract with the insurer, often leaving you out of control of your insurance destiny.

When you receive the policy or certificate, look for a clause regarding renewal premiums. See what the options for increasing the rates are. Does it say it can be changed on a class basis? If so, what's the class? If it's only fat, white-haired guys living in zip code 33065, you might be in trouble. You have a right to know how class is defined if it is to be the means by which premium is raised.

Look for cancellation clauses. How can the policy be terminated? Again, is it on a class basis? If so, what does the term "class" mean? All Floridians? All architects? All people age 35 that are bald? How this is defined is important. The looser the definition, the more vague, the more likely that you could receive a cancellation letter after your claims start to pile up. In other words, when you need the policy the most, it won't be there for you.

In the last chapter of this book, I've included a section on how to buy health insurance today, which consists of the right questions to ask so that you may avoid what has so often become commonplace among insurers today. Company stability, rating and cancellation practices, benefits and how they're determined are all important issues for you and this section addresses these to help make you a more informed health insurance buyer.

Cherry-picking. Post-claims underwriting. Sick-sorting. It's not an honor roll for insurers, to be sure. As an industry, we have done the unthinkable. The implied promise when a consumer buys insurance is that it will be there when needed. Instead, the industry has woven a pattern of broken promises, while leaving the public, the media and government furious, potentially leaving itself out of any future health care changes.

There is a place for the industry in a new health care financing system. It must be earned. We need to return to the basic principles of insurance, to large risk pools, to sensible rating, to accepting all risks, to being there when the insured needs coverage the most. Americans need to accept that health insurance is just that: a safety net against a catastrophic event. Routine health care is not an insurable event. As someone who's healthy, we must expect that our premium is going to be the same as someone who's not, to help subsidize that individual. If we argue that health care is a right, we must all be prepared to help ensure that everyone has a safety net. To do so might mean paying for something we may use little or not at all so that someone else may be saved from an enormous bill that none of us could afford to pay alone. Divided we fail, and we must all work together to improve our financing of the precious resource of health care.

Critics of health insurance carriers also assert that the administration expenses spent on the financing of health care through insurance is way too high. A look at PROFILES, 1992, published by the National Underwriter, reveals a wide variety of administrative costs as diverse as the insurers themselves. They range anywhere from 8% to 45% and, on the average are closer to 30-35%.

What is the administrative charge in this system? Since the insurer is being paid to finance health coverage, this amount should represent the charge for handling the money. Insurers collect premiums and pay claims. The administration expense, or load, therefore, shouldn't be much different than what you would pay to finance a car or the rate you would pay on a credit card. Isn't that what a bank does? Charge you to handle the money?

Clearly, in that case, 35% is absurd. You wouldn't pay that in credit card interest. Why should you pay that to an insurer to install and operate your health care financing? You shouldn't. Companies should easily be able to hold the administrative charges down to 15-20% at the high end and strive to bring it back closer to 10%. Insurance is still a legitimate way to finance health care, but insurers must do a better job of controlling their own costs or the public will look for a better deal somewhere else. Isn't that what you do when you look for a car? Or take out a credit card? We are all willing to pay a reasonable amount for companies to handle the money. The operative word, though, is reasonable.

Many insurance agents have told me that they're upset by what they believe to be a media and public bias against them because they make a living from commissions earned from the sale of health insurance policies. Why won't the public listen, they cry. Why won't the media give us a fair shake?

I hear you. Agents have taken a few hits. However, let's say I was able to find a reporter or anyone who was willing to listen to the insurance agent's side of the story. What could this reporter be told? Should this reporter be told how agents stood by while some companies took advantage of their clients by designing policies that took premium from them when they were predictably healthy and dropped them when they got sick or raised the rates through the roof?

Should this reporter be told about the 40-45% company retentions for agent commission and company profit? Should this writer be told about the rewriting of client's coverage every two or three years resulting in new acquisition expenses and pre-existing conditions limitations?

Is this the picture that should be painted? Yet every one of those circumstances happened and it's not enough to say, "hey, we didn't know what was going on." Why didn't agents ever question a high commission, low premium product as to where the money would be for claims? Why didn't agents step up and try to stop this practice of sick-sorting through the issuance of new policy versions designed to retain and attract only the healthiest of risks? Why didn't they blow the whistle on low-ball "usual and customary" practices that left clients with a lot less in coverage than they thought they had when they paid their premium in good faith?

What did agents do? They kept fighting for the status quo, to retain the health insurance system that failed people time after time after time, leaving them in the worst of all situations: ill or hurt, and stuck with the bill. What kind of press do agents deserve for that?

Shouldn't we agents have expected to earn commissions paid by playing the vital role of a financial advisor dispensing advice about a subject to which our clients have a limited amount of knowledge? Isn't this knowledge what our clients relied on? Where were we?

It's not enough to say it's not my fault, I don't sell health insurance. Your client buys it, though. If not from you, they seek it out from someone else. This act of omission makes all agents as guilty as those who knew what practices were going on, took the client's money anyway and held their noses, hoping for the best. Like it or not, the best of us ignored the worst of us, caring not about our clients, but about the status quo.

So now we complain that the agent may well be left out of any future health care delivery system. Agents have no one to blame but themselves, protecting the status quo in an environment where people were being placed in untenable situations. What right have we earned to be at the health care discussions table?

This really comes home to roost when you look at the acknowledgments in the beginning of the publication detailing Florida Governor Lawton Chiles' plan for health care reform. Throughout two pages of organizations listed and thanked for their help and support, insurance agent and company organizations are nowhere to be found. Why? Quite simply, they don't bring anything new to the table. Agents dominate discussion for their own purpose and pick apart the weaknesses of other proposals. Agents propose nothing new themselves, simply variations on a theme of building on a system they say insures 87% of the population.

The agent associations are most often composed of people interested in improving the well-being of our clients. But, even though it was known what was going on with cherry-picking and sick-sorting, if someone did raise it at an industry luncheon or convention, they were quickly dismissed. Agent associations didn't want to rock the boat and upset some insurance carriers who engaged in these reprehensible practices but whom also provided members to the association. Status quo was safe. Don't change anything. Instead, it was safer to go after targets where the bullets wouldn't ricochet back.

Agents do have a legitimate place in the health insurance world. There are many, many good insurance agents out there who, in every respect, do the best possible job for their clients. This group needs to unite and get rid of the circle of agents that are motivated only by commissions.

They need to get behind a position that makes sense. They should be the standard-bearers for people like the previously mentioned restaurant waitress who can't afford to buy coverage on her dependent child while her own manager, who makes three times as much, has his coverage paid for by the company and subsidized by the government. They need to propose solutions, not stand in the way of them. Even if the solution results in commission reductions, our only goal should be to insure everyone on a fair and equitable basis. Now is the time for change. Now is the time for insurance agents to lead that change.

Insurance companies and agents are necessary parts of the health care financing system. Companies can pool effectively if they standardize policies and rates and encourage all buyers to apply. Agents have an insight through their experience that can sort out the important fine print for the consumer and help them to rely on legitimate plans at legitimate prices.

The insurance industry is made up of, by and large, middle class, old fashioned, family values types of people. Throughout the last two decades, we have let down the people who need insurance the most: the middle class. The poor have programs or can, at least, secure indigent care. The wealthy can pay for health care if they need it. Insurance is uniquely a middle class problem, and by letting them down, agents have, in effect, let down themselves. Divided, we fail.

CHAPTER FOUR

MEDICARE AND THE ELDERLY

When Medicare was introduced to Congress in 1965, it was done so with an aim to help protect the assets of elderly Americans and remove one of the primary reasons for the poverty lived in by 1 of 3 senior citizens over age 65. Health care costs were a tremendous burden on our older generation and the retirement years for many were far from the blissful conditions everyone believed it would be. A Great Society, President Lyndon Johnson argued, does not forget its elderly.

At its inception, the Medicare program made several promises, chief among them the declaration that the government plan would never come between a physician and patient. The doctor/patient relationship would be preserved, we were told. The elderly would not be told which providers they had to see. The practitioners would not be told how to treat a patient.

Broken promises are a tradition for government and the Medicare program was no exception. Medicare assignment now definitely dictates choice of providers. The Diagnostic-Related Groupings (DRGs) and the new Resource Based Relative Value Schedule (RBRVS) which control hospital and medical treatment and costs has certainly influenced how providers handle their patients.

Moreover, as discussed earlier, Medicare has been a prime player in the deterioration of the financing of health care for all Americans. The initial reimbursements to hospitals and physicians in the program's initial years were an incredible windfall for medical providers. For most, this compensation was far removed from pre-Medicare days. Provider income went up as did provider expectations. All elderly benefited, even those that could pay for their medical services. Government bureaucracy kept pouring billions into the health care system. Everyone was happy.

When we go to a restaurant and enjoy food and beverage, it's usually a pleasant experience, until the waiter brings the check. But, like it or not, we settle up and pay for the wonderful time we had. That bill has long since come in for Medicare, only the diners that have eaten have left the table.

The costs have emerged in a number of ways. Government spending on Medicare has increased over the years, but the subsidy of its Part B premium has not decreased; it's actually gone the other way. Originally, participants in Medicare paid 50% of the plan cost; now, it's down to 25%. Insurance companies saw provider reimbursement expectations lifted by the government system and struggled to re-price policies and design new fee-for-service plans. Elderly poverty went from 35% of those over age 65 to 12.2% of today's 31 million seniors. That's a lower percentage than any group of Americans. While senior citizen life-styles improved as a group, the rest of the country has been slipped the bill, a check that has become harder and harder to pay.

The roll call:

- Private insurance was forced to absorb higher provider charges as hospitals and physicians shifted costs of treating Medicare (and Medicaid) patients to traditional insurance plans to make up for a shortfall as government reduced what it would pay them. Insurers in turn charged higher premium rates in anticipation of this cost-shifting.

- Employers who offered and paid for all or a portion of employee health insurance costs faced skyrocketing premium increases, which they moved either forward into higher prices for their goods and services, backward to employees in the form of lower or no wage increases and more responsibility for their own medical premiums. Hiring freezes were often precipitated by high benefit costs.

- Consumers found themselves paying more for items they purchased, while their income was subject to very little growth, causing a decline in purchasing power. Those who were in poor health found it difficult to find employment, especially with a small business, due to the problem of obtaining health insurance coverage.

- In 1990, federal state and local spending on Americans over age 65 amounted to $11,000 per person; for those under 18, $4,200 each, a reverse of the percentage allocation thirty years earlier when talk of Medicare was in its infancy. Seniors now command nearly 60% of federal social spending, mainly through Medicare and Social Security.

Medicare has accomplished its goal of reducing the number of elderly below the Federal poverty level. In doing so, however, they have created a safety net that some are using as a comfortable hammock while still others employ it as a trampoline. There are many elderly in this country that need neither Social Security or Medicare. Try and take it away from them.

In 1988, Congress passed the Medicare Catastrophic Act which improved benefits in areas senior citizens claimed were significant gaps, primarily long term care. To fund this program, a surcharge on income based on the amount of federal taxes paid was imposed only on the beneficiaries of the plan; those 65 and over. The maximum surcharge to be paid was $800 which, it was estimated, would only affect about 20% of the elderly population. For all, it would generally eliminate the need for a Medicare Supplement policy which cost, at the time, at least $800 annually, on the average.

A tremendous furor ensued, as the 20% most affected convinced the other 80% of our senior citizens that the Medicare sky was falling. Insurance companies stayed out of the argument presumably because repeal would keep them in the business of providing Medicare Supplements. Members of Congress dreaded trips home as they encountered, face to face, the wrath of the elderly. It was not a pretty sight.

It worked, too. Dan Rostenkowski, Pete Stark and others who had worked on this bill reversed the portions pertaining to Medicare and the surcharge was dropped. No thought was given to the possibility that, if the result of the Medicare Catastrophic Act was to reduce or eliminate the need for a Medicare Supplement policy, those having to pay the surcharge would have come out even at the highest taxed levels and ahead at all other incomes. Not only did the 80% unaffected by the tax lose the ability to re-evaluate their Supplement policy, so did the ones that had coalesced to lobby against this "unfair" tax. It was high noon for stupidity, fear and greed, and stupidity, fear and greed carried the day.

The elderly juggernaut is astounding. 31 million Americans and virtually all of them vote. Mess with Medicare or Social Security and you're destined to be a short-timer in the District of Columbia. Mention that Medicare and Social Security is almost entirely funded by those under age 65 who currently see no benefit from it and you're depicted as a brash youngster bullying grandma and grandpa. When you talk about the over age 65 population being the least represented in poverty and the highest represented in wealth, you're seen as an enemy of the state. The elderly want to be known as poor, signaling the need for entitlements, yet the facts aren't there to support that claim.

The elderly own 33% of all household assets and 40% of all financial assets. Yet programs designed specifically for the poor have ended up benefiting the richest segment of our society. Today, 40% of Medicaid benefits are paid to the elderly.

Medicaid is a program aimed initially at poor women and children, but has become a new playground for the elder care lawyers of the large metropolitan areas. If they reconfigure assets and income by transferring them out of a client's name, the client bypasses the usual spend-down requirements to qualify for long term care and other medical services under Medicaid. You no longer have to be poor to be eligible except "on paper". It has resulted in the abuse of a program funded through tax dollars paid for by working Americans. There's something wrong when 40% of those individuals, who reside in two of the wealthiest suburbs of Boston, Massachusetts, and who apply for Medicaid, are approved immediately due to a lack of income and assets.

Is this a reversible trend? Given the power of the wealthy senior voting bloc and its well-run organizations, it doesn't seem likely. Medicare was given to the elderly and the thought of reducing or eliminating benefits is nearly impossible. If you need any recent reference, recall the reaction early in 1993 when President Clinton floated the idea of minor Social Security Cost of Living cutbacks or an increase in the Medicare qualifying age. Newspapers were filled with quotable material about the poor senior citizens in this country and why should they be singled out for government reductions. The backlash was so initially heavy, Clinton withdrew the idea before even molding it into any kind of shape.

As costs continue to rise for these senior entitlement plans, the true losers seem to be the children. Three times as much per capita income is spent by government on the elderly versus children under 18. All elderly have health coverage while more than 12 million children slip in and out of the system or go completely uncovered. Operation Head Start has had to reduce its budget as Medicare and Social Security spending continue to increase, resulting in being able to reach only 25% of the 3 and 4 year olds who live below the poverty line. Between 1978 and 1987, spending on programs for the elderly rose 52% while spending on children dropped 4%.

Former Colorado Governor Richard Lamm argued, in 1991, that society has a higher obligation to our 9 year olds than it does to 90 year olds purely based on the remaining life expectancy of each. Medical costs to treat the elderly, he said, are clearly higher than for any other age group and any discussion about saving health care costs must start with rationing health services to the elderly. It's safe to say Mr. Lamm probably won't be invited to address any senior functions in the near future. Yet he has raised the question many have had on their minds. What exactly do we owe the elderly and should it be balanced with spending on other age groups to be distributed more equitably?

More to the point, should a waitress earning $10,000 a year have to sacrifice health care on her children while paying to provide medical care for a senior citizen who's earning more than that in a month from various investments? Should millionaires be on the end of a government hand-out? It's hard to sympathize with the person living in a $180,000 condo on the beach, playing golf daily, with $3,000,000 in various investment vehicles, who complains vehemently about the high cost of health care.

Yet the only social programs growing in the last couple of decades are those for senior citizens. We scream about "welfare queens" and there are many pictures on television that depict children in poverty, but they're not getting the federal loot. Overwhelmingly, wealth in this country is being transferred to senior citizens. They enjoy, as a group, the highest standard of living ever today; a standard that will likely be long gone by the time our youth reaches retirement age.

Not only do the elderly stand their ground on current benefit programs and fight every hint of cutback, but they believe what they have is not enough. Many elderly have campaigned for national health insurance because they believe government should also provide prescription drugs and long term care coverage, too. The AARP, a non-partisan, non-political organization, has recently authored their proposal for health care reform called Health Care America. It calls for universal access and tucked neatly inside the benefits structure is long term care and prescription drug coverage. For the funding of this proposal, among the suggestions are an 8% payroll tax and a 5% surtax on corporate income.

So this is where we are: the elderly are not pleased with the national health insurance plan they have now because it fails to include long term care and prescription drug coverage. It's hard to watch a senior citizen stand and argue the case for government-provided long term care and stipulate that the funding be done through payroll taxes, which wouldn't affect either him or a majority of senior citizens. They want long term care and they want someone else to pay for it.

There's more. Concealed within two lengthy House and Senate bills to provide long-term care for the elderly was a 20 line tax clause that called for cutting the estate tax exemption from $600,000 to $200,000, subjecting an additional $400,000 at a taxpayer's death to estate taxes ranging from 32 to 55%. The Wall Street Journal estimated that this would mean $67,000 in additional taxes for someone with a $400,000 estate and $138,000 for a $600,000 estate. The taxes would be inevitable; the need for long term care is not. Fortunately, the bills have not yet seen the light of Congressional day.

I don't object to a long term care program for the elderly. What I object to is that they don't want to pay for it. It's an "anybody but me" philosophy that is completely unjust. Why should the working poor be taxed to protect the assets of the wealthy elderly? If providing long term care coverage is an idea of merit, everyone should share in the cost of it. This continual abuse of power by the senior citizen voting bloc which penalizes the needy and rewards the greedy, must cease. Seniors tell us that it isn't fair to make people spend the money they've saved to pay for nursing care. They may be right. But is it fairer to force working low to middle income individuals to pay for it through additional payroll taxes? We already force them to pay for Medicare and Social Security. There may be nearly one million seniors who are millionaires. Why are we beating up on the working poor to provide millionaires with subsidized health care?

As a society, we should do everything in our power to ensure that every needy person is taken care of with dignity. But those that can pay for it should; not only for themselves but for those who can't afford it. We should be encouraging the working low to middle income earner to make more money to save for retirement and not rely totally on Social Security rather than further impoverish them, making it that much more difficult to get ahead.

Senior citizens today hold 44% of all U.S. passports. They purchase 34% of all overseas tour packages. They account for 70% of all cruise line passengers. And we pay for their health care. We pay for it at a time in this country when financial pressures will remain with people much longer than in the past. In the past decade, the number of first births to women over 30 have tripled. Parents of these children will be well into their fifties and still providing for their kids. At the time they'll be trying to save for their own retirement, when Social Security and Medicare may be long gone, they'll also be attempting to finance their children's college education.

There are Americans who truly need some assistance. Entitlement programs that assist high income retirees is not a prudent plan to provide support. The spiraling cost of these programs may actually jeopardize their presence for future generations. Is this what we want?

Medical costs for the elderly are dramatically higher than in any other age group. The Health Care Financing Administration reported that, in 1987, per capita consumption of personal health care was $5,431 for those age 65 + (12% of our total U.S. population) while just $1,274 for those under 65 (the other 88% of our country). The publicly funded portion of those dollars is even more skewed towards the seniors. Public expenditures represented $3,403 of the $5,431 per capita spending on the elderly, while accounting for only $356 of the $1,274 the under age 65 spend on health care, nearly ten times as much.

Like it or not, some tough questions, like those posed by former Colorado governor Richard Lamm, and others, must be asked. What do we owe an 85 year old who wants a liver transplant? Should we perform coronary bypass surgery for a 78 year old? When 20% of our nation's children haven't had a vaccination, should we be spending $35,000 in tax dollars to replace the hip of an 80 year old?

A tremendous amount of money is spent trying to keep people alive a few more weeks, months and years. Is this our society's goal? To beat death? Or is it in the name of a healthy society? Should this take priority over assisting our country's poor?

Why do Americans try so hard not to die? Death seems to be accepted with more calm in other countries, but here we demand all that medicine can give and later complain about how much doctors make. It's a uniquely American problem and one that must be addressed if we feel, as a society, that we spend too much on health care. 35 less bypass operations could provide neonatal care for 10,000 women living below the federal poverty level. Where should our priorities be placed? If we can't decide, or we say we should take care of both, health care costs will continue to rise. If we agree that this is the way we want to approach health care --everyone should get as much as they need -- than we should help absorb the cost of it. This idea of one segment of society shouldering the burden for another group that is capable of paying its own way is the ultimate hypocrisy. The needy should be helped; the greedy should not.

If national health insurance is the way society wants to move; if Ron Pollack of Families USA continues to be quoted as saying the high costs of medical care should be brought under control; if AARP wants universal access, long term care and prescription drug coverage and wants someone else to pay for it or have it paid by reducing overall costs; we will be a country, like the others in the world, placed in a position of having to ration medical treatment. The victims of medical cutbacks in every other society are the elderly. They spend the most, making them the largest targets. In Britain, limited kidney dialysis after age 55. In Canada, no bypass operation for several weeks if it is to be done at all.

What the senior organizations don't seem to realize is that they have argued themselves into an indefensible position. They may achieve prescription drugs and long term care, but lose major surgery and physician choice for its members. Is this their strategic move? Every society that has nationalized health care has had to trim costs to meet budget, and this conservation has come at the expense of the highest users of health care services.

Today, many seniors aren't aware of a pilot Medicare program, being tried in several states, that utilizes HMO medicine instead of the standard Parts A and B deductibles and coinsurances. There are first dollar benefits, small co-payments and prescription drug coverage, substantially reducing the elderly's out of pocket expenditures for health care. It's called Medicare Select and, after surviving a rocky start as the kinks were being ironed out, has achieved remarkable popularity here in Florida, one of the test sites for the program. I have heard some seniors complain about the lack of physician choice (they must use a provider within their HMO's network), but aren't they often confronted with the same issue when trying to see a physician who does not accept Medicare assignment? Besides, if it results in more savings, isn't the trade-off worth it?

I have little sympathy for the senior citizen who wants all the medical care one can possibly have, with little out of pocket cost, and complete physician choice, while someone else, who may not be able to afford it, is picking up most of the tab. Somehow the elderly have lost their ability to compromise. Health care is a finite resource and must be treated as such. Otherwise, the seniors stand to lose much more than an ability to choose their physicians.

We need to rethink our attitudes towards our older population. Many millions more will be joining their ranks (myself included) in the near future, so it makes sense to address future strategy for us today. We now provide every incentive to retire and considerable discouragement from working longer. The following is a list of federal legislation that encourages productive working people to sit on the sidelines and rust:

Date	**Legislation**
1935	Social Security Act is passed.
1940 - 1980	Legislation broadens coverage to include more workers. Percent of workers covered grows by 56% in 1940 to 74% in 1960 to 87% in 1980.

1950 - 1980	Social Security benefits are liberalized. The average benefit for a retired male (as a % of median male earnings) grows from 14% in 1950 to 28.5% in 1960 to 37.5% in 1980.
1956	Women can elect early retirement at age 62.
1956	Social Security benefits are available for the permanently disabled, ages 50 to 64.
1958	Benefits are extended to the dependents of the permanently disabled.
1961	Men can elect early retirement at age 62.
1965	Medicare, Medicaid and Supplemental Security Income (SSI) programs are established.
1972	Elderly who do not qualify for Social Security may buy into Medicare.
1975	Automatic cost-of-living indexing for Social Security benefits begins.
1983	Social Security benefits are subject to income taxes. The tax increases if wages increase.

Source: National Center for Policy Analysis, Dallas, Texas.

The government has encouraged people to retire by giving them early financial incentives (many do so at age 62 since it's not worth the wait for 100% benefits at age 65) and by paying for a substantial portion of their medical care, arguably the highest expense a senior citizen would face. In addition, we provide disincentives in the form of taxes on both benefits received and wages earned, enough of a deterrent to prevent healthy workers from continuing to be a productive member of the work force.

Where did the original goal of helping out the needy elderly go astray in these social programs? In 1980, the government per capita health care spending on the elderly as a percentage of the money spent on the nonelderly was an incredible 790%, vs. 419% on Britain, 361% in Canada and Japan, 345% in Italy, 270% in Germany and 176% in France. We encourage retirement, then pay for health care for the age 65 and older crowd, while a 25 year old, barely making ends meet, struggles to pay health insurance premiums or goes without health care coverage at all.

Is America truly the land of opportunity? For an answer, ask any senior citizen between the ages of 62 and 69. The ones that want to or need to work find themselves giving most of what they earn back to the government through special taxes that apply only to them. It's called a retirement earnings test and allows seniors to earn only a certain amount that varies between age groups 62-64 and 65-69 before reducing any Social Security benefits they are collecting by $1 for every $2 earned by the 62-64 age bracket, and by $1 for every $3 earned by the 65-69 group. It's a ceiling that discourages full-time work. Many older Americans have reluctantly cut back their working hours since it makes no financial sense to be employed.

This is misplaced taxation. Instead of asking wealthier older Americans to assist with the high cost of health care for their age group, we instead tell them that if they work and are financially successful, they will pay more in taxes than any other age group. We've taken some of the wisest people in our society and essentially told them to get lost. Productive, working people generally live longer and see less physicians. We clearly have this backwards.

Projections about the future of Social Security and Medicare are not optimistic. Medicare funds for Part A have been analyzed for solvency and given 5-8 years, depending on the study, before the money runs out. Social Security continues to run a surplus, but lends these dollars to the government to offset other spending programs in return for IOUs. As our population ages, the strain on Medicare along with the necessity, but not the probability, of collecting on those IOUs, means, under our present methods, significantly higher FICA payroll taxes. Is there any wonder the youth of America doubt the viability of the system to which they pay in money they don't believe they'll see? Given the government track record to date on social programs, the percentage of doubters in this country is on the rise.

There's more. The Financial Accounting Standards Board (FASB) has published standards for corporation's post-retirement benefits other than pensions, requiring them to reserve money for future retiree health benefit liabilities. This requirement of prefunding, which affected companies with fiscal years beginning after December 15, 1992, have forced companies to scramble to try to keep this number as low as possible. Managed care, wellness incentives, higher deductibles for employees, more premium responsibility for employees; all of these concepts are being tried to help pay for this retiree reserve.

Of course, we know how business pays for expenditures like this. The strategies above are backward movements. There is also every reason to expect that this cost will be moved forward into higher prices and upwards in terms of lower dividends to shareholders. In any event, it's still another example of someone else paying the tab for retiree health care.

We should encourage our older generations to delay retirement, especially since their ranks will swell as baby boomers start to reach retirement age. Let the seniors contribute. Don't take away their Social Security benefits, but, instead, tax them after their initial basis has been recovered. Wages earned should never reduce Social Security benefits and should be subject only to the usual federal, state, local and FICA taxes, depending on where you work. There shouldn't be any free rides, but we also need to remove the penalties that discourage our senior citizens from contributing. There are many people in this country that can and want to be productive into their 70's and 80's and we should provide every incentive to make that a reality. On the other hand, if someone wants to bow out of the work force at age 62, so be it.

The EqualCare USA system I'm proposing, when combined with the concept of taxing Social Security benefits beyond basis, will ensure that the needy do not impoverish themselves and prevent the greedy from gaining at the expense of someone else. Essential, necessary medical care for all Americans should be available and paid for by those that can afford it.

We can no longer tolerate situations such as the withdrawal by Sun City, Arizona, a wealthy retirement community, from a school district of 6,000 farm workers, with the expressed intent of moving to lower property taxes, by avoiding the debit for schools. Many vocal seniors in this country argue that they should no longer have to pay for public school systems since their children no longer use them. These same people argue for higher FICA taxes for Medicare, paid for by people not receiving any benefit from it. This vocal group dominates other quieter senior citizens who do assist others, old and young in a number of volunteer efforts.

Entitlements should be re-examined to be sure they are acting as the social safety net they were established to be at their outset. The retirement age for 100% Social Security benefits, being raised gradually to age 67, might be better placed at age 70 which more closely fits a healthier American life-style today. We can slow the growth of Social Security benefits and limit cost-of-living increases; moves that would generate billions of dollars in the system that can help stretch it without further taxation and make it more likely that younger people paying into the system will see some benefit from it.

It's time to step up to the line, senior citizens, and operate these programs on a sensible basis. Divided, we fail.

CHAPTER FIVE

GOVERNMENT BUREAUCRACY

Today, the conventional wisdom of media, politicians and academics is that a government bureaucracy can run things better than private enterprise. This has been demonstrated in the Administration's health care reform proposal. Trial balloons gauging public reaction to ideas such as mandates, global budgeting, and a basic benefits approach surfaced early in 1993.

The bureaucracy has decided they want to take health care over, playing a major role in its delivery. If government is to be involved, Americans should have the right to voice what we believe their role to be. I believe that government can be of assistance in a new health care system, but performing only those duties of which they are most capable. Their track record in running any type of social program or enterprise has not been favorable to date.

How about education as an example? Spending per public school child today is nearing $6000 a year. If a classroom averages 35 students, this would calculate out to $210,000 available for that class. According to the National Education Association, Connecticut has the highest average classroom salary in the U.S. at $48,850. If, say, $50,000 goes toward a teacher's compensation, that leaves $160,000 to operate the classroom. To run the classroom for the year for these 35 children with supplies, equipment and maintenance probably can be done for another $60,000. This leaves $100,000. Where did this money go? We've already paid the teacher, given the children books and supplies and access to technology. Where is that lost $100,000?

It's paying for bureaucracy, the people above the teacher. For every teacher, there's 3, 4 or more people who must also be paid in the name of administering the public education system. Government is filled with people who push paper around daily, trying to keep track of the laws that are passed. These bureaucrats don't teach a class, nor deliver a letter, or keep our borders safe, or stop cocaine from being smuggled into this country, or clean up the federal park.

No, these administration officials are part of a government growth that is reaching new highs in spending each year. This bureaucracy has become an integral part of the way our government functions today. They pass a law; if it proves ineffective or someone finds a loophole to bypass this particular legislation, they pass another law. Someone figures out a way around that law, so new rules are established, and the cycle starts again. Trying to administer this unwieldy maze of rules has grown government to an extraordinary size.

Government spends nearly $5 billion a day, running an annual deficit of $400 billion currently. Total government spending (federal, state, local) was 34.2% of our Gross Domestic Product (GDP) in 1992. This does not count the cost of federal regulation itself and federal regulation by litigation, which is estimated to be an additional 9% of GDP. Individuals pointing at the percentage of GDP that is health care spending should take a closer look at these numbers.

Bureaucracy rules and the cost is enormous. In the government, for every person on the front line, it is not uncommon to have 10 or 11 bureaucrats.

The purpose of bureaucracy is to monitor and regulate the production of others, not to produce anything themselves. Bureaucracies exist only to enforce the rules and are unattached to any result. They don't give you anything they don't take from you first. Just as in Russia, East Germany and other countries around the world who overthrew their bureaucracies, now is the time to overcome our own bureaucrats. The feudal serfs overthrew their masters because they had to give three months of production to them. Today, we give up 4-5 months of production to our bureaucrats. The civil servants have become the civil masters.

The following paragraphs are from a story that appeared in the March 22, 1993 edition of Medical Economics. Written by Frank J. Venuti, M.D., and reprinted here with permission, the article outlines the hazard of too much government involvement in private enterprise.

IF MEDICARE RAN BASEBALL

The scene: the television broadcast booth of a small but major-league ballpark in 1998. Three years earlier, the U.S. government, buoyed by its reforms of the medical profession, began regulating baseball to "assure the availability of quality sports at an affordable price for all Americans".

"Welcome to Pocatello, Idaho, baseball fans. I'm Jack Dinger of GFN, the Government Fairness Network, doing the play-by-play. And my broadcast partner today is Pete Fungo of the United States Baseball Administration, who's here to see that the game's played according to the rules, and to explain them when necessary. Brrr... It's plenty cold here, isn't it, Pete!"

"Sure is, Jack. They've only got two seasons here -winter and July."

"If these guys ever make it to the World Series, they'll have to snowplow the field between innings. They oughta play hockey up here, not baseball."

"Idahoans have as much right to see big-league ball as anyone else, Jack. That's why your government mandated a major league team in any city with a population of more than 50,000. Wait until we play the Eskimos in Anchorage next week."

"And that's another thing, Pete. These team nicknames are ridiculous. I mean, really, the Pocatello Palefaces?"

" I think it's a great idea. After the Cleveland Indians and Atlanta Braves won their lawsuits and were allowed to keep names that offended some Native Americans, it was only fair that some of the expansion teams be given names equally offensive to Caucasians."

"And now at the top of the 6th, the Palefaces and the Honolulu Haoles are all tied up, and we're headed into extra innings. Pete, I still feel strange calling the seventh an 'extra inning'. I miss the old days when ballgames went a full nine."

" Well, Jack, the games were getting too long..."

"That's because your regulations slowed the game down so much.

"Perhaps, but look at the skill level now. Fans deserve the highest quality of play when they come to the park."

"If they don't fall asleep first ... Okay, Pete, we're ready to go. Jackson steps in for the Haoles. Ruiz is on the mound for the Palefaces. He's got the sign. Here's the pitch. Jackson swings -- it's a long fly ball. It's going, going ... outta here, a home run! Ruiz hung a curve ball, and Jackson took him downtown."

"Too bad it won't count, Jack."

"Huh?"

"He swung at the first pitch. The rules say that a hitter leading off a late inning in a close game has to display more patience. You need base runners, not the Long Ball."

"But he hit a home run, for goodness' sake!"

"He got lucky this time. But what if he grounded out or popped up on the pitch? This is the kind of poor quality play the USBA is trying to weed out. The rules are crystal clear on this. Jackson's home run doesn't count, and he's out."

"When did this rule go into effect? I've never heard of it."

"The Committee for Reform of Athleticism in Baseball voted it in two weeks ago. Don't you read your USBA bulletins, Jack?"

"No. Each one is bigger than a phone book. All right, fans, you heard it. There's one away, bases empty. Miller's at the plate. Ruiz lobs in the first pitch underhand. It's a strike. Ruiz knew Miller couldn't swing at it. Nice rules, Pete."

"Hmmmm, I'll have to bring this to the attention of CRAB. Perhaps they'll have to make four strikes an out to compensate."

"Here's the next pitch. It's wild and hits Miller on the foot. He'll take first base."

"And Ruiz will take a shower, Jack."

"No way, Pete. He's working on a two-hitter. The Palefaces' skipper won't pull him out because of one hit batter."

"Maybe not, but the USBA rep in the dugout will."

"New rule again?"

"You've got to keep up with these, Jack. The pitcher must leave the game if he hits any batter with an average over .275. It's to protect the better hitters from beanballs."

"That's crazy! That pitch wasn't meant to hit him. It was in the dirt."

"The rules are crystal clear on this."

"For crying out loud, Pete, the Palefaces lose their best hurler on a technicality?"

"It's O.K., they've got better pitchers in the bullpen."

"Are you kidding? Ruiz has the best earned-run average in the Southeast Division of the Northwest Pacific Conference."

"But he has a very high GSTR."

"GSTR?"

"Generic screen trigger rate, Jack. We've had our eye on him."

"That's the most ridiculous thing I've ever heard of! Oh, well. Let's see ... Thompson has replaced Ruiz on the mound. Miller's on first, and O'Hara's at the plate. Here's the pitch. Outside. Wait a minute. Miller is being sent to second by the first-base ump."

"He's been rightly awarded a base, Jack. That's USBA rules, and I'm here to be sure they're followed."

"What the heck's the rule now?"

"The first baseman wasn't holding him on the bag. He was playing back too deep."

"Of course he was, Pete. Miller runs like a cow with a full udder. They were playing for the double play. That's good baseball."

"I'm sorry, Jack, but the rules ..."

"I know, I know. The rules are crystal clear on this. As clear as mud."

"Well, the Palefaces can appeal the decision."

"How?"

"In writing, to the USBA."

"Right. And has the USBA ever reversed a decision on appeal?"

"Not yet."

"Miller's on second, first base is open, and there's one away. Looks like they'll intentionally walk O'Hara and pitch to Sanders. Yep, ball 4. O'Hara heads to first. Hold on -the dugout rep from the USBA and the Palefaces' manager are arguing about something."

"This will cost the Palefaces a run, Jack."

"What?"

"They failed to apply for a certificate-of-need to walk intentionally."

"You're making this up."

"Of course, I'm not. The fans come here to see their favorite sluggers get hits. They're being cheated if the opposing team can walk batters anytime it wants."

"Intentional walks are part of the game!"

"Not anymore."

"You ever play baseball, Pete?"

"Well, no ..."

"Then how the devil can you decide arbitrarily what good baseball is?"

"Just because I've never played ball doesn't mean I can't protect the interests of the fans. They paid good money to get in, and it's costing them more and more despite our work."

"Because of your work! Are you serious? There are USBA reps in the TV booths, in the dugouts, and at the scorer's table. How much do they pay you guys, anyway?"

"Now wait a minute, Jack ..."

"Fans, you oughta see this weasel. Bug eyes with Coke bottle glasses and 90 pounds soaking wet. I'm not surprised he's never played the game. A sacrifice would knock him over."

"Hey, Dinger, I'll have you removed from the booth."

"Why, you little squirt, I'm gonna ..."

(Sounds of a scuffle. Momentary silence.)

"Hello again. Pete Fungo of the USBA here. Jack Dinger has-er-slipped out, so I'll guide you through these extra innings. Thompson steps off the rubber and wipes his brow. He's been having a lot of trouble with his breaking ball this year, and he's walked more batters than he's struck out. However, his GSTR is great, and his MAC - maximum allowable compensation - is among the lowest in the league. He's one of our favorites at the USBA. Here's the pitch ..."

More and more administration needed to handle the mountains of paper generated by legislation have led us to a cost of running government that is approaching social welfare countries like Canada and France. The U.S. and Japan have consistently spent the least for government. The U.S and Japan also have the largest output per capita and the fastest economic growth of all other nations. The numbers are clear: less government, better economy.

Yet the U.S. continues to head in the wrong direction. More government slows growth, and always spells bad news for our economy.

Big government isn't the school teacher, or the postal carrier or the Coast Guard worker. It's the bureaucrats trying to administer the laws they pass to regulate the productive. Reduce this portion of government, and the money spent on that 35 child classroom discussed earlier would produce higher SAT scores. Teachers aren't allowed to teach any longer as bureaucrats constantly peer over their shoulder, controlling the curriculum.

Until you've actually seen the effect of these bureaucracies up close, it's not possible to understand the costs. I have had at least twenty schoolteachers tell me that their own children would not attend public schools. Whenever I have offered any one of them a chance to be on my radio show, they have all declined, afraid of retribution from the bureaucracy. I spoke briefly with one teacher at a Chamber of Commerce dinner and the next day her school administrators asked her what was discussed. Most of the government employees I know are enraged by and terrified of their bureaucracy. Does this explain the recent Post Office violence?

Bureaucracy seems incapable of slowing their spending. The cost to operate Congress and its staff was $343 million dollars in 1970. In 1992, the total bill had increased to $2.8 billion, a 705% increase in 20 years. The defense budget, often the target for budget cuts, rose a mere 311% by comparison. $488 million is spent in the Senate, nearly $5 million per Senator on an annual basis. $722 million is spent on the House of Representatives, more than $1.5 million per Congressional individual. Can it really cost this much to run the government? What are we getting for our money?

Today's newly elected Representative or Senator often arrives in Washington today with a desire to serve their country to the best of their abilities. Suddenly, this individual is being treated as the most important person in the world. How does the ordinary human cope with this reality?

In addition, these new arrivals realize quickly that less than 50 powerful people actually run Congress. They either go with the program or risk getting voted out, so, finally, they compromise with the existing power structure. To get re-elected, they must raise enormous amounts of money. By definition, then, they must collaborate with special interest groups who represent a significant amount of potential campaign contributions. They must meet with senior lobbies, union lobbies, consumer advocacy groups, each trying to tell their story, with a promise to deliver the votes of their membership. A Congressperson quickly learns who they owe their power to and that congresspeople are merely pawns in an elaborate game of chess, run by the entrenched power brokers; and, thus, we the people end up with the following kinds of legislation:

- In the early 1980's, our duly elected officials decided that they could no longer let investors enjoy long-standing tax breaks on real estate, since some were said to be abusing these favorable circumstances. Rather than discontinue the tax break on future transactions, the Tax Reform Act of 1986, severely curtailing these breaks, was made applicable to existing real estate. Since most of the existing deals depended on the prior tax law for their viability, many of the investors were forced to walk away from the property and give the keys back to the bank. If Congress had grandfathered existing real estate transactions, would we have saved $250 billion dollars, the cost of the S&L bailout? We the people will never know. Instead, our Congress, and the media, chose to report the S&L story as entrepreneurial dishonesty. A better argument might be that it was bureaucratic bungling.

- Remember the 10% luxury tax, aimed at the rich? Entire industries were either hampered or failed as a result. What was our return on investment in that legislation? How much money did we raise with the tax versus revenue lost because of business failures? Who paid for this? The bureaucrats? The rich? Or, we the people? Who did finally pay for this envy tax?

- The 1988 Medicare Catastrophic Act added prescription drug coverage and additional long term care benefits for senior citizens. A few of the wealthy elderly lobbied hard for repeal. Now, the same selfish, wealthy elderly are back, lobbying hard again for re-inclusion of these benefits. The only difference is, this time they want these benefits paid for by the working young. If Congress had left the original legislation alone, it's unlikely we'd be hearing much from senior citizens in this current health care debate.

- In 1990, we the people were told we should support the largest tax increase in history in exchange for cuts in federal spending. The taxes went into effect, the spending cuts never came, and this legislation put the brakes on the longest peace-time growth economy in the history of the world.

This Congressional legislative bungling must cause us concern about any type of bureaucratic control in health care. The bureaucrats have proven themselves incapable of reversing their spending trends. Government revenues have been accelerating for years, but spending continually outpaces it, unable to downsize. When a project isn't working, they can't disband it. When a project has run its course, it can't be eliminated. The more money raised, the more money that's spent. We, the American people, can't budget this way, but, apparently our bureaucrats can and do. When forty cents of every education dollar is being spent on administration, you clearly have a business that's mismanaged. Yet the Administration's 1993 budget, passed in a close vote by Congress, called for further increases to the administrative portion of education. Where will it end?

There has been much attention drawn to the rise in the percentage of GNP accounted for by health care spending, increasing from 6% in 1960 to it's current 13% level more than thirty years later. According to the U.S. Department of Health and Human Services, total government social spending (Social Security, Medicare, Food stamps, etc.) has risen from 6.73% in 1960 to 14.4% in 1990. Can the government really do a better job than private enterprise with our health care system?

How has our government done with Medicare? After its introduction in 1965, the government poured billions and billions into the system, helping to finance provider overhead costs and raise their fees and expectations. Pay for everything! Question nothing! That was the strategy. If more money was needed, simply raise taxes. Then, with as much foresight, Medicare reimbursements were dramatically reduced, first with Diagnostic Related Groupings for hospitals and then with a Resource Based Relative Value Scale for providers. Providers, reimbursed now at a rate below expenses, shifted the burden of the shortfall to private insurance. For every dollar in Medicare fees cut, up went private sector costs. Presto! Millions uninsured! Does this experience qualify the government to handle the entire $900 billion health care system?

Medicare is not government's only involvement in health care. Medicaid was originally designed to provide health care for the needy, but, through waivers and the ability to reconfigure one's assets to ensure qualification, program spending is straining state budgets across the country. If Medicaid spending continues to exceed projected costs, further financial difficulties will surface as 33% of our states have less than 1% of general fund revenue with which to pay higher than expected costs. The likely result: higher state taxes and more budget cuts. It's not unlike what's happening in Canada today as each province manages its own health care plan and are independently struggling with their bottom lines to meet costs.

The Civilian Health and Medical Program of the Uniformed Services (CHAMPUS) is a government program that has been experimenting with managed care. The results, to date, have been disappointing, according to analysts. Test programs in Hawaii and California yield figures that show the program not saving money and actually causing about a 10% increase in costs to provide managed care. In addition, claims processing was so chaotic during 1989-90 that many providers and facilities dropped out of this managed care plan due to lack of reimbursement.

Government has been slow to react to the managed care trend to reduce health care costs. Medicare has not yet gone nationwide with its Medicare Select HMO program yet. Medicaid has rejected managed care, too, claiming we should not force the poor to use only selected providers within the network. Meanwhile, decreasing benefit reimbursements continue to restrict provider choices for the poor, anyway.

It's interesting that the people who pay the taxes to support this program are being forced by our employers to embrace the managed care concepts our government bureaucrats refuse to ask the beneficiaries of the program to use.

Veteran's hospitals are also a government-run health care program. This is national health care. Reports of treatment neglect and unsanitary conditions have become common. Even now, most experts are in favor of eliminating V.A. facilities and opting for use of empty hospital beds for veteran treatment. In Orlando, with a low hospital bed occupancy rate, heated discussions continue to take place over where to locate a new V.A. facility. If you like the way the Veteran's Administration handles V.A. hospitals, you'll love national health care.

Medicare. Medicaid. CHAMPUS. V.A. This is the current government record on health care as we decide whether or not to turn the rest of the system over to them. The idea that government can do it better than private enterprise is clearly misguided. To date, what the bureaucrats have done best is to escape accountability. If they didn't have private practice medicine to scapegoat, who would they blame?

Even Thomas Jefferson understood this. He once said that a democracy cannot exist if government cunningly robs the people of their control under the ruse of correcting a problem an individual cannot. Further, he noted, government's responsibility is to inform our discretions so that we can make enlightened decisions, not take away our control by saying we aren't capable, but government is.

There are many concerns if government took the helm at the head of a new health care system. One that immediately comes to mind is the idea of the separation of church and state. What would government-run health care mean to the Holy Cross Hospital, or the St. Joseph's Hospital, or Mt. Sinai or Baptist Hospital? Would we be allowed to have chapels in these facilities? Would we be permitted to pray in any government medical building? Or in a hospital that receives government funds?

Would priests, ministers and rabbis be allowed in the halls of these government-run hospitals? Would a physician be able to pray before starting an operation? Would a dying patient be able to receive last rites? Would a patient in pain be allowed to ask God for comfort? The answers to all of these questions is an unequivocal "no", if we accept the doctrine of separation of church and state.

When government took control of public education, we never dreamed these would become essential issues. But these questions were answered when government opposed school prayer. Now, these ideas have to be considered as we debate the health care issue. Will these hospitals continue to function as usual? Or will these questions be raised again?

Where government is involved, rules abound. What about parental consent laws? If a girl, age 12, needs surgery, does the hospital have to notify her parents or risk civil rights violations?

Global budgeting is seen as a panacea for cost control by the current administration. But this concept directly conflicts with the principles of a free market economy and will introduce rationing on a grand scale to America. Remember the gas price controls? How well did those work?

There will be a limit on what you can pay for any item, which will eliminate all of the higher-cost, high technology we've used to provide the best health care in the world. Even if you wanted to pay more, you couldn't. Some treatments would simply be off limits. Sorry, can't pay for that heart bypass for a 75 year old, it costs $35,000. No kidney dialysis for you 68 year old; we can't afford the $25,000 for this treatment. Forget that $60,000 liver transplant or the $40,000 bone marrow treatment since it will take us over the global budget.

That would make these types of treatment illegal. Does that mean they won't be done? What happened when abortion was illegal? Did that stop abortions? No. People found a way to have them, and they'll find some way to obtain the medical treatment they need, too. The demand for service doesn't go away simply because you placed a financial ceiling on it. What it creates is a black market for the treatments. Global budgeting may push the best of our providers offshore, or make criminals of the ones that remain here. Perhaps our best providers will set up facilities in Nassau, Bahamas, or Juarez, Mexico, or Windsor, Ontario. If you need a bypass and can't get it here, it's off to the Carribean, Mexico or Canada. What's the cost of a plane ticket when you're fighting for your life? Many foreigners come here today for treatment they cannot receive in their homeland under their national health insurance program. Is this what we want for Americans?

It's time to re-evaluate how we work with bureaucrats on this type of social program. We have the opportunity, with a new health care system to create a partnership that utilizes the strengths of both government and private enterprise. Let each do what they do best.

Private enterprise cannot guarantee that young, healthy people will participate in the system, but government can. This is critical to the program's success as there must be non-claimants as well as claimants to effectively spread risk. By creating a public health plan, government provides the compulsory requirement that all Americans be in it. Secondly, government is best at collecting revenue. This they can also do with a new health care system. What will be different is that the money will be distributed to private enterprise for health care services. No government bureaucrats. No layers and layers of massive regulation. Only pre-negotiated administrative costs and entrepreneurial efficiency.

Compulsion and collection, two areas of government excellence can be put to work for us. More involvement than that will doom the entire venture. Government should work for us, not the other way around. This is an opportunity to use the strengths government has to construct a social program that will work.

The front-line Federal employees, I believe, will be supportive of this plan. They don't like the bureaucrats, either. The hard working government employees work for us and are, in effect, riding in a cart that we pull as taxpayers. They, too, would like to see the people pulling the cart have the same access to health care that those riding in the cart enjoy. This will be possible through a social program combining the unique qualities of government and private enterprise. If it works in health care, we can move on to education and other necessary social programs which have the potential to function far more effectively than they currently do.

Managed properly, these social programs can serve the needs of the American people and properly compensate those doing the actual work. Health care is our golden opportunity if we stand together and tell government how we want it to run. Divided, we fail.

CHAPTER SIX

THE PROVIDERS

Today, when you are a candidate for surgery and you ask how much the operation is, you are asked a question in return. The provider says,'' what kind of coverage do you have?'' The patient replies, ''private insurance, Medicare, PPO, Medicaid, or, perhaps, no coverage at all''. Knowing that, the provider tells you the price.

That's like going in to MacDonald's and saying, ''I'd like two Big Macs and a large drink, how much is it?'' and the cashier saying, ''how much do you have?''. You say, ''$11.00'' and they tell you the two Big Macs and large drink will cost $10.50. Would you buy food that way? Would you buy anything that way? Yet this is, generally, the health care system we have; one where how much you pay is based on how much you have.

This is clearly a bad system, but it is the end-result of the history of third party payments which we've discussed earlier in sections about Medicare and insurance companies. Medicare's introduction and the billions of dollars that were thrown into providers' hands changed expectations for them. What they were getting from Medicare was more than what private insurance had been paying, so fees increased to the latter and private insurance paid. Medicare finally tightened up 15-20 years after its introduction, so providers, rather than reduce expectations, charged insurers or cash-paying patients more. HMOs changed fee structures again and insurers started to put together networks of providers to render discounted services for their insureds.

Thus, today's system is overrun with different reimbursements depending on what type of coverage the patient possesses. Hence the question, ''what have you got?'' before telling you the price.

I'd like to propose that we limit our discussion of the providers into these categories: physicians, hospitals and pharmaceutical companies. They all contribute to improving our health while creating and reacting to an entirely different set of circumstances which challenge them each day on the front lines of medicine.

The Doctor As Scapegoat

Currently absorbing much of the wrath being unleashed on the health care industry today, the physician continues to function as the key person in dictating medicine. They are, as a group, dedicated, hard working, and, in many cases, an idealistic gathering of people who can mean the difference every day between life and death. This is not meant to be overdramatic. When you are on the table for bypass surgery, and that physician has your heart in his or her hands, that person is closer to you than anyone has been or ever will be. This individual literally holds your life in his or her hands.

We complain constantly about physician fees, but would we trade places with them? Would we want to be the person who sees thirty-five patients a day and whose beeper goes off at 4:00 A.M. because there's a bleeder in the emergency room? On call Saturday, Sundays, holidays, listening to our aches and pains, having to be alert on three hours sleep because of an emergency operation; is this the job we would like?

Instead, we gripe about their Mercedes, or their vacation in Rio that we insist we paid for, or their five bedroom house overlooking a lake. These criticisms have reached a crescendo of late because we are less insulated to the costs of medicine now than before the third party payment system went out of whack. Private insurers have absorbed the bulk of higher fees in reaction to Medicare cutbacks and passed these costs on to the employer through increased insurance premiums. The employer, struggling with the bottom line has raised policy deductibles, increased the coinsurance responsibility of the employee, and even passed some of the premium accountability through payroll deduction. Finally, the price of medicine is there for all to see.

As consumers, we don't know how to turn off the tap ourselves. If one of our family members is ill, we want all the best tests to be run, do anything possible, whatever it takes, and not worry about the bill. Now that we have to pay more of the bill, we're upset when it does come in.

The physician must react when the patient arrives. The individual has had the opportunity of leading a lifestyle that might have avoided the current symptoms being experienced. The physician can't worry about that any longer. Working with the ever-present threat of malpractice, that doctor orders all of the tests appropriate for the condition, looking for a way to reverse the tide of ill-health. Fees are not likely to be on the doctor's mind at this juncture; the possibility of a lawsuit, however, might be reflected in the actions taken.

The physician is an easy scapegoat in the public response to health care today. One can conveniently blame the high cost of medicine on them. That we choose to vent our frustration on a surgeon who works 80 hours a week to earn $500,000 per year rather than on a baseball player who makes $7,000,000 for a seven month season is due to the notion that we have a health care crisis, not a baseball one.

For physicians, medicine is not likely what they thought it was going to be when they were studying all night for exams, working double shifts in the emergency room as an intern, barely making ends meet as a resident, only to enter private practice with a medical school debt of nearly $100,000 and a malpractice premium of $50,000, $75,000 or higher staring at them before they open their doors. Idealism suddenly gives way to financial reality and can permanently alter the outlook for a few. Despite this, they forge ahead, playing a role in our society that we can't do without, and which we have now taken for granted.

Like it or not, these are the medicine front-liners. Whatever changes we make to our health care system will have to be carried out by the physicians. Ultimately, they are the standard-bearers for medicine, ones in whom we place our trust and, often, our lives. Yet the media and consumer associations have labeled them as a special interest group whose motives are suspect and barred them from all but the most superficial role in the discussions of health care's future. When it comes to health care, though, isn't everyone part of some special interest group? Don't we all have something to lose or gain from the health care discussion? Don't we all have rights, and, if so, aren't doctors part of the "all"?

The physician's main concern has been the integrity of the doctor-patient relationship, a concept that has been eroded in recent time as lawyers, hospitals, the government, insurance companies and unions often stand between the two. Current cost-containment procedures are no more than someone standing and peering over the physician's shoulder as treatment is prescribed. Fees are questioned, cut and even deleted as third party roles have grown. This is not the way health care was intended to be delivered.

Dr. William E. Goodman of Toronto, Canada, in a speech given in June of 1992, quotes Swiss medical philosopher, Dr. Ernest Trufer, saying, "The real danger of collectivist state medicine is that the patient becomes a tool in the hands of the holders of power and is dispossessed of the protection afforded by Hippocratic principles. This amounts to a rejection of the Hippocratic medical ethic which is to care for the patient according to the latter's specific medical requirements, in favor of the veterinary ethic which consists of caring for the sick animal not in accordance with its specific medical needs, but according to the requirements and dictates of its master and owner, the person responsible for any costs incurred.'' If we allow someone else to pay the bill, have we now given someone else the right to dictate our health care?

The physician seems less and less in control of the patient's destiny and is concerned with new health care changes which might further dismantle the practice of medicine. The general public, however, assisted by the media and consumer groups, continues to express outrage at the incomes the doctors earn. The magazine, MONEY, called for M.D.'s to undergo a ''radical cashectomy''. But, when you're the patient, do you really want cheap health care? As one physician put it, '' a heart attack today does not merely mean a bit of watchful waiting, but rather a stay in the coronary care unit, cardiac catherization, myocardial imaging, and often, coronary artery bypass grafting.''

Before we begin hanging doctors in effigy, we should know that physician fees represent only 22% of the health care tab, half of that going to overhead, including malpractice premiums and administrative personnel to handle required cost containment procedures and third party claim forms. If we cut all physicians' incomes by half today, we would save only a little more than 5% of the overall $900 billion we spend on health care.

Is fee for service the problem? Should doctors be salaried? This would run contrary to all we know about the free enterprise system. Many salaried workers today function on the basis that they will do as little as possible to still receive their salary. Is that what we want for physicians? To do as little as they can? If they're going to be paid a flat salary, they will likely arrange to keep their patient load to a minimum. Where's the incentive to see 35 patients in a day when you can see 10 and receive the same income?

Doctors are free-market professionals and should operate that way. If you rein in what they can earn, you take the incentive out of the career. Today, the more patients they see, the higher their income. They can control what they earn. Any system that tried to change an incentive based job to a salaried one, has failed. What happened to insurance companies that put their agents on fixed salaries? What happened to cab companies that put their drivers on salary? Some occupations in this country aren't suited to salary renumeration and physicians are in that category. Providers cannot and should not compete on the basis of price. They should compete on the basis of outcomes, services and efficiency.

When doctors have to raise fees, we notice, and we're unhappy. But do we want them to select less ethical choices? We force doctors to lose money treating Medicare, Medicaid, and indigent people, and then we complain because they raise fees? Some doctors, rather than raising fees, look to practices such as unbundling, upcoding and joint ventures to help cover the rising cost of practicing medicine today.

Physicians are commonly reimbursed through a coding system contained in a Current Procedure Terminology (CPT) handbook. There is a usual and customary fee assigned to each code. By manipulating the codes, physicians can receive a higher fee reimbursement per procedure performed.

Unbundling is taking a one-code procedure and breaking it down into several codes, the sum of which generates a higher reimbursement than using the single code. This is more common with surgical services. For example, the code for a hysterectomy can be unbundled into separate procedure codes like abdomen exploration, ovary/tube removal and scar tissue removal to effect a higher payment.

Upcoding is a simple upgrade of the procedure performed. A limited office visit which is reported as an intermediate visit generates $10-15 more renumeration. Removal of a mole coded as three centimeters in diameter is paid at nearly $200 more than a two-centimeter removal. A lumpectomy billed as a partial mastectomy doubles the fee received. It has become a very common practice for some to work the codebook in one's favor.

Joint ventures are physician investments in diagnostic and treatment centers to which they refer patients. Accusations of over-charging and over-utilization are common. Studies (and by now you are hopefully all tuned in to statistics released that are exactly right and absolutely wrong) show that tests done on a self-referral basis are performed more often and cost more then if the doctor had referred to a non-interested party. Regulators, both state and federal, have called for a halt to doctors referring to clinics or centers in which they have an interest.

To me, this is more of the same whining about how much physicians make. Why else would there be complaint? So who should own the labs and clinics and make the money instead? A group of investors? A group of malpractice attorneys? The local AARP chapter? You tell me. If the physician discloses that he or she has a financial interest in the center, what's the beef? You can go somewhere else or even change your physician if you don't like it. As to over-charging and over-utilization, at no time in history do third party payers scrutinize the medical bills like they do today. If there is over-utilization or higher charges resulting in any unnecessary tests, they won't pay for it. Limiting doctor investments in clinical labs, physical therapy centers, diagnostic imaging centers and radiation centers will more likely reduce the frequency of preventive tests, raise the costs of all tests, reduce the availability of these tests to inner cities and the poor and force physicians to raise their own fees to make up for this lost income source. Doctors will still make more money and it is the consumer who will pay for it. Why is this so hard for some to understand?

The physician today must also cope with a malpractice system that punishes the wrong physicians in the form of skyrocketing liability insurance premiums. If we had to pay the bill the doctor does to protect against a lawsuit in the event of a bad result, we wouldn't stand for it. Not only do we fail to empathize with the physician, we're upset about what he or she does to increase income to pay for it.

Today, we sue if something goes wrong, regardless of circumstances. We become involved with a tangled legal framework designed to pay the attorney no matter what the end result. If the court determines a mistake wasn't made, little or no settlement is given the injured party, while thousands of dollars are spent on legal costs. If it's an honest mistake, the insurance company pays and malpractice rates go up. If it's a criminal act, the same settlement is made and the physician often continues to practice.

So what's happened? If a person loses the use of one's legs as a result of a medical procedure, the settlement can range from -0- to multi-millions in monetary retribution. Does either result change the bottom line for the individual, that of loss of use of legs? Why should one person receive nothing at all for that result while someone else is awarded $5,000,000 in damages, and, in both cases, attorneys are well compensated and a bad physician continues to operate?

No health care changes can effectively be made until malpractice changes are enacted. Good physicians are forced to put patients through an extraordinary amount of testing to cover themselves at a cost estimated to be running at several billion dollars annually. What other choice do they have? A bad result means a lawsuit so everything possible is done to avoid potential repercussions following a bad result. No physician ever wants a bad result. They didn't choose to become a doctor to do a shoddy job. They know, more than anyone, how important it is that they do all of their homework. They also know how uncertain medical science still is, so the appearance that everything possible was done in the form of more comprehensive testing is inevitable, since those actions could mean a substantial monetary difference in settlement and, of course, their malpractice premium.

Again, consumer expectation runs high and there has been a subtle transfer of faith from what the physician can do to what new medical technology can perform. If that technology doesn't meet expectations, the search is on for someone to blame. So, doctors do tests they know aren't necessary under the guise that they have to live up to the highest standards of care, but then recoil for the impending backlash of lawsuits if it goes wrong and cries ofhigh fees if it goes right. The rate of professional liability claims, even in this litigious society, have declined in the last five years, yet premiums continue to increase.

One reason for this seeming anomaly is the high amounts awarded when judgements are made. Punitive damages have escalated the cost per settlement to the insurance company. Unlike compensatory damages, they are determined by the perceived need to punish the defendant, no matter who it is among physician, insurer or manufacturer, or all three. These awards often run well out of proportion to the real harm done to the patient. For example, a five year-old boy pokes his eardrum with a Q-tip and injures his inner ear. His family sues the manufacturer for marketing the product without providing safety-warnings or child-proof packaging. The plaintiffs get $21.5 million dollars, $20 million of it in punitive damages. An airline crash that kills 112 people leads an attorney, on behalf of 45 of the victims, to sue the company that built the plane, the company that built the engine, the company which supplied the engine builder with a part, and two other companies who refined the primary element contained in that part. As one observer put it, ''if the ground were incorporated, you can bet Mother Nature would also have been sued''. Where does it stop?

The present system does not equitably provide retribution to those hurt nor does it usually punish the proper individual. The real winners are the attorneys, numbering some 700,000 in this country today with another 135,000 of them on the way. Despite this apparent glut, many of them enjoy a more comfortable lifestyle than the average physician. Legal fees are increasingly rapidly, but no one calls for lawyers to be placed on salary. Can you imagine the outrage of the American Trial Lawyers Association if the wife of the President of the United States began conducting closed meetings of 511 physicians to discuss whether or not to continue the use of a contingency fee for lawyers? After all, we are the only civilized country in the world that does use it. These indirect legal costs contribute to the increase in health care prices, generating anger aimed in the wrong direction.

Third party cost-containment procedures have also saddled physicians with an administrative expense none of them envisioned while in medical school. Staff has been added simply to keep up with the varying requirements of contacting the third party payor before administering any treatment. It is a system trying to control medical costs from the outset; an arrangement that drives up costs without achieving a similar result in savings. It may achieve some avoidance of a test here or an operation there, but amounting to far fewer dollars not spent than in the increased salaries and office equipment necessary for compliance. Overall, however, there seems to be no evidence that this utilization review reduces the cost of care.

It often ends up being a vicious circle for the physician. An OB/GYN orders a Caesarean Section, widely regarded as a safe procedure, with very low complication and mortality rates, which, while costing far more than a normal child delivery, ensures a measure of relief from malpractice repercussions. However, insurance companies see no need for the high number of C-Sections being performed and are beginning to cut down on them, arguably exposing the doctor to a higher possibility of malpractice. The patient seems to be left out of these arguments.

While C-Sections are on the rise, so too are higher risk pregnancies of older patients, many of whom waited until later in life to have children. C-Sections are almost always performed on women that have previously had one, as well as in 27.1% of premature deliveries, 47.7% of cases of fetal distress, and 54.9% of multiple births, all cases where risks are running higher than the norm. But now a doctor must choose between patient risk, what insurance will pay and the threat of malpractice in reaching a decision. It truly is a system that subverts the doctor-patient relationship.

The EqualCare USA system proposes a new handling of malpractice damage awards based on equitable settlements and punishment of the real wrong-doers. It is a vital step towards returning the practice of medicine back to the providers.

Another contributing factor to increasing health care costs has been the over-specialization of medical providers. As I see it, we need to build a different kind of doctor today. Due to the complexity of medical practice coupled with a higher monetary reward accorded a specialty rather than a general practice, we have an overabundance of costly specialization concentrated in metropolitan areas, a scarcity of primary physicians and a limited number of physicians practicing in rural areas.

We shouldn't be surprised. The health care system pays much more for specialized care, higher fees in urban centers and no incentives to either work as a primary care physician or live in a less populated area. If you could live in New York City and be paid five or six times more per procedure with the likelihood of seeing five or six more times the number of people, why go and practice in a rural area where the demand and the payment schedule is far lower?

The attractiveness of a specialty is evident in the number of medical graduates choosing primary care; only 14.6% in 1992 versus 36.1% ten years earlier. This trend is such that some individuals believe that Americans will have to look to non-doctors for primary care in the future. Nurse practitioners and physician's assistants may well be the beneficiaries of the specialization glut. With supervision, these occupations can often perform a majority of general physician services at a much lower cost.

Several years ago, family practice was elevated to a board-certified practice and currently accounts for 12% of all medical practitioners with a similar number now in a residency status. This specialty has done well at placing physicians in rural areas, but is currently struggling to increase its share of residents as academia still tends to reward experts in narrower fields with research money. This must be changed to encourage medical students to pursue general practice.

A health care system that continues to reward specialties will widen the gap between the primary care physician and the specialist. The more specialists available to perform expensive medical procedures, the more that are performed. It's almost a self-fulfilling prophecy.

One of the ideas I propose is to change qualifications for those who would like the opportunity to attend medical school. To be accepted today, one needs both high grades and money. Yet there are many individuals who would make great physicians (and primary care ones) who never get the opportunity because they either aren't the best student or don't have the financial resources to attend medical school. The best physician isn't necessarily from a wealthy family nor the individual with the highest grades in school. We can certainly modify medical school acceptance standards to let in students with a low B average rather than a high A one if this person truly wants to attend. They may wash out or they may become the physician that finds the cure for cancer. Right now, we never find out. I'm not suggesting lowering state medical board standards, but simply giving a few more average students who want the opportunity the chance to enroll in medical school. Scholarship programs for students can be arranged in exchange for agreeing to a primary care practice and/or eventual location in an area that needs physicians. Without encouragement, some of our potentially best physicians never get the chance to become one.

There is much to be done to improve our current health care system.

Directing our anger at physicians solves nothing. Doctors should be more than willing to accept positions in primary care, rural area location and lower fee reimbursements if we could cure some of the headaches they face, such as malpractice fears, fluctuating third party payments, expensive and misdirected cost containment procedures and other obstacles which undermine the doctor-patient relationship.

High consumer expectation must also subside as we remember that physicians are only human. As one doctor recently said, "we were there when you were born and we will be with you when you die. Between those two events, we serve you to the best of our abilities." Doctors do not give life. Neither do they take it away. But, at some time in your life, one will be closer to you than anyone else on the planet. They deliver health care.

Hospitals and Cost-Shifting

If any further evidence is necessary that the financing of health care is where the real crisis is centered, look no further than some of the bizarre billing practices of hospitals for more proof. The meltdown in the third party payor system that began with the introduction of Medicare has expanded the practice of cost-shifting by hospitals. In most cases, it makes up for shortfalls in reimbursements. Here are some examples:

- The Idaho Hospital Association reports that, in 1989, privately insured patients paid Idaho hospitals an average of $2,041 more for services to cover losses from Medicare, Medicaid and charity care.

- The Colorado Hospital Association advised that each bill sent by hospitals in the second quarter of 1990 was increased $2,710 (36%) to cover uncollectible charges from Medicare, Medicaid, charity care, bad debt and discounts.

- At Christian Hospital in St. Louis, the average charge per patient is $7,400; 41% of that (approx. $3,000) was added to cover lost charges from fixed-price payers, including Medicare.

- The Prospective Payment Assessment Commission released a study in October of 1991 that showed, on average, Medicare paying hospitals only 91% of the amount it costs these facilities to care for Medicare patients, and Medicaid paying only 74% of actual costs. To make up for it, private payers paid 128% of costs, or $3.3 million per hospital.

The original goals of cost-shifting are noble and most often done out of necessity and compassion. It's about those that can afford to pay making up for those that can't. It has long been the way we paid for indigent care.

However, cost-shifting also opens up opportunities for abuse, and it occasionally results in profiteering that is both unethical and unacceptable. Therefore, all cost-shifting must be eliminated because of the few who damaged a system that enabled us to deliver charitable health care for years.

When lawmakers slash Medicare and Medicaid reimbursements, or when big business negotiates discounted fee for service plans for its employees, both believe they are containing health care costs. And they are -- for them. But it doesn't change the fact that the services are being performed and if the providers can't collect for them, they will try and take it from someone else. When government doesn't pay enough to cover the health care treatment of the elderly and the indigent, the rest of us end up paying twice: once through taxes for these legislative programs and a second time through cost-shifting. This amounts to a second tax for all of us; hidden, perhaps, but a tax nonetheless.

The practice of having to shift costs has simply widened the inequities in the health care system. Insurance companies, forced to shoulder higher than expected charges due to the inflated provider bills, raise insurance premiums, putting the financial squeeze on small business and middle class taxpayers. As more and more of them cannot afford the premium, they drop the coverage and add themselves to the uninsured rolls. This leaves fewer and fewer people to bear the extra burden, leading to a further deterioration of the third party payment system.

Since Medicare introduced the Diagnostic Related Groupings (DRG) system of payments in 1983, hospitals now function in a system of price controls. Essentially, the government allocates a hospital so much money for treating a patient for a specific condition; a victim of a stroke accorded more in reimbursement than an individual in need of a tonsillectomy. Fees per diagnosis are established, imposing a revenue cap on the care of each Medicare patient. If the hospital can treat the patient for less than what the government is paying, a profit is made; if not, it loses money. Yet another promise was broken when the government pledged to give hospitals equitable rate increases to account for inflation and new technology. As we all know, reimbursement rates have been chopped, not increased in recent years. Between 1989 and 1991, one California hospital lost $20 million on Medicare alone and an additional $6 million in Medicaid (called Medi-Cal in California).

To make up for it, this hospital has increased charges to non-government customers, charging commercial insurers $24 million dollars over and above actual costs, giving the hospital a profit two of the last three years. This $24 million was passed on to those of us who were privately insured.

Some major insurers have switched to DRG type reimbursements as well, rendering the actual charges a hospital incurs for a patient nearly inconsequential. In 1992, a South Florida family was forced to put their daughter into the hospital for an overnight stay. Total charges on their bill were $885, including $285 for the room and $304 for a bone scan. They were told the insurance company was being billed for the charges and they would be billed later for the 20% balance due following the insurance settlement. To their surprise, the hospital actually billed the insurer $2,003 for the stay, the amount allowed for their daughter's condition under the DRG schedule. (Remember, if the facility can do it cheaper than the DRG specifies, it gets to keep the difference.) The insurance company cut the bill back from an 80% reimbursement of the $2,003 to a 60% payment because the hospital failed to notify the company of the hospitalization under its cost-containment notification procedures. So, the insurer paid the hospital $1,201 instead. The hospital billed the family the 20% balance of the actual $885 charges, or $177. All things being equal, this is what would normally have been the case if the $885 amount actually mattered.

What kind of system virtually disregards the actual costs of the health care delivered? It readily becomes apparent that it's not a health care crisis that we have. It is not surprising that there are studies such as one done by a business-sponsored research group where 7,000 families were asked to rate the value of 50 different products and services, and hospital charges were rated as the worst buy. Health insurance was fifth, trailing hospital costs, lawyer's fees, credit card fees and premium pay T.V. Doctor and dentist fees were rated much closer to being an average buy.

The practice of cost-shifting can, and in some cases, is being used to mask profiteering. Any company, hospitals included, should be able to operate on a for-profit basis. When that profit moves from reasonable to unreasonable, I get angry and you should, too. When an aspirin costs $12.00, the actual cost (including labor) may be $1.00, with the need to overcharge insured patients another $5.00 to make up for government and big business shortfalls, for a total of $6.00. The other $6.00 in the bill may be used to pay for other overhead. It may be valid and needed, but how do we know? This type of discretionary pricing has become a problem for consumers trying to understand what part of the overcharging is necessary and that which is not.

Hospitals also endure bad publicity when studies are released showing them to run on a less than efficient basis. One example would be a 1992 review that said, on average, hospitals spend $53 on clerical and communications task and $25 on administration for every $100 spent directly on patient care. Better run hospitals spend $21 to $42 on clerical and communications costs and $8 to $15 on administration for every $100 spent directly on patient care. A 31% improvement in operating efficiency could save an average of $60 billion annually.

All of this leads to helping out our legal system. Patients sue hospitals because of bills that reflect $2.53 for a disposable razor and $4.61 for one pain-killer tablet. Hospitals, in turn, sue the government for higher Medicaid reimbursements. A settlement is reached here, a jury verdict there, and hospitals go on with cost-shifting and Medicaid continues to cut back reimbursements to avoid more red ink. The shift goes on.

Bed occupancy is down for hospitals nationwide and the cost for these unused beds must also be passed along through billing practices. DRGs, to a certain extent, have reduced bed capacity by only allowing so many days reimbursement per health condition. The goal of the hospital under the DRG system is to discharge a patient as soon as possible. This premature discharge can lead to a re-hospitalization, or a stay in a skilled nursing facility. My EqualCare USA proposal makes use of those unoccupied beds by adding "recuperative care" to the DRGs, thus avoiding premature release of patients and unnecessary nursing home stays.

Hospitals must also cope with the overuse of the emergency room by individuals who have no insurance, either by choice or by lack of the means to afford it. From 1985 to 1990, emergency room use was up nearly 20%. This has diluted the delivery and quality of health care as the ER physicians and nurses try to distinguish the true emergency from the person just wanting to see a doctor. Waiting times have climbed to an average of 3 1/2 hours and obviously some individuals who need attention faster than that slip through the cracks.

This jamming of the ER has resulted in a number of people leaving without ever seeing a doctor, a situation that alarms those that consider community hospitals to be the safety net for the medically indigent to obtain care. A General Accounting Office study revealed that 57% of ER patients in 1990 had a condition that was not urgent. Devising a system of patient evaluation in the ER setting when overcrowding is prevalent is nearly impossible to get right, but continues to generate more bad publicity for the providers as another study revealed that 11% of patients leaving one hospital's ER due to a lengthy wait were hospitalized within one week.

We're told that a Canadian style health care system will solve this problem. It won't. It will make it worse. In Canada, walk-in clinics have sprung up in response to the overwhelming demand for services. These clinics see patients after hours when private practice physician offices are closed. Canadians don't want to lose a day's pay at work to take off and see the private physician during regular business hours.

We must devise a system that encourages providers to be open in the evenings and on weekends. Even a higher fee reimbursement would probably be lower than ER costs. Primary care physicians must be available for ER work at all hours since people come to the ER to see a doctor. Like it or not, some Americans want their health care at 11:00 P.M. or on a Sunday afternoon, and we should be prepared to handle this demand.

Hospitals must also deal with malpractice rates, further adding to the costs of delivering health care. Professional liability insurance, for example, for Jacksonville, Florida's largest hospital, Baptist Medical Center, increased in cost from $300,000 in 1983 to $3,000,000 in 1987. This boost was given, despite the fact that no appreciable lawsuits or settlements as a result of professional liability were brought against the hospital. But the malpractice threat will always hang over the medical profession until the system for awarding damages to injured parties is overhauled. Higher malpractice premiums result in more cost-shifting, yet one can still read an article entitled, "Attorneys call cost-shifting a national disgrace". Talk about having it both ways. Malpractice rates remain high as attorneys sue for damages on behalf of a patient; then, when higher overhead is passed along in the form of $4 painkillers, they sue again on behalf of another patient. What a system!

Finally, something needs to be done (and will be done with EqualCare USA) about the way hospitals bill. A hospital bill is not all-inclusive for the stay. It does include specific hospital charges (or overcharges), but a week later you receive a bill from the surgeon. Two weeks later you receive a bill from the anesthesiologist. This is like going to a restaurant and receiving separate bills for salt, pepper, and steak sauce, condiments you expect to be included in the bill. As bills keep trickling in separately, it makes it more difficult to determine the actual cost of a hospital stay.

Hospital reimbursements and billings must be improved to make the health care system function properly. The varying amounts of reimbursement must be levelized, making it simpler for all to understand and saving billions in administration costs devoted to separate billings. Moreover, the hospital bill must become all-inclusive, so that the payor remits one amount to the hospital and the hospital is left to distribute it to its various providers. The surgeon, the anesthesiologist, the ER physician, all of whom are attached in some way to the hospital overhead, must cut their deals with the hospital, not separately with the payor. Simplicity must be the new status quo or our health care financing woes will continue.

The Drug Companies

Another current, easy health care target for government and media marksmen is our pharmaceutical industry. They are called "price-gougers", "obscene profiteers" and "rip-off artists". Pointing to the cost of a child vaccination, the politicians lay the blame for millions of children not receiving the immunizations they need squarely at the feet of the pharmaceutical companies. The American people, alarmed at these "sound bites", rally around in crying for reform of the pharmaceutical industry.

But where is the story about the millions of dollars spent annually giving free medication to the indigent? Where is the story about drug therapy that keeps patients off expensive operating tables or out of nursing homes, resulting in a substantial overall savings in health care? Where is the story about prescription drug prices rising more slowly than any other health expenditure? Where is the news story about an industry that is universally acclaimed as the most competitive and technologically advanced in the world and remains a leader in both exports and innovation?

Instead, some want to torpedo one of our economic star performers. We do the Research & Development for the rest of the world. Who do we want to do it instead? Canada? Japan? Germany? What's wrong with America doing it? If a cure for cancer or AIDS is found, it will be because these American research giants will have funded it. Drug companies will invest more than $13 billion dollars in 1993 to discover and develop new medicines, an amount more than the entire government budget for health research. This $13 billion is all earmarked for R&D, not marketing.

The reason people are now more aware of prescription drug costs is that not every health plan covers drugs and individuals must pay the cost out of their own pocket. The elderly constantly lobby for more free health care in the form of prescription drug coverage because Medicare won't pay for it. Individuals who change from PCS (Pharmaceutical Card System) coverage under an insured or HMO plan, to one not offering this feature, suddenly must pay $20 for the prescription they paid between -0- and $5 for in the past.

Pharmaceuticals aren't cheap when viewing price alone. It currently costs about $231 million dollars to research and develop a new drug. Only one in every 5,000 compounds mixed in a lab ever becomes a marketable drug, according to the Pharmaceutical Manufacturers Association. Yet out of this research comes an impressive array of new medicines designed to save lives and, ultimately, health care dollars.

Substantial money is also being spent on lawsuits, with much of the cost passed along in the price of the drug. Tort reform could save all of us money on prescriptions, too.

We can't afford to think short-term with health care. Drugs developed and in development are estimated to reduce leukemia mortality by 20%; to reduce lung cancer cases by 1,000,000/year: to reduce colorectal cancer cases by 300,000 per year; all generating a savings by the year 2015 of $425 billion. A 1991 drug that saves your life may cost more than the 1980 equivalent that left you dead, but, according to the director of economic research at the Hudson Institute in Indianapolis, Indiana, this is qualitative progress that costs money to achieve, not pure inflationary pricing.

The rest of the world recognizes the advancements American manufacturers have made in developing drugs to cure world-wide illness. U.S. manufacturers account for over 40% of the major pharmaceuticals marketed throughout the world. Even so, drug companies must contend with price and profit controls in European communities which limited pharmaceutical price increases to less than half the general inflation rate over the last 20 years. A strong U.S. dollar does not help the cause, either. Widespread piracy of product and process patents also affects the industry and little progress has been made in dealing with the largest country offenders. Still, the industry forges ahead, continuing to do the R&D for the rest of the world. In 1992, the pharmaceutical industry spent nearly $11 billion in R&D, some 16% of its revenues. Contrast that 16% with other industries like computers (8%), electronics (5.5%) and all manufacturing (2.9%).

The drug industry is criticized for the amount of money it spends on marketing, but how else to make physicians and other providers aware of new drugs, their value and potential side effects? All other industries are allowed to advertise; why not pharmaceuticals? In addition, major publicity campaigns have been devoted to patient compliance in the use of prescription drugs.

A 1991 study revealed that 7% of patients fail to have their prescriptions filled; 15% fail to take it for the prescribed time; 32% fail to obtain necessary refills; 50% of all prescriptions dispensed are taken incorrectly and 10% of hospital admissions are due to this non-compliance. When the failure to follow recommended prescription usage results in higher overall medical costs, the drug industry reacts accordingly, since the drugs will only do what they are supposed to do if compliance is generally followed.

As for adding to the health care bill, the Organization for Economic

Cooperation and Development, compared pharmaceutical expenditures as a percentage of total health care expenditures for several countries. The U.S. ranked below Britain, Canada, Japan, France and Germany in this percentage as well as per capita expenditure.

This may not necessarily be good news. There are many drugs which can be used in place of more expensive medical procedures. If we're using the procedure and not the drug, we're saving drug costs and boosting the overall amount of money spent in our health care system. More education needs to be done of consumers and providers as to the value of drug therapy in place of other forms of treatment. When that knowledge hurdle is cleared, we will spend health care money more effectively and efficiently and continue to look to pharmaceutical manufacturers to come up with the cures to our largest medical woes.

Conclusion

We all owe a great debt to our health care providers. We are the healthiest nation in the world. In a country with a failed education system, a failed police system, a failed welfare system, health care is getting a bad rap. Providers have created an industry of which we can all be proud; one that will soon be our first trillion dollar business. If we don't engage ourselves in the health care industry, which one will we select for our future? Why not health care? Why shouldn't we continue to build on our progress to date?

Instead of cutting back in health care, we should be expanding beyond our borders, exporting our medical expertise to everyone. If mankind has any hope at all in the world, America will provide it.

The providers of American health care have earned the right to treat patients without the interference of either business or government. We must preserve the doctor-patient relationship by changing the way we pay for health care and through tort reform. The health care industry should have banded together over the last few years to fight the bad press they received. Divided, we fail.

CHAPTER SEVEN

HEALTH CARE FRAUD

The previous chapters in this book have been largely devoted to discussing the breakdown in the financing of health care in this country. The present third party payment system, where a wheelchair seat cushion can be reimbursed by Medicare at $248.96 in Pennsylvania, but only $41.93 in Tennessee, is full of fraud possibilities. Fraud is a hazard in any type of business, but the opportunities presented in health care with the wide disparity in fee reimbursement make it a special target for those who want to cheat the system.

Why is this important? It's the final link in a chain of failure for the financing of health care. It adds between $50 and $80 billion dollars to the overall health care tab, a significant number for those that believe we already spend too much as it is. Even if what we're spending is right, the savings that could be generated by cutting the fraud number in half could be used in ways to improve such things as the child vaccination rate or neonatal coverage for women.

Health care fraud has become such an art that investigators have developed their own vocabulary to describe some of the practices that occur. Among them are:

- Pingponging: Medicaid patients see General Practitioners, who then refer them to several specialists to generate fees for everyone.

- Pill mills: A term for pharmacies that knowingly enter into schemes to illegally fill prescriptions.

- Non-con men: Individuals, often drug addicts, usually on welfare, who obtain prescriptions for non-controlled substances such as heart medications or antihistamines. Once they obtain the "non-con" substance, they sell it to a middleman or a pharmacist who then resells it to the pharmacy.

- Unbundling: Described in the chapter on providers, this practice involves doctors who do a single procedure, but then bill Medicare or a private insurance company for several procedures.

- Upcoding: Physicians bill Medicare or an insurance company for a one-hour visit that actually took 15 minutes, with the one-hour visit naturally being paid at a higher rate. Podiatrists, for example, may bill for toe surgery when all they did was clip toenails, generating a substantially higher fee.

- Family ganging: A billing practice where a doctor sees one family member during an office visit, but advises the government or insurance company that several family members were seen, too. It is not uncommon for these M.D.'s who sees a mother to bill for seeing the children as well.

- Sink test: This is how labs run tests on blood or urine. They throw the samples down the sink without testing and bill the third party for payment anyway.

- Screening: An illegal enrollment procedure used by some HMOs to prevent high-risk patients from joining.

- Rolling labs: Vans, trucks and even horse trailers visit senior centers, malls or health clubs and attract patients by promising free lab tests ranging from cholesterol checks to blood pressure readings to more complex heart and lung measurements. The tests might be free to the patient, but Medicare, Medicaid and private insurance companies are billed for them.

Many of these schemes go on for months and even years before they are discovered. Today, the Health Insurance Association of America believes health care fraud to be distributed as follows:

- 43% for services not rendered
- 33% for fraudulent diagnosis
- 14% for deductible waiver
- 10% for other frauds including employment falsification and brand/generic drug substitution.

Fraudulent diagnosis: How many times have we, knowingly or not, participated in this practice with our physician? Many physicians today report a diagnosis for a routine physical to effect reimbursement to the patient since regular exams are not often covered by insurance. If you went in for a physical and left with a slip of paper that said "stomach cramps" on it to submit to your insurance carrier, you have participated in health care fraud. You might not think of it as such, but if the coverage you have does not reimburse for a routine physical exam, the policy is not priced to do so. Submitting a claim in these circumstances increases the number of actual (versus expected) claims for the policy, resulting in higher premiums at a later date.

Co-payment waiver is another way the average consumer co-operates in health care fraud. Here, the provider agrees to waive the insurance co-payment, commonly 20% under most traditional indemnity plans, advising that what the insurance company pays will be enough. That practitioner then bills the insurer for a higher fee than normal to cover the lack of co-payment from the patient. If the inflated fee is still within usual and customary charge limits, the money is often paid without question.

So what's the problem? The insurance company paid the usual and customary fee, right? It was higher than what normally should have been paid and this practice will continue and multiply as the patient is more likely to use that same provider in exchange for no "out of pocket" costs. If the patient had responsibility for 20% of the bill, there is a greater likelihood that individual would seek out a provider with lower fees. Lower fees means smaller insurance claims, less out of pocket costs for the patient, and a probability of more reasonable insurance rates. All of it is intermingled and to believe that something as small as a co-payment waiver has nothing to do with the overall cost of health care is naive at best. The more frequent this practice, the greater the effect on insurance premiums.

What's alarming about health care fraud is that it's mostly an insider game. Patients and providers alike are the biggest perpetrators of these criminal offenses. The better one understands the system, the easier it is to rip it off. As usual, everyone ends up paying for the few who try to make a few extra bucks off the government or the insurance industry. Many claim forms contain the following statement:

" Any person who knowingly, and with intent to defraud any insurance company or other person, files a statement or claim containing any materially false information, or conceals for the purpose of misleading, information concerning any fact material thereto, commits a fraudulent insurance act, which is a crime."

Despite the warnings, health care fraud is everywhere. In Illinois, a diet clinic operator was found guilty on fraud charges for operating a diet clinic which billed Medicare for bogus tests. In addition, this individual was selling a manual for $50,000 that was a blueprint for ripping off Medicare.

In Georgia, a physician was rebating as much as $100 to patients for an office visit and billing insurance companies for extra office visits and other charges amounting to more than $3 million. In another case, a minister who was also a doctor visited members of his church at home and then, unknown to them, billed the visits as psychotherapy to their insurance companies.

Health care fraud can leave an individual with a medical record that may torment one for years. Let's say you have been solicited to come down to your local shopping mall this Saturday to get a free blood pressure and cholesterol screening. You go, have the tests, hear the results and leave, believing you are in good health. What if the lab owner turns around and bills your insurance company (reading what you wrote on the innocent-looking questionnaire you completed when you showed up to obtain the screenings) for reimbursement by claiming you came for the tests reporting angina and shortness of breath. The company pays the claim for several tests (even though you only had a couple done), all related to those which would normally be administered for these symptoms. The company then reports your symptoms to the Medical Information Bureau, which stores the data for future reference. The next time you apply for insurance coverage, you are asked about a past history of angina and shortness of breath. You think the company is crazy, but they won't issue any coverage until it is clarified, so you might have to take a battery of tests to disprove it, at your expense.

Think it doesn't happen? Ask a Californian, an active athlete, who spent two years trying to remove diagnoses of obstructive pulmonary emphysema and heart defects from his medical record.

Another common area of fraud in health care is the billing for medical equipment to Medicare. The government estimates that it is likely being bilked for more than $200 million annually in payments to marketers of overpriced and unnecessary equipment for senior citizens.

In this scheme, boiler room operators call Medicare beneficiaries to ask them how they're feeling and if they've had any physical complaints. It doesn't take long to ascertain that type of information from some people and the problems told to these "telemarketers" was noted and assessed for equipment needs. Seniors were assured they would receive the equipment at no cost to them (under Medicare, they are supposed to pay 20% for durable medical equipment). These operators circumvented the necessary doctor's signature to obtain the equipment in a variety of ways. In addition to outright forgery, they obtained stamped signatures (not an uncommon practice for a busy doctor) or real signatures signed by a physician in a hurry, often without reading it. The equipment was purchased as inexpensively as possible and shipped off to the patient, with a bill for the highest possible Medicare reimbursement sent to the government. For example, a bed-size chunk of foam that cost $28 was billed to Medicare as a "dry flotation mattress" at a reimbursement due for $900. Another high profit item is called a transcutaneous electronic nerve stimulator (referred to as a TENS unit) which is legitimately therapeutic for some patients. You can buy the components of it for $50 at a Radio Shack store, but Medicare is more likely to be billed $500 for it.

Another example of inflated billings can be found in the home health care industry. This is very difficult to trace because home visits to infirm elderly may be billed for a variety of reasons other than or in addition to the service the nurse or aide performs. Verification of the services by the patient is often impossible. So, longer visits can be billed, visits that never occurred, services that were never administered, and so forth, and Medicare pays off in reimbursements like a slot machine.

Psychiatric fraud is a cornucopia for those that would misuse the health care dollar. Common practices here include inflated billings such as $1,100 per person for three hours of group therapy, charging for services never rendered, or billing for group therapy when a woman was actually on her lunch hour. Worse, this area of medicine commits fraud using children by having them admitted to psychiatric hospitals for unnecessary treatment and keeping them there generally against their will until the time or dollar limit in their policy runs out.

Trying to combat fraud has only been moderately successful to date. The government has been forced to reduce their budget allocated for fraud detection and enforcement. Only a few of the larger insurance companies have fraud units. Many companies do not allocate much time to check the validity of the claim at all, focusing instead on trying to get it paid to either or both the provider and insured as soon as possible.

The best detectors of fraud are us. We know whether a bill is correct or not and can alert the company if inconsistencies exist. An insurer will always send out an explanation of benefits form and if something doesn't look right about it, we should contact the company immediately. It's not much fun to review hospital charges especially after a stay of several days creates a bill pages and pages long. But one can often spot services that weren't rendered, medications not taken, or charges that seem unusually high (the $12 aspirin).

We can instruct our doctors not to put a diagnosis down for treatment if the visit was only for a check-up. Remember, false diagnoses can come to haunt you later as you try to explain away medical conditions you don't have.

Medicare eligibles should be particularly careful about various common activities. Beware of free tests! Some other ways you can avoid being an unwilling part of a fraud scheme are these:

- Do not pay your $100 yearly Part B deductible in advance regardless of what anyone, providers included, tell you.

- Be wary of anyone who offers you a free gift or some other form of renumeration in exchange for conducting free tests on you. Medicare has no provisions for free tests nor are any approved providers permitted to give them.

- Always check specifically with your own doctor concerning any medical equipment someone believes you should have. If they're promising no 20% co-payment, it's guaranteed to be a scheme.
- Doublecheck your Medicare statements against those of your doctor to prevent any overinflated billings for services you never had.

Fraud is prevalent throughout the current health care system whether its the woman who falsely claimed herself as a dependent under her friend's medical insurance or another person who claimed to be an employee of an alarms system company in order to collect health insurance benefits or a provider who charges the insurance company for several office visits on a patient when that patient was known to be travelling out of the country. It's a system where cheating is easy and the practice of it adds billions to the overall health care bill we must pay.

It is one more reason why the current third party payment system no longer works. A different method of financing health care is in order, and EqualCare USA attempts to make changes for the better; changes that will remove many of the fraudulent opportunities that exist today. No system is completely fraud-proof, but with the empowerment of the consumer as end-user, the best prospect to stop fraud in the system has been recruited. Divided, we will fail.

CHAPTER EIGHT

CANADA AND OTHER NATIONAL HEALTH INSURANCE MODELS

So far, we have identified the various parts of our current health care system that have contributed to the situation we face today; a puzzle that signals changes to be made to ensure the continuation of the finest health care program in the world. There are several solutions that are under consideration now to solve these problems and correct the course in which we are headed.

They won't work. While all of them have some merit, the drawbacks inherent in each doom it to overall failure. As you now know, not everything is broken. Attempts to correct failings that also negatively impact the positive aspects of our system will ultimately be considered unacceptable by the American people. What looks good on paper may not possess the practical reality to work in real life. One part of the system is entangled with another and a decision made for one section invariably will affect some other area, making the right solution a difficult challenge.

The next two chapters review the current proposals to fix health care, beginning with an analysis of national health programs in Canada and elsewhere and continuing with a look at ''employer-mandated pay or play'' and ''managed competition'' models which have been presented as panaceas for us. While each have some strong points we should consider, they do not offer the right mix of ingredients, in my opinion, to take our health care system to its next level.

The Canadian System

For some time now we have been hearing from both the political and media arenas about the success of the Canadian national health care system and how it should serve as a model for us in our efforts to solve our own health care problems. ''Look to the north!'' they proclaim. ''Everyone's covered equally. The system has been around for years and it really works.

Canadians love their system. They have better infant mortality and life expectancy numbers. They spend one third less than we do on health care. They know how to control costs.''

Exaggerations, of course. But Americans have not been as easily fooled as these pundits had hoped. Regardless of the poll you review, despite the way in which the question is carefully worded, it is rare when more than a third of those polled believe a single-payor, government-run, national health insurance program is the best direction for this country. Despite the almost constant barrage of positive information about this type of system, two-thirds of the country wants to hear about something else.

Without knowing anything about the Canadian plan, common business sense would tell you that this is not likely to be the plan on which we should base our health care future. Canada has about 30 million residents, the U.S. over 250 million. In preparing a business plan, a CEO would not likely consider copying the plan of a company eight times smaller than his or her own. Logistics, circumstances, market share, personnel, they're all different. You would be more apt to review the plan of a company more similar in both economics and demographics.

When you do review the nationalized health care systems of the world, you discover that Canada is the second most expensive per capita (behind us). If we were to select a plan to imitate, why pick the second most expensive plan in the world? Why not look at Portugal or Greece or Turkey, some of the cheaper ones? If size isn't a factor (and I contend that it is), why go to the second costliest plan anywhere? Surely we can find a program more cost-effective than that.

Proponents of the Canada plan have said that ``special interests'' like the insurance or medical community, have used scare tactics to dissuade people away from a Canadian solution. They are accused of taking isolated articles about problems in the Canadian system and inflating them into tabloid style headlines to make their point.

The primary contact Americans have with Canada is either through our own media or with Canadian citizens who visit or vacation here. Those Canadians, by definition, are better off than the average Canadian, since they can afford to come here for often substantial periods of time. These are people who have prospered under their system and not likely to complain much about anything, including health care. Our media rarely carries a negative article about the Canadian health care system. Thus the picture Americans have of the Canadian system is extremely distorted.

Honestly, you don't have to search long and hard in Canadian media (although rarely published here) to find discord about the Canadian system. Everything you might expect to be wrong with a government-run "free" health care plan has emerged in Canada. Every week, feature stories discuss the deteriorating position their health care system is in. I will give you several examples of what Canadians actually think about their own system. As you read their thoughts, remember this about Canadians: they are a people very proud of their country, individuals who want to believe more than anything that the way they do business is better than the way we do it down here. For them to criticize their own health insurance program is very difficult. I know. I used to live in Canada. As a Canadian, it's accepted that the two things you do not criticize is health care and hockey. While it may be American to criticize America, it's not Canadian to criticize Canada.

It is not easy for a Canadian to write an article such as that which appeared in the February, 1993 edition of Canadian Business magazine. It runs contrary to what we are normally told about Canada through the press and our own personal contact with Canadian citizens:

"When was the last time you felt good about Canada's economic future? When was the last time you believed that Canada had a truly splendid economic future -- a better future, for example, than the United States?"

This is the country after which we will pattern our new health care plan for America? Is this the model to which we aspire? Should we rethink this?

Canadian provinces are struggling to maintain positive fiscal balance sheets, worsened by having to manage the government-mandated health care plan. One of the common misrepresentations we hear from our own press and politicians is that the Canadian plan is one national health insurance program. It's not. It's ten separate plans. Each province administers a different set of benefits for its inhabitants. Some are currently worse off than others, but none of these provinces has been able to check health care spending. They are now coping with a new cap on what their Federal government will spend on health care, causing a downward pressure on their own financing of it for their residents. Here are some of their most recent health care records:

- British Columbia: Charges a monthly premium to residents for its health care plan on top of the federal taxes already taken; the provincial government has suggested euthanasia to hold down medical costs.

- Alberta: Cash-strapped Calgary hospitals are looking for alternative sources of income; many towns do not have long term care services and force residents to be shipped to Edmonton, often separating elderly couples towards the end of their lives.

- Ontario: Covering fewer items and using generic drugs are two actions the provincial government will take to lower the skyrocketing costs of the Ontario Drug Benefit plan; woman wins battle for bone marrow transplant that the hospital said they were declining to give her as it would mean running a deficit.

- Quebec: Caps on Quebec's out-of-country benefits will go into effect May 1, 1992, expecting to raise the cost of the out-of-country insurance travelers purchase to cover this medical necessity.

When we focus on the Canadian health care system, we must remember that each province controls its own benefits and budget where medical costs are concerned. Each one operates somewhat differently and has a different set of problems to handle. But it is not ONE plan.

We have been frequently told through our media that the Canadian health care system has been around for years. Not true! The current system, as it exists for both hospitals and doctors, has only been in existence since 1984-85. Here is a brief history:

Canada's federal government became involved with provincial health care in 1957, passing legislation that enabled the provinces to receive federal funding for around 50% of hospital costs. In 1966, more legislation was tacked on to include physician fees in the reimbursement. It wasn't until 1984, though, that the latest legislation was passed which banned unauthorized hospital user fees and eliminated extra billings by the doctors. Ontario physicians reacted to that by going on strike, but eventually gave in and the final piece of the Canadian system fell into place; a program which ostensibly provides free health care to all its citizens.

Although existing less than a decade in its present form, it has helped to create serious economic problems for its provinces, forcing them to re-evaluate coverages, out-of-province costs, expensive procedures and to even contemplate euthanasia as a way to hold down costs.

Costs. Very common rhetoric from the media and consumer groups, the political proponents of government-run health care, is that Canada spends one-third less than we do and has better infant mortality and life expectancy than the U.S. We already know that these vital statistics are social and not health-related. Since we started measuring costs, however, back in the 1960's, Canada has always been one-third lower than we are. They've never had and probably never will have the technology we do. Even the present low levels spent on research and development continue to decline. Crime, AIDS cases, car accidents, alcohol and drug problems are significantly fewer than here in America. Even if we adopted a Canadian-style system, Canada would still spend one-third less. So what's the point of this comparison?

Canadians have lower expectations and different attitudes than Americans do. If an American goes into a restaurant in a foreign country and the air-conditioning isn't working, he or she endures it and enjoys the meal. If that same person went into a restaurant in America and the air-conditioning was broke, that person would either complain or leave. We expect all the conveniences in this country and we're usually willing to pay for them. Given that attitude, we will always spend more than our northern neighbors for health care.

There are more accurate ways to measure costs. Since Canada has been spending one-third less than we have for a significant length of time, how do they compare with us since 1970, the time many believe health care costs started to multiply rapidly in the U.S.? According to the Spring, 1991 edition of Health Affairs, per-capita spending in Canada, between 1970 and 1989 grew at a rate (8.97 times) that is actually higher than the U.S. rate (8.12 times). Even though this Canadian spending rate is rarely mentioned in our media, it has not escaped the Canadian press.

Columnist Diane Francis of Canada's MacLean's magazine (their version of Time/Newsweek) said in 1990, "The patient is sick. Canada's gold-plated medical system is a serious financial drain." Later in 1990, that same magazine also advised, "Weighted down by budget deficits, Canadian governments can no longer afford the ever-rising costs of medicare. The result of tightened budgets is evident at Montreal's venerable Royal Victoria Hospital, where about a dozen rooms and laboratories have been closed for years because the hospital does not have the $1.5 million needed to fix a leaking roof. Said hospital president Phillip Aspinall 'The money just is not there'." Same magazine, later still in 1990: "The Ontario Hospital Association announced that 224 hospitals in the province are facing massive job cuts and bed closures because the provincial government cannot provide the $630 million needed to maintain the current level of services." In another article: " In what is seen as a disturbing trend, Manitoba's largest hospital has temporarily halted elective surgery to replace hips and knees after it went over budget." MacLean's, January 13, 1992: "In Canada, where the cost of medical care has risen by 20% during the past three years alone, deficit ridden (provincial) governments no longer can afford to pay the increased cost and have been forced to search for ways to run the system more cheaply."

Would you say there is a pattern in this reporting? Or is the Canadian media making it up? Why, after a clear picture that the Canadian system is coming apart at the seams as provincial governments can't afford to fund health care to its current extent any longer, do we have to read a Business Week article, published in March of 1992, that says, of Canada's system, "It's not perfect, but it works"? That's open to debate, especially after reading what Canadians have been saying in print for some time.

Instead, we read about per capita spending, even though you now know that both countries have paralleled each other in per capita spending for twenty-five years. In 1991, our per capita spending rate was listed as $2,868 while Canada's came in at $1,915 which, incidentally, is higher than several of our individual states. What does that number mean to the average individual? What percentage of our discretionary income is spent on health care versus a Canadian's?

In an article entitled "Want a Big Raise? Move to America", Canadian journalist Peter C. Newman quoted the results of a Price Waterhouse-Canada report about the difference in disposable incomes between the U.S. and Canada. What he found was disturbing to Canadians.

According to their calculations, a married taxpayer with two children earning $100,000 would pay taxes of $37,700 in Calgary and $38,300 in Toronto versus $16,400 in Chicago and $21,300 in Houston. Thus, after-tax disposable income in Ontario, in this example, is $61,700, as opposed to Houston, where it's $78,700. $1,915 per capita health spending is 3.1% of disposable income for the Canadian in Calgary. For the individual in Houston, Texas, it's 3.6%, not an appreciable difference and certainly not the one-third difference we're consistently told. In Calgary, the number is 3.07%; in Chicago, 3.4%.

The truth is Canadians pay a lot for their health care and are going to pay much more or end up with much less as provincial governments grapple with finances. They pay in higher taxes to support social safety nets like health care. Taxes are everywhere to see, including the morning newspaper that actually details what portion of the paper's cost is the newspaper's and what amount can be attributed to the federal government. According to a Canadian Tax Foundation study, the tax burden for Canadians increased by 25% between 1980 and 1991. By 1991, taxes paid by individuals and companies had jumped to almost 40 cents per dollar of GNP. Additionally, two provinces, British Columbia and Alberta, charge an additional monthly premium for their health care plans.

Canada faces today what other countries that operated social welfare nets have been forced to undergo: economic disaster. These nets are traditional for Canada, whose difficult climate has long caused Canadians to look to their government for some assistance. It's a system that encourages you to view the government as one's father. The common belief is that he'll take care of us. But what happens when Dad runs out of money? Canadians are finding out now as they shoulder one of their worst recessions ever. The news is bleak. As one journalist noted, "Most of the jobs lost in the last recession (1981-82) were eventually filled again; this time many are gone for good. Since 1989, employment in manufacturing has declined by 14%, nearly 500,000 jobs." Unemployment is nearly twice what it is in the United States. MacLean's columnist, Barbara Amiel, said, in 1992, "Socialism has brought every country that has had it to its economic knees. Like any statist system, which centralizes power and regulates human affairs much more than is necessary, socialism stifles enterprise and productivity. The British have rejected socialism because they know what it leads to. Canada has never really lived under it, and only now in Ontario are people beginning to discover what it means. It means that the very best people try to leave the country for the United States while business simply bypasses the province, or relocates". Another story: "In the mid-80's I was so gloomy about Canada's future that I looked for a nice U.S. university at which to teach Canadian history. Then I realized that I couldn't and can't go, and am willing to pay a considerable price to stay Canadian. But I have always told my children that they had best keep their options open".

This is the country "experts" tell us we should be looking towards and becoming more like if we are to face the health care future. It's a scary thought. If we continue to foster more dependence on the government to take care of us in some way, we will walk the same economic path every other country who "grew more government" did. We're at that crossroads now. An earlier chapter in this book outlined the phenomenal growth in government services here as a percent of our Gross Domestic Product. It is a situation we must reverse, or face drastic consequences.

Even as lame-duck Prime Minister Brian Mulroney's mother undergoes heart bypass surgery in Florida or Quebec Premier Robert Bourassa has experimental cancer treatment in Bethesda, Maryland, we are still told great things about the Canadian system and how it really isn't socialistic at all. On American television, at a church in a suburb of Boston, Phil Donahue hosted a show which spent a lot of time on the Canadian system and included a guest, academician Jane Fulton who was quoted as saying, "we Canadians believe in fairness and equity and, to a degree, mediocrity". She went on to say that the health care system is free market and entrepreneurial, except, when asked what the one thing she could do to improve the system was, she responded by saying, "put doctors all on salary". I guess you can't have those doctors being too entrepreneurial. Interestingly, this comment was met with silence from the audience, a group that had been cheering her earlier. When it comes down to it, Americans rightfully don't like being told there's a ceiling on what they're allowed to earn. With regard to paying higher taxes for a health care system, we threw tea into the Boston harbor and founded our country on just the opposite principles. I hope these beliefs are still alive and well in this country.

We know Canada's system is in trouble. What are they doing to hold costs down? Rationing. It is the only answer to preserve a finite and valuable resource. In Canada, we are told, you can see anyone you want, when you want, free of charge. There are no disincentives from seeing providers. The end result, however, is overutilization of the system and incurred costs greater than anticipated. Holding down utilization will lower costs, a must for provinces to have any hope of balancing their budgets. Holding down utilization means rationing treatment in some way. It could be a delay; it might be an outright denial for a service. It may also be increasing out-of-pocket costs for certain highly used services to discourage frequent utility. Limiting medical services by some method is rationing, but when costs run higher than the province can afford, their choices are few.

Normally even-tempered Canadians are becoming irritated with their system as a result. Cutbacks forced by growing costs and shrinking budgets have caused some Canadians to turn on those they feel "abuse" the health care system. In Alberta, the Minister of Health, Nancy Betkowski, talked about 20% of Albertans who "consume a disproportionately high number of health care services and can be grouped into five general categories: psychological disorder, vague symptoms, suspected drug abuse, alcohol abuse and major illness... It is important that all of us diligently examine the use of resources available for health and to ensure that we are making the best use of these precious resources". In British Columbia, limitations are in place for identification of high users. Moreover, in the province of Saskatchewan, a series of newspaper articles entitled, "The Road to Recovery", ran one story headlined: "Silver threads threaten to strangle the system", that discussed the implications of Canada's aging population and its impact on the costs of health care. In it, the comments included, "Statistically, the older the elderly get, the more they cost" and "Many believe the problem is not the number of elderly, but the fact that they are overdoctored, overmedicated and overhospitalized".

Should senior organizations in this country rally behind a government-run plan? Do they really think that, in the final analysis, when health care budgeting is necessary to control government costs, they will not be the first group to whom the axe is swung down on medical treatments? If a country like Canada, known to be one of the kindest and gentlest nations on earth, can run articles about the elderly and other high users of the health system as if they've committed some terrible offense, what makes you think it wouldn't happen here?

Rationing (yes, the "R" word again) is a reality in government-run programs. Canada is no different. Witness the case of an Ontario woman stranded in Texas where she sought medical treatment for a condition that caused her to be allergic to everything she touched. When admitted to a Dallas hospital earlier this year, she weighed less than 80 pounds and could not keep food down. She came to Dallas because there were no facilities in Canada to treat her condition. Her province, Ontario, finally agreed to pay 75% of her bill for treatment in the U.S. She made steady improvement and is currently undergoing outpatient treatment for her condition. However, Ontario has now stopped covering her at all, citing new rules that place limits on medical spending in other countries. The portion of the bill she had to pay has left her in difficult financial circumstances and she may have to stop treatment herself because she couldn't afford the care at 100% of the cost. Another recent article said, "Across Canada, 25% of those surveyed had problems getting immediate access to health care for reasons that included long waiting lists, inconvenient service hours, and problems arranging child care. Sometimes the service wasn't available."

Waiting lines are not just "special interests rhetoric" as proponents of a Canadian system here will tell you, but a harsh reality. The Fraser Institute in Vancouver, British Columbia published a list in 1990 of average waiting times for certain procedures, such as:

- varicose veins, 8.4 months
- coronary artery bypass, 5.5 months
- cataract removal, 4.2 months
- hysterectomy, 3.8 months
- hemorrhoidectomy, 6.4 months

In Newfoundland, CAT scans take two months, first time mammograms can take 4 months. In Quebec, in 1989, the wait was 6 months for angiograms, 9 months for coronary bypass surgery. In Toronto, Ontario, the waiting period for cardiac surgery was 3-9 months in 1989.

Some say money can move you up. Canadians are loathe to admit it, but if you're a member of the House of Commons or a big-time hockey star, it is rumored you can obtain treatment quicker. If you're an Eskimo in Northern Alberta or an unknown senior citizen it's probably a different story. A couple of years ago, in British Columbia, residents were outraged when some individuals waiting for heart surgery passed away. This province finally worked out an arrangement with the University of Washington hospital in Seattle to do bypass surgery for 50 of those on the waiting list, at a reduced fee. Another discounted batch of 50 surgeries would be purchased if it went well. At the time the news story about this appeared in 1991, only nine British Columbians were willing to leave their home and family, make a trip to a strange city, and undergo a serious medical operation. For some reason, the provincial officials were quite disappointed at the low sign up rate, as they believed this could have reduced waiting times down to 4-6 weeks for this procedure.

Traveling Canadians are now faced with tougher rules and regulations. Ontario now requires their Canadian citizens spend 183 days in their province to render them eligible to receive out-of-province coverage. They've also placed ceilings on spending and cut out some of the treatments they cover. This year's plan hopes to save $178 million in out-of-country hospital payments.

Ontario is also the new home for what is being termed "fast-food clinics". These resemble our own walk-in emergency clinics that boomed over the last decade. They are popular because they provide "quick, convenient health care". One of the patients said that the attraction was not needing to schedule an appointment or worrying about whether or not one would be seen. Convenience can be expensive and the article notes that it "has cost the province's taxpayers $44.5 million in 1990 alone". This has now become the true pattern to any reaction about health care in Canada. It no longer can be reviewed without a look at what it costs provincial taxpayers. Cutbacks are so much in evidence, utilization of "free" care so high, revenue shortfalls getting larger and larger, that everything done in health care must now be viewed with respect to cost. They have no choice. With these walk-in clinics, defenders of them say that they replace the use of the emergency ward, a more costly visit. Opponents say the patient comes back to their doctor again for the same symptoms, thus doubling the cost of the health care. Stay tuned.

This is the health care system we are being encourage to adapt. In Toronto, it was reported that a man who'd been waiting two months to obtain a CAT scan was upset when he learned that his facility of choice uses the CAT scan machine on dogs at night for $300 per test. The dog doesn't need to wait.

The individual was understandably upset and said he'd gladly go at night for a CAT scan since his headaches were getting worse, but, no luck. The hospital justified veterinarians' use of the CAT scan machine for dogs in the evening since it would otherwise sit idly.

In Calgary, hospitals are trying anything they can to raise money to cover shortages. One hospital considered offering a charge card whereby each purchase generated income for the facility, estimated to be $36,000 annually. Also in Calgary, Holy Cross hospital is conducting a "Holy Lotto" to raise about $325,000 to buy operating room equipment. Still another Calgary hospital is sponsoring one night's production of "Phantom of the Opera", hoping to make $250,000 in net receipts. If you're a Calgary resident and you receive a call from your local hospital, asking you to buy tickets to a local theater show to help raise money for the hospital, what do you say? Do you worry that, if you didn't contribute and later needed bypass surgery, you might be placed farther down a waiting list than someone who did kick in some money? Does this contribution count in calculating what the average Canadian spends on health care each year? Canadians are forced to think about that more than our liberal pundits would like us to believe.

As I said earlier, money might move you up in line. Much as we think the practice of rationing health care by wealth is reprehensible, the Toronto Star reports, in a survey responded to by 3400 doctors, that "well-connected patients receive better health care than those with lower incomes". In addition, it was also mentioned that "a high profile union boss was put at the top of the lineup for a heart transplant, and a noted baseball player was rushed in for a specialized test that lesser mortals would have had to wait weeks for".

In that same survey, nearly half the doctors said they had seriously considered leaving Canada to practice elsewhere, mostly in the United States. In fact, according to Reader's Digest, September, 1992, some 8263 Canadian doctors were practicing in the United States in 1990 despite tight visa rules. One such doctor could be an Ontario dermatologist who had been a vocal opponent against limiting doctor fees. He was accused by a government minister who said she had seen confidential files confirming that this doctor was overbilling the province for his fees. He endured the wrath of local Sudbury, Ontario citizens until the minister admitted to lying about seeing any files. He was considering Denver, Colorado in his move to the states.

Everyone is supposed to be covered in Canada. However, since two provinces, Alberta and British Columbia, charge a premium to have coverage, if you do not pay this assessment, you are technically uninsured. Does this mean you aren't eligible for medical services? As some states do in this country, Alberta reimburses providers anyway. But, in British Columbia, only the hospitals are reimbursed. The doctor is left to decide how to collect from the patient, or to simply absorb the loss. This might create difficulties for uninsureds seeking treatment.

The March 7, 1993 Sunday edition of the New York Times addressed Canada's health care problems in a story entitled, "Now Patients Are Paying Amid Canadian Cutbacks" and subtitled, "Spending Outstrips Government's Ability To Pay". It discusses a Toronto man who took his kids, both of whom had colds, to a medical lab to have their throats swabbed. A few weeks later he received two bills, $19.80 each, heretofore unthinkable in the Canadian system. But this is going to be the norm now, not the unusual. The other option to charging patient fees is a reduction in covered services. For example, in Ontario, an employment physical must now be paid for by the individual.

Canada, in fact, has looked to the U.S. for some ideas. Several provinces have launched pilot programs establishing a type of HMO medicine called CHOs (Community Health Organizations), emphasizing capitation payments instead of traditional fee-for-service, wellness programs and reliance on nurses and nurse practitioners rather than doctors for some services.

This look at the U.S. may also be a wave of the future. Ontario's Health Minister said last year "The consensus that virtually every major study or report on health care reform has reached over the past several years is that we must fundamentally restructure and reorient the health care system if it is to survive". That restructuring is in full swing, folks. This is not the best time to be viewing Canada as a model to solve our problems. Even a General Accounting Office report which largely complemented the Canadian system in 1991, summarized its findings by saying, "It is not, however, clear that the United States could or should replicate the Canadian system in every dimension." In fact, there are only one or two things about the Canadian system that are worth noting for us. Most important is that all are in the system without choice(except the non-premium payers in Alberta and British Columbia who still get most of the care they want anyway). A major drawback to many of the proposals for health care change here is that young, healthy people are not mandated to be in the system. In a single payor system, that problem is eliminated.

Canada is not the place for us to learn about health care. A February 24, 1992 MacLean's edition pointed to the role government plays in providing social safety net programs to all Canadians. The writer says, "Until Canadians realize that socialism is the problem, not the solution, they will simply go on stabbing themselves in the gut''. Two weeks later that same magazine ran an article encouraging Canadians to ''kiss off the universality myth that all Canadians are created equal''. The article further notes that, ''every federal budget, and most provincial ones, document the severe fiscal strains we face. It's no longer an idle threat that unless economic conditions change and the revenue side of the balance sheets get a significant boost, we may end up as a Third World country, run as a colony of the International Monetary Fund''.

While we all empathize with our neighbor to the north, we can certainly do better to find a health care solution that more aptly addresses the problems we do have and need to fix in our system.

Other National Systems

When calling for national health insurance in this country, many use the argument that the rest of the world provides health care for all their inhabitants, why not us? They point out how much more successful their programs are than ours and use that as leverage to lobby for a government-run plan providing universal access here.

The only truth to these comments is that other countries provide universal access and their governments spend less on health care than ours does. What's really happening, though, is far from the success stories these advocates would have you believe. What national health proponents are good at doing is using the best examples from each country as if the world were all one health care system. To prove that a national health insurance system works, these individuals will point to the infant mortality rates in Japan, the universal access of Canada, the employer mandate in the Netherlands, life expectancy in France; all as if this proves these systems are great successes, instead of isolated statistics. For a more interesting overall picture, an Associated Press report from the February 28, 1993 edition of the Daytona Beach Sunday News Journal had the following comments:

''Money is not the only measure, however. Patients in some countries do without sophisticated care or a choice of doctors, and wait months or years for nonemergency surgery. Many health systems require partial payment by the patient.

''None of the systems is without problems and some countries are making significant reforms, among them Germany, the Netherlands, Italy, Sweden, Argentina and Zimbabwe.

''Several nations are turning to the free market to encourage competition and greater efficiency.''

What's this? The free market? You mean, like our system? Why in the world would people want to copy us? I thought we had a lousy system that needs to look more like one of their programs. We know now Canada's out, but what about Germany? Or Sweden? Are they turning to the free market? We're told that won't work in health care. Doesn't anyone in these countries read our press or listen to our politicians and consumer advocates talk?

What the free market hasn't been able to do here is get everyone covered, including the young, healthy people who would rather spend their money in other, more glamorous ways. A single payor system would require everyone to be in it and EqualCare USA will do that. What other countries are realizing is that the free market does the rest of it far better than the government can and when we wake up to that fact in this country, we will go a long way towards solving our health care problems.

A closer look at health care plans in other countries will reveal a pattern I believe you'll find interesting and, not surprisingly, quite different from what you've been hearing. If we can learn what these countries have learned, we can save a significant amount of time used trying out systems that don't work. I've also added 1990 population figures for each country as we must remember there is a difference between national health care systems that have been established for 30 million people and what might work for a population base of over 250 million.

GERMANY (Pop: 79 million)

In this country, workers pay anywhere from 8 to 16% of their salaries (the average is 13.1%) to belong to one of the country's non-profit sickness funds, of which there are around 1,200 from which to choose. Those covered at government expense are the retired, those on welfare and the unemployed. Wealthy individuals can opt out to join for profit private plans. Roughly 50% of the population, especially blue-collar workers, have no choice about which fund they can join. Employers also contribute the same proportion to the sickness funds.

The funds negotiate rates with providers and it is here that their Parliament has had to handle recent difficulties. In 1992, the funds were running at a deficit of $7.7 billion. The government voted to cut provider reimbursements to make up the difference. The problem is over-utilization. Germans see their doctors twice as often as Americans do, so the fee per visit was dropped to handle the increased demand (the average German visits a doctor once a month).

You don't hear much about Germany with respect to the usual useless vital statistics information. That's because, despite a low infant mortality rate (for social reasons we've already enumerated), life expectancy for West Germany isn't much different from the United States. In the demonstration earlier in this book when we measured remaining life expectancy from ages 55 and 65, we found that West Germany wasn't even close to the U.S. Worse, West Germany will probably now be measured (unfairly) as just Germany, incorporating East German statistics, numbers which approach Third World margins.

Forbes magazine notes that Germany has its current economic problems, blamed as much on the escalating cost of their social democracy than on reunification. Social services eats up 29% of Germany's gross national product. In 1990, for the first time in a decade, Germany ran a merchandise trade deficit with the United States. Businesses pay out up to 53% in retained earnings in corporate taxes. Their 1992 growth rate was expected to be a minimal 1.8%. Reforms will be coming and how this will affect their health care system is not currently known.

The success we can utilize here is that everyone (except the wealthy) has been mandated to join the health care system. It costs, though, and the typical problem of overutilization in any national plan is causing deficits that are being financed in lower reimbursements to doctors. Hospital and ambulatory care physicians cannot deliver care outside their respective locations, leading to service duplication and a growing population of physicians already larger per capita than here in the United States. It's not all free choice, either, as many workers have no say in what plan they can choose.

BRITAIN (Pop: 57 million)

Operates a National Health Service which is financed from general revenues (about 80%) and from payroll deductions. All are covered. Rising costs, as they are everywhere are a problem and the government is pushing free-market reforms (surprise!) leaving local authorities to contract with hospitals now and doctors to negotiate with the hospital in arranging patient care.

There is a tendency to divert funds from expensive care for the small number who are seriously ill toward the large number who seek relatively inexpensive services for minor ills. For example, more than 19.5 million ambulance rides are given each year (1 for every 3 Brits), but over 90% of them are non-emergency in nature, amounting to more of a "free" taxiservice where someone is transported to a local pharmacy to fill a prescription or trips of that nature.

This is a key element to understanding how national health insurance works. It takes care of inexpensive basic services for the masses quite well. This is critical to its public reception for it is the masses who vote. There are fewer people who need complex care and it is politically feasible to ration that care without an uproar since the majority of people are relatively healthy and don't cost the system much. The sick are labeled as high-users (like Canada), but they don't amount to much of a political base, so they wait for care, helping the system to stay within it's budget.

This is why you see glowing letters written from abroad by Americans in other countries talking about how wonderful health care is because you can just walk in to any doctor and get two aspirin. But they aren't sick. They aren't 58 and in need of kidney dialysis, which you almost always cannot have at that age in Britain. National health care plans are great at clipping your toenails and comforting your colds, but when you need serious health care treatment, you're in trouble. That's not really what Americans want, especially as our population continues to age.

SWEDEN (Pop: 8 million)

Universal access exists in Sweden with health care run by the local city councils. Patients pay about $20 for a visit to a doctor. Swedes are not all that happy with their health care system and other social programs which generate tax costs, that in 1991, equaled 57.7% of their GNP, the highest measure in the West. Unhappy, the Swedes booted out the Social Democratic party in 1992 elections.

Sweden is in economic and social turmoil. Just over 6% of Swedes are on housing waiting lists and, despite enormous subsidies, the housing crisis worsens. Their public education systems is one of the most expensive in the world, but academic standards are declining rapidly. Given prohibitive tax rates, employers find it impossible to get anyone to work overtime. Daily absenteeism has soared to 25% of the work force in some sectors.

Health care is more of the same. A 64 year old Swede reported to a city hospital with a serious heart condition and learned that it would be 14 months before he could have an angiogram to pinpoint the problem, with another seven months to wait if he needed surgery. He went to Norway instead, where he was told he would be dead in two months if he didn't have bypass surgery. Back in Sweden, he found a rare, private clinic that was willing to do the surgery. In 1990, the city of Stockholm had some 28,000 people waiting for surgery.

Newly formed political parties are bowing to Swedes' requests to open up social services like health care to more competition from the private sector. They also complain about the anonymity of their system, so promises have been made to bring back the family physician.

NETHERLANDS (Pop: 15 million)

Universal access for the Dutch is achieved by the use, like Germany, of sickness funds. Some 62% of the population pays 3.15% of payroll (employer contributes 4.95% in addition) as they earn less than $30,000 annually. They also pay an annual premium to belong to one of the 30 regional funds and low-income and unemployed are asked to contribute nominal amounts to the system. The 32% that make more than $30,000 must buy private health insurance. The other 6% work for the government in some form and are covered under a separate plan (sounds familiar?).

The Dutch government wants to eliminate employer-based health insurance (so do I, under EqualCare USA). Under a new proposed Dutch system, each individual would select a health plan from competing insurance organizations during an open enrollment period. Insurers would be required to offer a basic benefits package. Individuals would pay into a central fund based on income, as well as an additional premium to the plan of their choice. Insurers could not deny anyone coverage, although those companies who enroll a substantial number of high-risk people will be compensated accordingly. Managed care and limits on the use of expensive technology would be used to help control costs and emphasize free market competition to give the Dutch the best insurance plans from which to choose. Here again, free market capabilities are recognized as being far more effective for the individual and the government serves only to collect the money into a central fund. The Dutch have recognized some of the obvious corrections we can make to our system such as using a single premium collection center and turning it over to the people, rather than employers. We read very little about the Dutch in articles written that promote a national health insurance system. I wonder why.

FRANCE (Pop: 56 million)

Their national health insurance plan is part of its social security system. It is financed by the government revenues and by a 6.8% payroll tax (employers contribute 12.6%). The national plan covers about 70% of the costs for doctor's fees, drugs and other prescriptions. The 30% balance can be covered by private insurance, partially subsidized by employers, and nearly 80% of the French participate in these plans.

All is not necessarily well with the French health care system. In late 1991, 200,000 health care workers took to the picket lines to protest government budget cuts due to rising health care costs. Doctors, pharmacists, dentists and others turned out to formally make known their displeasure with the socialist government. This group was another in a long line of protesters in present day France as farmers, nurses, social workers, teachers and others have led demonstrations in recent months. As health care costs continue to rise globally, government-run programs will continue to suffer cut-backs.

Recent election returns in this country marked defeat for the incumbent socialist party, signaling change for the future. This change is certain to affect the health care system.

RUSSIA (Pop: 290 million before the breakup)

The granddaddy of all national health insurance plans, the former Soviet Union often held up its state-run medical system as a model of how health care should be run. With its collapse, the deficiencies in the system are there for all to see. 40% of Russia's hospitals lacked hot water, 18% had no sewage systems and 12% had no water at all. Much of the equipment is obsolete or broken. Doctors complain of having to reuse disposable syringes after cleaning them with bleach.

This last alarming fact has caused a sharp rise in AIDS cases, simply because of this shortage in disposable syringes. Reuse of the needles has spread AIDS at a rate that threatens the entire country. Some analysts believe that the number of AIDS victims in the Soviet Union could reach 20 million by the year 2000 and by the year 2010, up to 40% of the nation's younger generation may be threatened. The costs of combating the epidemic is greater than their current gross national product.

Russia is turning to private health insurance as part of its reforms because it can no longer afford to subsidize hospital costs, currently growing six times faster than their general inflation rate. What if America had socialized its health care system 70 years ago as Russia did? Would we be facing these incredible troubles, too?

ITALY (Pop: 57 million)

This country is embarking on a three year program to reduce costs and improve services through increased competition and some privatization. Starting in 1995, Italians will be permitted to buy their own health insurance coverage and will receive tax refunds if they do. This is another country beginning to introduce U.S. style health care even as we discuss turning it upside down here.

SPAIN (Pop: 40 million)

A 6% payroll tax, matched by the employer provides health care for all. In January, the socialist government reduced costs by trimming 900 drugs from the covered list, while Spaniards already pay 40% of the costs of drugs as it is. In this country, 20% of its inhabitants have private insurance but, here, public hospitals are often better equipped than private ones. Still, the normal complaints about waits for surgeries and check-ups are inherent in their government-run system.

JAPAN (Pop: 127 million)

Providing health care for all for the last 30 years, Japanese today pay an average of 8.2% in payroll deductions for medical care. About 70-90% of services are covered and patients pay the rest up to $484/month.

The Japanese are struggling today with an aging population and an increasing number of unemployed individuals who are costing them substantial amounts under the health care system. Growth in Japan's economy is currently contracting as its 1992 growth will come in under 2% along with Germany's. Again, social programs continue to take their toll over time and health care will undoubtedly undergo reform here to cope with the elderly population and the new, higher unemployed people who do not contribute via a payroll tax.

* * *

Turning health insurance over to the bureaucrats to run is clearly not in our best interests and virtually every country around the world is experiencing difficulties with their health care programs. The answer for them is to try free market approaches and slowly shift it out of bureaucrat hands. Why would we want to go the other way?

Bureaucrats have already broken promises with Medicare. What would they do with the entire system? Yes, health care costs are increasing here, but they're obviously rising everywhere. Is that the reason to nationalize it? Have you checked the price of a haircut today versus what it costs 25 years ago? This increase rivals health care's jump, but I don't see anyone calling for a national hair care plan.

We do hear, though, from people like Ron Pollack of Families USA, who's been quoted as saying, "We know there are effective solutions because every country in the democratic Western World has solved this problem''. Wrong, Ron, they're grappling for answers just as we are, and turning it over to the government isn't an option for most of them -- the government already has it, and can no longer afford your solution.

The call for national health insurance, especially among seniors, is entirely misguided. Seniors are the losers in any government-run system because they are the ones most often rationed for health services. It's the best way to keep costs down in other countries; why would it be any different here? National health insurance is about people believing they will get something for nothing. Let's make government responsible and we won't have to pay. If you believe that, check some of the tax rates in these other countries.

The call for national health insurance really isn't about getting medical care for the indigent, either. The poor in this country have access to care and, despite their inability to pay, can and do get treatment. They don't have to endure waits of several weeks or months to obtain it. Stalin led a revolution supported by the poor because he told them he would equalize the country between the wealthy and poor. He just didn't tell them how. The poor thought he meant he would make them all rich, or, at least, comfortable. Instead, he made everyone poor. He equalized it not by bringing everyone up, but by knocking everyone down.

A compassionate, entrepreneurial American health care system would assure that all Americans everywhere, at all times, would be guaranteed access to essential, reasonable and necessary health care. It would also guarantee the right of those that can or want, to do more for themselves and their families as they see fit. Wouldn't that be a great American system?

The more government takes on, the less it does well. Paul Johnson, author of the book, Modern Times, talks about New Zealand and the lessons learned about socialism the hard way. They set out years ago to take care of those that needed it, providing free health care, unlimited unemployment benefits and high welfare payments. The welfare state grew and suddenly everyone, regardless of wealth, was dipping its hand into the government's grab-bag.

The result was a devastated economy, with nearly as many people receiving welfare (1.1 million) as workers (1.4 million), the lowest level of productivity of any developed country and a declining GNP in 1990. They had to change. Welfare spending was slashed, state-owned enterprises sold off, trade barriers lowered and price and wage controls lifted. It's beginning to work and their inflation rate this year may be below 1%.

Most governments are moving away from managing things and

giving it to free enterprise. Johnson believes the question future historians will pose is not why people finally turned against the welfare state but why it took so long. There are three things that government can do better than we can do in private enterprise: providing for national defense, internal order and an honest currency. Beyond that, there is an inverse relationship between the size of government and its effectiveness.

With most of the world moving in the direction of the free market in health care, it's time to take that lesson and apply it to health care here. We already have free enterprise at work. If we focus on the specific problems we have, as already noted, and figure out the best way for us to fix them without jeopardizing the free market essential to their long term success, we will move health care to its next evolution and have a model the world will continue to look to, as they do now, for solutions to their own health care crises. Divided, we fail.

CHAPTER NINE

OTHER PROPOSED SOLUTIONS -- THE BIGGEST PROMISER GETS THE DEAL

It has been rumored that First Lady Hillary Rodham Clinton, chairperson of the President's special task force on health care, is in the middle of evening prayer when she suddenly exclaims, "God! Please tell me! This health care problem is driving me absolutely crazy! Will it ever be fixed?" God replies, "Hillary, I have some good news and some bad news". The First Lady says, "I don't think I can take any more bad news right now. What's the good news?" "The good news", God tells her, "is that, yes, the health care problem will be solved." Hillary Clinton cries, "That's great news! What could possibly be your bad news?" God replies, "It just won't be solved in my lifetime."

Hillary Clinton has publicly stated that she understands why people have thrown up their hands in frustration over trying to work through the maze of the health care puzzle. We know that the problems in the system didn't happen overnight, making them difficult to untangle. We also know that many Americans are pleased with the system and not necessarily motivated to solve a problem they don't have.

State legislatures do want action, as they face tight budgets and increasing health costs, as Medicaid assumes the position of the fastest growing entitlement program we have. In some states, Medicaid accounts for 20% of the overall budget. Since each state is in a different financial position with regard to health care, their individual solutions to the problem are exactly that: individual. There is little uniformity and, at this pace, state reforms may give us 50 different solutions across America.

The federal government is waging their own war against health care and have almost as many varieties of proposed solutions as the states have created. A government-run single payor health care system has been proposed again in the 1993 session. Senator Nancy Kassenbaum has introduced a bill called "BasiCare", which would provide a basic benefit package of health care to all Americans. Republicans, angered at essentially being left off the President's health care task force, worked out alternative proposals of their own.

The elderly want prescription drug coverage and long term care added to the Medicare program. Federal workers are not enthusiastic for any change themselves since they have the best health care plans in the world today.

The media, political and academic rhetoric associated with the proposed health care solutions, suggests that this is a class war, a struggle between rich and poor. It's not. It's a struggle between the people in the wagon vs. people pulling the wagon. A new health care package that is based on who votes in this country will be skewed in favor of the elderly and government employees, leaving the average tax payer (the wagon-puller) at the bottom of the deck again. So far, all of the solutions being proposed favor someone over somebody else. This is not the way to approach changes in health care.

Nor can the changes be piecemeal. Our present third party payment system is a complete failure and any solution that suggests retaining aspects of it is doomed to failure. We should no longer have a basic health care system that is different, for example, for those over age 65 versus those under age 65.

None of the solutions on the table truly empowers the end-user, the actual consumer of health care services. No one can hold down costs better than the individuals themselves. If you give the power to someone else, we will still be complaining about costs next year, five years from now, twenty years from now. If a person has to spend some of their own money, they likely will not overutilize health care. If a third party is paying, overuse is rampant. Every other country in the world is confronted by overutilization because there hasn't been any incentive not to go and obtain all the free health care you believe you deserve.

Most individuals want some kind of health care change in this country. They just don't know what kind. The pattern in the polls over the last couple of years is that each different solution has a small force backing it, with no clear majority winner. This is one of the reasons for the frustration many have felt in trying to address the whole issue of change. People are protecting their own turf. No one wants to give up what they already have. Those that want radical change do not seem willing to pay much for it.

Still, the health care task force developed its own solution to send to

Congress. Some of the reports you read suggests that the plan has been ready for some time, but the necessary political posturing has kept it from being revealed until the timing is right to send it to Congress. Rushing into a solution to try and deliver on at least one campaign promise is not necessarily the wisest decision.

Which solution will be chosen? I hope that, by the time you finish this book, you'll agree with me that EqualCare USA is the only real solution that will work. I suspect, however, that we may end up with something else, a result which I call "the biggest promiser gets the deal". You can promise the American people anything as long as you reserve the right to break that promise. Medicare broke its promises; public education has broken its promises; do we really want to live with another program of promises that guarantees a similar end-result?

There is talk in Washington, D.C. of even higher "sin taxes" to help pay for the new program; a popular tax with a majority of voters who, of course, wouldn't have to pay it. This sin tax is aimed at cigarettes, which is also represented as a reason for higher medical costs. But who decides what is a sin to be taxed and what isn't? Poor nutrition adds to our health costs, too. Should we have a Twinkies tax? A pizza tax? What about gambling? Is that a sin? Should we impose a lottery tax to help pay for health care? Auto accidents cause higher health care costs. Does this mean we should assess individuals who spend substantial amounts of time in their cars? There are many people who consider homosexuality a sin. Should this be taxed? Where do we draw the line? Who gave us the right to draw that line in the first place? Moreover, the administration's proposal phases in mental health and substance abuse coverage, meaning we will make those smokers pay for health care reform up front, but we'll still help them out on the other end when they need health care to kick their habits. But if we do cure them and they no longer "sin", thus avoiding the tax, where will we get the money to pay for their treatment? Conversely, smokers often die early, thus drawing little or no Social Security benefits, saving us valuable tax dollars. If cured, they might not pay the tax, while living long enough to now collect a substantial Social Security benefit.

Preventive care is high on the list of many of these proposed health care solutions. Preventive care is not an insurable event. The routine cost of care should be paid by those that can afford it, with insurable assistance coming with higher cost health conditions. Providing preventive care for all will be expensive. I'm not saying it shouldn't be considered, only that it doesn't save money in a global health care budget. It costs more to give annual mammograms to women over 40 than it does to treat each woman that comes down with breast cancer. If preventive care is to be part of any solution, let's be honest about the costs involved.

This chapter reviews the principles of the major solutions that have risen to the top in recent discussions. While each attempt to solve a part of our actual health care problems, all of the ideas either leave too much unsolved or create an entirely new set of problems that we will face now or at some point in the future.

In Chapter 8, we reviewed the single-payor solution, which is jeopardizing national economies worldwide due to overutilization, bureaucracy and a lack of sufficient revenue to pay for it all. This chapter explores the other proposed solutions.

The Employer Mandate

Virtually all talk of health care changes continue to center on employer-provided coverage. Since many of the current uninsured in this country are employed, experts speak of an absolute mandate on business to provide health care for their employees.

That employers are even in the business of providing health care benefits at all is the result of wage freezes in the 1940's. Labor unions lobbied heavily for some other form of compensation since incomes couldn't be raised, and ended up settling for health insurance and a variety of other employee fringe benefits.

It's been nearly 50 years since businesses began offering health coverage, but the economic times are changing. Back then, we were rooted in the industrial age, a historical era rapidly passing. Just as the agricultural age was replaced by the industrial age, so too is the industrial age now being replaced by a service-oriented economy. The entire world is moving towards using "contingent" workers in this new service economy, and the old employer-employee relationship will quickly become the exception rather than the norm. Any health care solution that uses the employer as the primary source of health care coverage will not be addressing the needs of many of us in only a few short years.

You read weekly about another Fortune 500 company laying off a few thousand workers, yet our unemployment has remained stable over the last couple of years. That's because a lot of these individuals are being hired back (or working for someone else) on a contract basis. Part-timers, self-employed, freelancers, consultants, temporaries, these are all part of the new contingent work force and many of them are on their own for health insurance.

Charles Handy, author of "The Age of Unreason", says, "It's not going to go back" when discussing the growth of this new type of worker. Why, then, should we cling to Industrial Age ideas?

Immediate implementation of an employer mandate will seriously hurt small business, and proponents of this solution suggest it be phased in over time. Approaching the problem in this piecemeal fashion will not provide an effective solution. Knowing a mandate would hurt small business should lead us away from employer involvement in health care, rather than requiring even more from business.

Businesses can't, and shouldn't bear the entire burden of health care. Small business, in particular, will suffer. The National Federation of Independent Business estimates that 26% of small businesses will fail under an employer mandate, while costing between 650,000 and 3.5 million jobs. Small businesses that offer coverage now are losing business to competing firms who hold costs down by not offering coverage. Small business, ironically, is being asked to lead the country out of its recent sluggish economic growth, as it struggles, even now, to cope with the high costs associated with providing health care.

The March 29, 1993 issue of Business Week, estimates that business pays for $17.2 billion of health care today for uninsured or underinsured patients, in the form of cost-shifting. This added burden makes it difficult to survive as business tries to hold their enterprises together while being asked to pick up the costs of heart bypass surgery, transplants, AIDS, cancer, kidney dialysis and any number of other expensive health care treatments.

The Clinton Administration is walking on eggshells around anything that might be perceived as a middle class tax increase. Yet, an employer mandate, would drive the cost of goods up, paid for predominantly by those same middle class wage earners. Not taxing them directly doesn't mean standards of living won't be adversely affected as higher prices further tighten household budgets.

The concentration on employers is, as mentioned, the result of a high number of uninsured being employed. There are many reasons small businesses do not purchase health insurance. Their costs, for one, are estimated to be anywhere from 10 to 40% higher than large businesses, according to the Department of Labor. They have less access to managed care products, a strategy used by larger businesses to hold down costs. They are too small to self-insure. One large claim could severely impact the business or shut it down entirely, as there aren't enough employees around to spread the risk. This not only raises insurance costs, but prevents any serious thought of self-insurance.

If one business offers coverage and another doesn't, employees in less than average health may be put into a position of "job lock", where they can't leave their firm to go somewhere else as they would lose their health insurance (even with COBRA requiring continuation of coverage for 18 months in those firms with 20 or more employees, the benefits will eventually expire), a situation many couldn't afford. If another company offers coverage, but requires medical evidence of insurability, the same problem exists, as it is likely coverage will not be issued.

One of the ideas about employer-mandated benefits that floated to the surface a couple of years ago was that of "pay or play". It was hot for a time, but I believe many have seen through the fallacy of this approach, and it probably won't surface again.

The thrust of "pay or play" was to require the employer to either purchase health coverage for all employees or pay into a government-run system. To "play" was to purchase health insurance while to "pay" was to contribute a flat percentage of payroll into a government health plan.

The percentage of payroll that would be paid into the system was estimated to be between 7 and 12%, depending on who was doing the talking. In all of the major metropolitan areas of the country, these estimates definitely made it cheaper to pay than to play, as insurance costs were running above even the high-side 12% estimate. Why would an employer buy health insurance for the employees at a cost of 15% of payroll when a much lower contribution would put them in the government plan? You don't need to be a business genius to figure that out.

What you'd end up with eventually is Medicaid for the middle class. A bureaucrat-run program based on underfunding can already be found in the form of Medicaid. Neither government or the states can afford to reimburse providers for health care at actual cost in that system today, leaving beneficiaries to overcome obstacles such as non-acceptance of Medicaid patients, lower cost hospital services and, as in the Oregon plan, prevention from obtaining the more costly medical procedure. While the poor dominate Medicaid today, the middle class would join them in the pay or play plan.

Analysts that examined this concept believed it likely that firms with younger, healthier employees would opt for providing health coverage while those with older, sicker people would join the government system, thus guaranteeing that the plan would be short in funds. Single women, on average incur higher medical costs than single men, while being paid less wages. Basing the fund contribution on payroll means a smaller contribution, in this example, for a higher user of health care.

An article in the January 3, 1992 edition of The Wall Street Journal stated that the "play or pay" approach would likely lead to surging costs, hiring discrimination against workers with large families or medical problems, endless lawsuits brought by job-seekers who think they're the victims of such discrimination, and eventually to the kind of nationalized health system none of us really wants". The start of another government program combined with Medicare and Medicaid is one more step in the process of taking it all over, a plan we know can't work. That same Wall Street Journal article advised, "most business leaders currently reject the wholesale nationalization of American health care, knowing full well that it hasn't worked in any other industry and won't work in medicine, either". Yet, once in control of more health care dollars, succeed or fail, it is not likely to be returned to private enterprise. Medicare and Medicaid are third party payor failures today. Have the bureaucrats returned them to the private sector? You know the answer.

Bureaucrats, for some reason, don't believe themselves subject to the same downsizing rules the rest of us play by. If a subsidiary is not working, a business either shuts it down or, more likely, tries to sell it to someone else who might be able to turn it into a profitable venture. Not so with our government. What will happen when pay or play can't pay its rightful share of health bills? Will they cut the program back? Or raise employer taxes, driving more out of business and adding more to the uninsured population? Or will they try to control it by "global budgeting"? Which of our Congressional members will be the one to come down here to Broward County, Florida and pull an MRI machine out of a hospital? Which hospital will they select? Will it be like the military base closing choices being made today?

Why spend any time or effort on a plan that would weaken our economy and move farther away from solving the accessibility problem in health care today? Why not look to the obvious idea that comes to mind when we look at a work force becoming more and more independent? Remove it from business entirely. Any health care solution that doesn't spread the inevitable pain associated with reform evenly will seriously hamper the people with the most need. In this case, the group assuming an undue share of the burden is business. It's time to remove it from their hands entirely and let small business lead the way in economic growth.

Big business isn't completely unaffected either, although size helps them with solutions small business can't utilize. A number of large businesses are coping with the high costs of providing employee health care with varied methods.

Xerox, for example, has given its employees strong incentives to join HMOs by providing larger premium subsidies and, due to its large employee base, forcing competing HMOs to be as price-conscious as they can to attract a large nest of enrollees. For the lower premium, the employee gives up doctor choice, but, for the majority (nearly two-thirds of the employees enroll in HMOs), this is the preference.

DuPont's per-employee health care costs have risen 50% since 1989, faster than the prices of their products, so they have responded by increasing the worker premium contribution. It is the quickest way to save health care money, while other strategies, like managed care and wellness programs, take more time to realize cost reductions. Even so, DuPont is also working with these approaches, attempting to stem the tide of rising health care costs which make it difficult for them to compete globally.

General Motors is paying more today in health care costs than it spends on steel. Further, they, like other companies of their size, are taking an enormous hit in the required budgeting for future retiree health care costs. Its 1992 tax return reflected a nearly $21 billion dollar write-off for this health charge. Businesses have the right to spread the one-time charge (to get their reserves up to acceptable levels) over a 20 year period, but G.M. elected to take the hit all at once.

Big businesses have banded together to contract with providers and attain health care at a discount rate. This is one of the few options open to them to bring costs under control, although small business continues to lack a consistent way to accomplish the same thing. And small business is still the one in trouble. You don't see horror stories about health insurance and health care on television citing the problems of an employee at IBM or a postal worker. Invariably, it's the tale of a small business person who ran into affordability and/or insurability problems.

Why should business, big or small, devote time, money and effort towards our health care? Wouldn't a better use of their talent be within the framework of the business they're in? Every individual has their own needs for health care and passing the buck to the employer means giving up your own choice about the type and quality of health care you want. As more and more workers go contingent, individual decisions will become the order of the day. A system strapped down by an employer mandate only creates more problems than it solves.

Supporters of employer mandates point to Hawaii as proof that this type of health care system can work. But is Hawaii truly a model for the U.S.?

In 1974, Hawaii passed the Prepaid Health Care Act, which requires employers to offer health insurance to their employees that meets or exceeds a state-defined package of benefits. Included in the package is 120 days of inpatient hospital care, outpatient surgical, medical and emergency care; home, office and hospital physician visits, most common diagnostic services, maternity (if not pregnant when enrolled) and medical and surgical consultations. Employees contribute no more than 1.5% of gross income for the cost of their coverage, while employers pay the balance. Dependent coverage is not required, although many are included as the state is heavily unionized.

Those not covered by employment health insurance are eligible for SHIP, the State Health Insurance Program for the unemployed, dependents, people working less than 20 hours per week, seasonal workers, students and low-income/self-employed workers. This program targets the uninsured and emphasizes preventive care rather than more costly forms of health care which, if they occur, are passed along, if possible, to Medicaid. In effect since 1990, it has signed up 10,000 of the estimated 30,000+ uninsured (3% of the state's total population).

Interestingly, a federal study notes that 95% of the civilian population was already covered in 1974 when the law was passed, rendering the employer mandate as a requirement to do what employers apparently were already doing. How many employers would have dropped insurance over the years if they were not mandated to offer it is difficult to quantify. Businesses that don't comply are subject to fines, held liable for the health bills of their workers or shut down.

The majority of the insured market is controlled by two major entities, Hawaii Medical Service Association (HMSA -the equivalent of Blue Cross) and Kaiser. These two companies also provide the coverage for SHIP. Many businesspeople believe this lack of competition has driven insurance premiums to double over the last five years, although rates still remain lower than those, on average, on the mainland.

Physicians don't have much say as to whether they will or will not participate in the fee structure paid by HMSA and Kaiser. Since these plans dominate the market, there is little choice, enabling a better control over physician fees. Further, plan benefits and lower malpractice premiums give less incentives for physicians to do unnecessary tests, further holding the line on costs.

Proponents point towards the healthiness of the average Hawaiian versus the average American as a byproduct of the employer mandated system, but there is not much evidence to support this claim. In fact, Hawaii's death rates from heart disease and cancer have actually worsened since passage of the 1974 Act. Its relative health can be more likely attributed to the type of population mix (white and Japanese are 50-60%, Hawaiian and Filipino 36%), less big city violence, lack of inner cities and smog, a warm climate, and less workers exposed to the hazards of manufacturing and construction since many of their jobs are grounded in agriculture, trade, tourism, government, communications and finance.

But would it work anywhere else? Aside from the fact that ERISA (federal law passed after Hawaii's Prepaid Act and from which it is exempted) forbids employer mandates, Hawaii can attribute much of its success to where it is located. An island 2000 miles from the U.S. West Coast doesn't leave businesses or individuals with much choice, if they wish to escape the system. Tourism taxes are high, and tourists keep coming, giving the state more surplus revenue than other states are able to generate. Standard of living is high and real wages are low, but there is little for the islander to do short of moving east.

I have no hard data, but, in visiting Hawaii, I talked to a number of workers who were employed off the books. Given the choice between adding an employee and paying wages plus health insurance, companies trying to survive slim profit margins balanced against high standard of living costs, simply alter their hiring practices. Many do comply, of course, and pass the increased cost along in their services or in low wages, a real problem for residents there. Higher prices hit both tourists and residents, but where else can you go for a hamburger when the mainland is a three hour flight away? End result: you pay whatever they charge for the hamburger.

Many of the medical services have been moved to Oahu, where residents of other islands must take a day off work to go visit a physician. Wealthier people fly to California for major surgery. SHIP is not popular with physicians because the fee reimbursement is similar to Medicaid with corresponding paperwork. Thus access to care still remains a problem for the poor covered under this program. Fee shortages are ripe to be passed along to businesses that are insured under the state's other programs.

What works in Hawaii does so for a combination of reasons having to do with geography, population, and type of industry. To presume this is a model for the remainder of the country is to base this on assumptions not applicable to the mainland. Requiring employers to provide coverage puts employees at a severe disadvantage in their jobs, passes their health care fate along to the employer, and drives up costs in all goods and services while reducing wage increases and hiring. Employer mandates will not solve the problem.

Managed Competition

One of the newer terms in the health care language, this apparent oxymoronic phrase could well be the centerpiece of the health care task force's proposal. At it's roots are a complete embracing of managed care and a strengthening of the buying position for both individuals and small business. There would seem to be a contradiction in terms in the phrase ''managed competition'', but proponents argue that it will foster much lower cost and more competitive insurance programs than are available today.

Conceived by think-tankers known as the Jackson Hole group and now enveloped by the Conservative Democratic Forum into a blueprint for federal legislation, the plan is to create large buying groups of individuals and businesses with less than 1000 employees to negotiate for better insurance plans built around the concepts of managed care. Small business has been on the losing end of any buying power in health insurance. This proposal would make the type of health insurance programs that a Xerox, for example, can offer its employees, available to small business and individuals.

In a sense, it extends the federal government health plan across the country. Federal employees can choose each year from between 300 and 400 plans, depending on their needs and those of their family's. Anything from traditional indemnity plans to PPOs to HMOs are there from which to make a selection; a choice you can change from year to year.

Managed care plans like HMOs and PPOs do seem to be controlling costs better than traditional plans because of the discounted fee for service medicine provided. Allowing everyone to take advantage of this, supporters of managed competition argue, will help everyone save money.

But will it? New Congressional Budget Office director Robert Reischauer says managed competition will not only be costly but won't achieve savings for at least 5 years. His estimate, along with others, puts the price tag at $270 billion dollars before health care costs begin to drop.

Managed care generally means no choice of doctors for the average individual, a requirement many consumers are heartily against. But, in order for managed care to hold down costs, they must control the health care delivery itself. The more the savings, the less control for the consumer.

Managed care has also been less successful in the rural areas where there are fewer doctors around to compete with each other. There is little incentive, as we have already shown, for doctors to live in rural areas based on today's third party compensation system.

In this plan, you could join individually, or through your employer, in a Health Insurance Purchasing Cooperative (HIPC). Upon joining, you would have the opportunity to select from a menu of insurance programs, called Accountable Health Plans (AHPs). By forcing insurers to compete for buyers in this fashion, it is believed premiums will come down.

In actuality, the opposite effect may occur. The more successful plans will be those with the largest network of providers. Only the largest of carriers can be consistently successful at attracting a substantial group of doctors and hospitals. Reducing the number of carriers, or "managing the competition" if you will, transfers a tremendous power to only a few companies. Given the possibility of a controlled market, upward pressure on premium rates is bound to occur. This leaves HIPCs less in control than believed if participating AHPs choose to raise rates at the same time. You can't toss them all out of your purchasing group or you'd have nothing left to offer your members. Trying to manage competition just doesn't work.

There could be one or more HIPCs in your state, leaving us with maybe 100 or so HIPCs across the country and perhaps 1500 to 2000 AHPs nationwide. Federal employees have enough problems now trying to understand the excess number of plans they have to select from, and these are generally well-educated people. If they struggle with the complexities of managed care, how will us average Americans cope?

We won't be able to ask our insurance agent. They aren't part of the system. Employees of the purchasing cooperatives will explain your choices to you and you will pay an administrative charge in your premium for that right (sounds a lot like a commission to me). Federal employees in Washington, D.C. seek help from the insurance agents locally, who offer advice as a favor. Removing the insurance agent from the equation to save money takes away the one individual who has served as an interpreter of these plans for years on behalf of all Americans. Complexity is the name of this game, though. Academics of the think tank variety, who came up with managed competition, live by the axiom, it's no good unless it's complicated.

Complexity diffuses energy. Businesses operate under an entirely different approach: keep it simple. That's why lasers work so well -- they're focused. Complicating the health care process will not empower the end-user. Under managed competition, the end-user passes their right to select a health plan to either their employer who may choose the program (much as they do now), or to the HIPC, who is selecting the plans they believe best for the membership.

The people behind managed competition say they are crystal-balling the whole concept of health care in this proposal. It's too late for crystal-balling. A system that takes 5 more years to rein in costs is unacceptable. Many government officials have said that managed competition is the last chance for private enterprise to get health care right. If that's the case, private enterprise should hand it over now.

Managed competition still does nothing about requiring younger, healthy people to be in the plan. The 23 year old sole proprietor or unemployed individual who has to make a $280 monthly payment on a Mustang and now is asked to pay an additional $100/month for health care is going to opt for the Mustang payment every time, as long as they're healthy. What can happen to you if you're 23 years old? Nothing! So, health care premiums are put off. How many sole proprietors exist in America today and are not required to be part of this proposed solution? How many are college students coming off their parents' health plan who don't yet have a job? The one advantage of a single-payor method is to require this individual to be covered and contribute. It's the only way to effectively spread the risk.

The other aspect proposed in managed competition is that it leaves Medicare and federal employee coverage as is without change. This means that Medicare will continue its regular and HMO alternative plans, federal employees will retain their 300 health plans, and other under age 65 Americans will have, as noted, some 1500 or so AHPs, all of these programs paying in a different way. How does this save administrative costs and uncomplicate health insurance?

Managed competition may eliminate job lock but creates a new set of problems -- HIPC lock, or even state lock. Every HIPC would have their own plan, meaning each state would be different. Some states may have better programs than others, perhaps creating an influx not possible in Hawaii, where the expense of moving is great. But, in the U.S., if you hear Florida has a great health plan, why not move?

If you live in Fort Lauderdale, Florida and move to Orlando, Florida, would your rates change? Would they be better? If so, would you pay the lower rate? If you do, what's to prevent you from going back to Fort Lauderdale for more expensive health care? If you offer out-of-area service coverage, costs are going to be high if the individual seeks treatment in more expensive areas. If you don't allow out-of-area coverage, you've now created HIPC lock where people are forced to stay in a certain location for health care. One of the failings in Canada is that each province maintains a different plan.

For example, Ontario requires residents to stay within its borders for at least 183 days per year to continue eligibility for their health benefits. What if some of our states began to require the same residency rules? If they don't, what will prevent an individual who lives in Chicago from establishing a Central Florida residency to enroll in Florida's HIPC to attain lower rates. This person then returns to Chicago, where medical care, if needed, will be sought most of the time. This medical care is more expensive then the rates under which coverage was issued in Florida, but that's the whole point. With fifty different states, a hundred or so HIPCS and thousands of AHPS from which to choose, word will get around as to where the price bargains are and when it does, Canadian rules will have to be instituted to prevent people from flocking to lower rates.

We're too mobile a society to restrict movement. We change states, jobs and families on a regular basis now. The traditional family unit is less common today. The potential for abuse under a Managed Competition plan is as high as under our present system which has too many premium collectors, too much variance in fees from region to region, and too many loopholes for those that wish to slip through. Managed Competition takes virtually everything that is wrong with our present system and institutionalizes it. It will only delay a true solution to our health care problem.

Adding an additional layer of bureaucracy in the form of purchasing groups (HIPCs) can only add to administrative costs even though insurance agent commissions are removed. Someone will still be needed to enroll. Someone will still need to stay abreast of market changes. Someone will still be needed to market the purchasing group to potential customers and try to retain the business of existing clients. This costs money to do and will be passed on in the form of administrative charges to the enrollee.

Buying groups for small business and individuals is not a bad idea nor is it a new one. Multiple employer trusts and association group plans are the same type of arrangements and they are a nightmare for insurance regulators. There are few good ones and since most are established to avoid difficult state regulations, it is not uncommon to see coverage lost when the insurer who initially backed the venture decides to pull out. The enrollee is not contracted with that insurer, but, instead, with either the association or the trust which often has little behind it. Who will your contract be with under Managed Competition? The HIPC? The insurer? The U.S. Congress?

Managed care, the key element in the Managed Competition proposal, has held costs down in the past, due to their negotiated fee for service discount. HMOs and PPOs have merit for many seekers of health care and this option should be part of any health care proposal. Remember, Managed Competition can add to costs initially as they get up and running and proponents admit that cost savings won't be realized for five years (at least). By that time, the few insurers left in the market will likely have determined how to price the AHP in a market of limited choice for the individual consumer. New problems will be created as people seek additional choices outside their residency realm.

Crystal balling is not what we need to be doing today. The task force didn't seem as interested in solving the health care problem as much as trying to achieve a politically palatable consensus on who will pay for it. We need to shift away from the old bureaucracy, not embrace it further. A greater erosion of the doctor-patient relationship is not in the best interests of Americans. The continued inability to attract younger, healthier people into our health care system will drive prices inevitably higher. You can't empower consumers by giving their choice away to the purchasing group. Growing government is the lesson other countries are learning and are now electing to reject. Heading in that direction ourselves would clearly be a mistake.

Medical IRAs

Another idea that has been promoted off and on for many years is that of the establishment of medical IRAs for individuals. This concept gives more control to the consumer to watch one's health care spending.

Here's how it works: Individuals or their employers could set up tax-favored accounts in a manner similar to IRAs to be used only for payment of medical bills. They would then purchase a high deductible health insurance plan ($25,000, for example) which would dramatically reduce their premium outlay and could, in fact, help to fund the medical IRA. The account would accumulate without taxes and would always be the individual's, even as they moved from job to job, from city to city, or state to state. A system of tax credits would be created for low income people to set up these same accounts.

Insurance was initially meant for catastrophic events and high deductible policies lend themselves to that concept. Check-ups, x-rays, common cold treatments, and the like are not insurable events; open heart surgery is, and the high deductible policy would save the insured from financial catastrophe by paying all bills beyond a certain point. The money in the medical IRA would be used to pay for the routine care people needed. Since it was their own money being spent, the average individual would probably not overutilize the system. They wouldn't be discouraged; the expense would simply be coming from their pocket.

If this idea had been promoted fifteen to twenty years ago, it might have worked. Today, it's too late to solve the complexity of our health problems with these accounts. The problem now is that many people no longer have the ability to put $25,000 away into a medical IRA. While the individual can control the small bills, the larger ones are often out of one's control. If you have a heart attack, you aren't going to be thinking about cutting back on some of the tests to avoid wiping out the money you've accumulated in your medical IRA account. Once it is depleted, though, you have to replace it, a task that may not be performed easily if you are recovering from heart problems and may be experiencing a loss of income. Trying to rebuild it may take a long time and you will undoubtedly need some medical services during your recovery.

Medical IRAs are the right idea -- at the wrong time. Americans are used to having someone else pick up the majority of the bill when they see a doctor for any reason. The savings account concept is too drastic a departure from that to work now. The time has come for us to accept that we must all pay for health care.

State Reforms

States have been hard at work on their own health care problems for some time. Arguably, they are in a better position to know what works and what doesn't in their states. Several states have recognized the problems inherent in the small group insurance market (the cherry picking, sick sorting practices we discussed earlier) and have taken steps to fix them. Other states have addressed the problems of the uninsured, applying for Medicaid waivers, which are currently being granted by the Clinton Administration. Still others have looked at universal access for all in their states and actions have been taken to implement plans to try and ensure such access.

This creates additional problems when fifty different states institute fifty distinct health care plans. If Oregon rationed and California did not, where would you live? What if rates for individuals and small groups could not exceed a certain level in Florida, but could in Alabama? Would that affect a residency decision? If all are eligible for health care coverage in Minnesota, but not in Michigan, will this enter into a decision about where to locate for people in poor health?

While the efforts are worthy, they should be considered mere stop-gap measures pending the delivery of a consensus national plan where the site of your job or home or status of your family does not matter. Equality will neutralize the ills of a system with too much disparity. States can then focus more on their unique economic and social problems rather than health care. A health care system where every hospital, every doctor, every American and every administrator are reading from the same page will be of immense importance for our states.

Conclusion

The proposals being considered today address only certain aspects of the true health care challenge we face in our country. As such, they are destined to fail, some sooner than others. To act just to act and prove to the American people that something is being done is typical of policy that has faltered in the past. A "solution" that fixes one or two areas but creates newer difficulties will be a step backwards.

It is the consumer we have to empower. Employer mandates empower the employer. Managed Competition empowers bureaucracy. Medical IRAs empowers the well-to-do. Giving this power back to all Americans is step one towards meeting the challenges of access and cost. There are many other pieces of the puzzle that need alteration to make it all work, but any plan that takes a different approach then empowering the consumer is not a solution at all.

EqualCare USA is a system that addresses the health care challenge directly and provides a new, workable plan for a new American program. It repudiates the old ideas of socialism and capitalism by recognizing and incorporating the need for a social safety net through the efficiency of capitalism. Such a system could be best described as bleeding heart capitalism. Americans helping Americans, motivated by self interest for the good of all. If not this, then what? Divided, we fail.

CHAPTER TEN

EQUALCARE USA: THE NEXT EVOLUTION IN HEALTH CARE

Now that you understand what the real areas of concern are in our health care system today, it's time to propose a solution. We know that our present third party payment system is no longer reparable. We know that the doctor-patient relationship must be freed from intrusive micromanagement in the form of prospective cost containment procedures and a lottery-like malpractice system. We know that continuing to tie health care coverage to one's employment is a dinosaur of an idea grounded in an economic age that is rapidly changing.

The following 21 point list outlines a framework for a valid, honest, workable health care program for all Americans. The successful health care solution will address and include these concepts.

1. Every American must be able to obtain the same essential health care delivered anywhere in the world, without regard to any other factors.

2. Non-claimers, usually the young and healthy, must participate without choice so that there will be money available to pay the claims of the unhealthy.

3. The new health care plan must be up and running quickly, with its primary cost saving measures having immediate positive effects on the businesses of America.

4. Everyone must be taxed to pay for the health care system equally. Taxes assessed for this social program must not be allowed to punish production or penalize American business, as in the past.

5. Providers must be able to negotiate their own fees.

6. Employers must not be required to provide health care for their employees. We need to stimulate business development, not set it back further. Costs for providing health care are always passed on to the consumer, one way or another. Business has not, does not, and will not ever pay for health care.

7. Any reform plan must prevent job lock, state lock, country lock, marriage lock and welfare lock. Job lock occurs when employers provide coverage, insurability questions may be asked, and pre-existing conditions may not be covered. State lock is best illustrated by Hawaii's program where residents who need care are restricted to their state since coverage outside the borders would either not be reimbursed, or would be reimbursed at very low levels. Country lock is best exemplified by the need of Ontario residents to live within their provincial borders for 183 days. Many of Canada's other provinces have similar requirements. Marriage lock happens when a spouse is stuck in an undesirable marriage because of a personal health condition or that of one's child. Finally, welfare lock is the inability of recipients to work because it would mean losing Medicaid benefits.

8. There must be a limit for public spending on essential health care utilizing some form of medical efficacy list like the Oregon plan.

9. Provider utilization cost containment must be done retrospectively to avoid the overmanagement and endless paperwork for providers, thereby reducing unnecessary administrative costs for all concerned.

10. The system must be designed to emphasize access through primary care, utilizing physicians in general or family practice fields and in conjunction with Registered Nurses, nurse practitioners and Physician's Assistants in delivering this primary care.

11. Physicians must be encouraged to reduce overhead expenses by locating in rural and other low cost areas.

12. Government's role must be reduced to collecting funds and providing compulsion for all Americans to participate in the health care system.

13. The plan must not build up either a surplus or deficit of funds that government could use or divert to further empower itself.

14. Health care consumers must not be deprived of the services provided by professional insurance advisors, or the availability of supplemental insurance benefits.

15. The plan must pay for prescription drugs to facilitate drug therapies, often a low cost alternative to expensive surgical procedures.

16. The plan must ensure that consumers have the option to choose their own physician, and to select the benefit plan that best suits them.

17. Short-term recuperative nursing care benefits must be incorporated into the basic health care plan benefits. For long term care, a public/private sponsored cooperative benefit plan should be available to all.

18. The plan must pay for all essential and necessary medical

expenses in the most effective, cost-controlled way.

19. The plan must provide treatment for non-residents and tourists. Reimbursement for such services must be collected by the government, who would, if necessary, pursue collection from the foreign patient/country. We would actively encourage residents of other countries to avail themselves of our modern, high-tech health care services and facilities, and develop this into a full-fledged medical tourism industry, to include the export of American medical products, providers and expertise.

20. The plan must control tort costs for participating providers by re-defining the way a bad medical result is handled for both the injured party and the provider.

21. Just as we have prohibited the State from being involved in matters of religion, we must insist on the separation of health care from the State, too. Government bureaucrats must not be given the life and death control over the amount and quality of health care services delivered to all Americans.

The other health care proposals we've examined do not measure up to all of these ideals. The enthusiasm for them among consumers has dwindled significantly over time, further proof that these plans would not provide positive long-term results. Single-payor health insurance has been a catastrophe in other countries, plagued with overutilization, fraud and greed. The "pay or play" arrangement transfers an excessive burden to small business and would send our American economy sliding backwards. How long can we beat up on our businesses and expect to have America? The new darling of many politicians, media and academics, the so-called managed competition plan, sounds very stylish, but it is a complex system that only college-educated bureaucrats could love.

These solutions wouldn't have emerged if they were completely without merit. Some of their principles conform to the 21 point outline detailed above. What America needs is a system that utilizes and puts into practice every one of our 21 parameters, taking the best of our current system, and disposing of the parts that don't work.

The ideal health insurance plan will involve both government and private enterprise, doing what each does best. As the old saying goes, "when you come to a fork in the road, take it". There is no one path we can walk down that holds the solution to our health care difficulties. Either path, government or free enterprise, holds some of the answers. The time has come for us to recognize that neither government or private enterprise alone can provide on effective solution. It must be a joint effort or, divided, we fail.

Capitalism is the economic future of the world. That being said, capitalists should understand that certain social needs must be addressed. If the truly needy are ignored, our free enterprise system will ultimately fail. Conversely, socializing the health care system will ultimately fail. Taking the health care system away from private enterprise will create the same set of problems all countries with socialized health care programs face and which we are currently experiencing with our government-run public education system; namely that per capita student costs have been increasing as fast as health care since the 1970's, while education performance standards have dropped through the floor. We can and should utilize both government and private enterprise to create a unique American health care system that will be the envy of the rest of the world.

It could be our first venture into "bleeding heart" capitalism. Business (capitalism) furnishes funding, energy, imagination and goals. Government would provide the force to compel all to participate. Business and government would function jointly to provide Americans with the health care we all need, and a healthy, viable health care industry we can all support.

My solution, EqualCare USA creates a single buyer system in which all Americans are treated equally. It utilizes the most effective strengths of both government and private enterprise. Together, they employ the power of capitalism to meet the social objectives of covering all Americans for essential and necessary health care in an affordable manner. The components of our EqualCare USA system that will be examined in this chapter are:

- single buyer, one group plan for all Americans
- the role of government
- the role of private enterprise
- our benefits and plan choices
- cost containment features

One of the primary concerns of any health care proposal is how it will be paid for. EqualCare USA's funding comes from an idea I call the "One Cent Solution", where our health care program can be funded with our small change. This idea is so vital to the plan's success that I have addressed it in a separate chapter (11) called "Paying for EqualCare USA".

A Single Buyer System

The time has come to make essential health care available for all Americans, both in terms of benefits and how we share in the cost. Today's third party payment system rewards some and penalizes others. There is too much disparity in provider reimbursements; too much fear that the insurance plan you have will not pay off when you need it; no control in premium charges for the consumer; and no guarantee that your health insurance plan will always be there when you're sick.

A single buyer system would eliminate situations where one person has comprehensive health care coverage without having to pay for it, while another individual has no coverage for health care at all while paying for the person who does have health care. All resident Americans would belong to our EqualCare USA plan. Every American would have exactly the same benefits, paid for in exactly the same way.

If we truly believe in equal access for all Americans to essential health care, our EqualCare USA system would be our one chance to prove it. A single buyer system would guarantee access for all and remove the current complexity which allows better benefits for some Americans than others. Health care is not and should not be an over age 65 thing, or an under age 65 thing, or a big business thing, or a small business thing. It's an American thing and united, we the people can make it work. We must all possess the desire to solve the problem of access. We must accept that all of us should be treated equally, that no one group of us is entitled to better benefits than another. The time has come for all of us to sit at the same table, be dealt the same cards and to ante up equally.

A single buyer system can accomplish the objectives of equal access, equal benefits for all, equal contributions from all. We should be able to understand what we have and what it costs, and know that our fellow American is covered for the same benefits and paying for it in the same way. Our EqualCare USA system is a single buyer program with both government and private enterprise serving the American people.

The Role of Government

In our EqualCare USA system, government's responsibilities will be to do what they do best, namely:

- Compel all Americans to be covered. This is critical to EqualCare USA's success. Everyone has to be in the system on the same basis, whether young, old, healthy, sick, whatever. This is the only way to effectively spread the insurance risk, something private enterprise has been unable to do and will never be able to do.

- Collect all necessary premium to pay for our EqualCare USA plan. Revenue gathering is a function government performs well and it can properly enforce the payments required to make EqualCare USA work.

Compulsion to participate and collection of the money needed to fund EqualCare USA are the duties our government can best handle for our system. Any further bureaucratic involvement will destroy health care. Government programs foster too much bureaucracy which consumes an inordinate amount of their funding. An earlier chapter of our book detailed the dangers inherent in the growth of bureaucracy.

EqualCare USA would be a model social program with which we can go back and restructure our other government bureaucracies. Government should work for us and they should not forget that. Too often bureaucrats lose sight of the mission in delivering our social programs. In education, bureaucracy is destroying the system. The objective of teaching reading, writing and arithmetic is buried underneath a myriad of rules and regulations that have nothing to do with the original goal. We must not allow that to happen to our health care system.

The purpose of government is to act as the referee, enforcing rules that we the people establish. Too often in recent history, bureaucracy has become the quarterback instead. We need to remind the bureaucrats that they work for us, that people and business provide the tax revenues that pays their salaries, expenses and perks. The bureaucracy increases while their accountability decreases, a dangerous formula that has destroyed many governments around the world. America was founded on the principles of a democracy, where government would not control the people, the people would control the government. So it shall be with our EqualCare USA single buyer system.

The people would mandate and government would ensure all Americans to be in the EqualCare USA plan, and that everyone pays. The government would then distribute the money needed to provide health care. That's it. They wouldn't run the system. They wouldn't global budget anything. They wouldn't establish special rules of privilege and access. They would have clearly delineated duties, while our American free enterprise ensured delivery.

The Role of Private Enterprise

Government would distribute the revenue to private enterprise. Private administrators would be invited to bid for the privilege of administering EqualCare USA. This is similar to the system Medicare presently employs. Each state would have at least one administrator, depending on its population, who would receive the revenue dispersed by the government. The private administrator must be able to perform four key functions:

- electronic fund capability to enable processing and provider reimbursement within 48 hours;

- issuance of cards to all state residents certifying them as being part of our EqualCare USA system;
- maintenance of a database which can furnish benefit information on any specific individual; and
- maintenance of a database which can provide retrospective provider utilization review.

The administration of EqualCare USA would be streamlined considerably by a universal fee schedule. This universal reimbursement schedule would save substantial administrative dollars. There will be one fee set per procedure irrespective of geographical site or what licensed provider performs the services.

The present third party payment system has wide-ranging fees per service. For example, an appendectomy is reimbursed at an average of $1,934 in New York City, $1,216 in Chicago, $964 in Atlanta, and $909 in Denver, a difference of 112% for the same medical procedure. Under our EqualCare USA system, one fee for an appendectomy would be pre-negotiated and would be the same in Denver and New York.

Doing the pre-negotiating would be an EqualCare USA Board, overseen by a Health Commissioner. This Commissioner would be elected nationally by the American people to a four year term in office. The Commissioner chairs an annual meeting of the Board to discuss and set provider fees for the following year. On this Board will be five members each nominated through the professional associations of the following industries:

- primary physicians
- hospitals
- nursing care
- physician specialist
- insurance administration
- pharmaceutical

These 30 individuals represent a cross-section of the health care system, sharing an insider's knowledge in delivering medical services to all Americans. They would meet to set fees as well as to hold annual hearings on the state of our EqualCare USA system.

The Board would receive input during these hearings from consumers appointed by their Congressional representative for their district. This translates into 435 Americans giving feedback annually to our EqualCare USA National Health Board. Collectively, this group would hold the power of a tie-breaking vote on any measure deadlocked by the 30 person Board.

These 435 Americans, in turn, would invite comments from anyone desiring to express them through means of district town meetings. Following these sessions, these selected representatives would attend the annual Board meetings to pass these insights along to our Health Commissioner and other Board members.

Consumer suggestions might affect the type of procedures covered, the price of medical services, or any other system specifics for which improvement might be made. EqualCare USA is every American's health care program and how it functions will be largely up to us. The utilizer of health services, the end-user, can certainly add invaluable information to assist the Board in its annual planning.

Thus, the government would perform the two functions it does best: enforcement and collection. Private enterprise would do what it does best: efficiently manage resources. This partnership would lead us where no social program has gone before and should finally provide a social safety net managed through the efficiency of free enterprise.

EqualCare USA's Benefits

All Americans would be eligible for EqualCare USA by virtue of being a resident of the U.S. Americans would enroll in their home state and receive an ID card with their Social Security number as their health care identification. Americans would have a choice of two benefit programs: a Preferred Provider Organization (PPO), and a Health Maintenance Organization (HMO), both of which provide essential, necessary medical care, covering each of us from birth to earth.

The PPO program would allow Americans to choose their EqualCare USA provider, and would contain deductibles and coinsurance. Under the HMO plan, you, as an American, would select a primary care provider. This provider would manage your health care needs and no additional out-of-pocket costs would be needed to pay for the essential benefits included in coverage.

The PPO Choice:

The current Medicare system for American seniors age 65 and over would be expanded to include all Americans under age 65. Medicare is a well-established basic benefits package of essential, necessary care, and it would be offered through any participating EqualCare USA physician. Just as in Medicare, there would be two parts to this PPO plan, an inpatient hospital program and reimbursement for physician services.

The first part, inpatient hospital care, carries a $696 deductible which would be paid first. The plan would then pay 100% of covered hospital expenses for up to 60 days for any one hospitalization. After 60 days, a co-payment of $174 per day would be necessary, with EqualCare USA paying the balance of covered services. After 90 days, the copayment increases to $348 per day.

Inpatient services would include semi-private room and board, nursing services, use of regular hospital equipment, supplies and appliances, drugs ordinarily furnished by the hospital, operating room costs, anesthesia services, blood transfusions, x-rays, radiology services, lab tests and rehabilitation services.

The second part of the PPO plan would cover physician services, after a $100 deductible. The coinsurance required would be 20%, with our EqualCare USA paying 80%. Services covered include physician and surgeon services, diagnostic x-ray and lab tests, outpatient physical therapy and speech pathology, ambulance transportation, durable medical equipment rental, maternity, prescription drug costs, screening pap smears and mammograms, and mental and nervous conditions (with coinsurance required increased to 50%).

You would select any EqualCare USA provider you want. There will be, as mentioned, no regional variation in fees between providers for a procedure, regardless of where it is delivered. You would hand the provider your EqualCare USA ID card which would be run through a computer connected by modem to your state's EqualCare USA administrator. Information would be displayed, showing your current deductible and coinsurance status. The provider would know, as would you, what part of the bill is your responsibility, and make appropriate arrangements on the spot. EqualCare USA would reimburse the provider within 48 hours after the medical care is furnished.

If your wish is for no out-of-pocket costs (in the form of deductibles and coinsurance), you, as an American, would be able to opt instead for an available HMO plan.

HMO Plans

This benefit choice would reduce your out-of-pocket cost to -0-. No deductible. No copayment. No coinsurance. The reason for that is simple: you use the providers within the Health Maintenance Organization (HMO). Under the PPO plan, you would select your own EqualCare USA providers. Under the HMO program, you would choose a Primary Care physician from a list you receive when you enroll. This primary care physician would coordinate all of your health care for you. If you need a specialist or hospital care, this doctor would arrange it. If an emergency arises and you can't contact your physician immediately, you would obtain whatever medical care you need, and contact your primary care provider as soon thereafter as possible.

While you give up the flexibility of using whatever EqualCare USA provider you wish, you would not incur any additional costs for treatment provided. The HMO providers would be paid directly by the various state administrators. Your ID card would be necessary for this purpose, but you would have no further fiscal responsibility.

Included in the benefit structure for the HMO option, would be the following:

- primary care physician office visits
- participating specialist office visits
- periodic health evaluations
- x-ray, laboratory, and other diagnostic services
- health education
- professional counseling, nutrition, and medical social services
- semi-private hospital room and board
- surgeon and physician inpatient services
- anesthesia services
- inpatient drugs and medications
- use of intensive care unit, operating and recovery rooms
- maternity costs
- radiation, inhalation, physical and rehabilitative therapy
- emergency room services
- prescription drug coverage
- mental health care outpatient visits
- mental health care inpatient days (limit: 100)
- outpatient surgical, radiation, physical, and rehabilitative services
- rental of durable medical equipment

The administration of this plan would also be simple as HMOs would be using pre-negotiated fees like PPO providers, or capitation payments, and would know what reimbursement to expect for each health care service they render. These providers would also have electronic fund transfer systems to enable them to be reimbursed within 48 hours. There would be no additional costs to you as a patient.

If you initially elect the HMO plan and decide that you would rather have the PPO program instead, you may change your selection by contacting your closest EqualCare USA administrative office through a toll-free number. The reverse, changing from a PPO to HMO plan, would be done in the same manner.

Both the PPO and HMO plans would include 100 days of short term nursing care that would provide services either in the hospital or at home. Many of the elderly patients today are discharged early from the hospital resulting in an increase in nursing home admissions. Many of these nursing home stays could be avoided with extra care provided in the hospital or at home. Our EqualCare USA system will build in 100 days of short-term recuperative nursing care to help avoid these often unnecessary nursing home stays. Individuals could utilize specific hospital beds designated for nursing care to receive their recuperative treatment, or elect to have the recuperative care done at home.

Beyond 100 days, an expansion of the long term care program currently available in Connecticut and a handful of other states, would enable each American that wishes to buy into a public/private sponsored long term care benefit plan. Every individual could design their own long term care program based on their individual needs and budget. A lump sum benefit amount would be available for purchase. The joint sponsorship between the public sector and private enterprise would help to keep the program affordable. All Americans, of course, would still be entitled to the first 100 days of recuperative care under EqualCare USA.

These are the benefit choices from which you, as an American, would select your preference under EqualCare USA. On the one hand, you'd have the PPO system, with freedom of provider choice and some fiscal accountability through deductibles and coinsurance. On the other hand, you might prefer the HMO program, with no additional costs for medical care and in which you choose a primary care physician from a list of choices. This physician would then coordinate all of your medical treatment. There is something to appeal to virtually everyone in these two benefit choices.

Every American resident would be covered under EqualCare USA. Each American would be issued a personal I.D. card with his or her Social Security number on it. Children would be covered from birth and the hospital would notify the proper state administrator following birth, to generate the child's own EqualCare USA I.D. card.

This system would immediately improve access to health care coverage. No qualifying health questions. No pre-existing conditions. The risk would effectively be spread as the young and the healthy people are compelled to participate in our system. EqualCare USA is the only proposed solution that brings every American into one single buyer free enterprise system. Our younger Americans currently represent a high percentage of our uninsureds in this country simply because they don't see the need to secure coverage, given their youth and likely good health. Their first exposure to a health care system is usually the birth of their first child. Up to that time, health care isn't a priority. In their youth, they may not have as much money to spend, and it's easy to justify foregoing health insurance and make the rent and car insurance payment instead.

Regardless of one's age or circumstances, each American would be eligible for either benefit choice as outlined: the PPO plan with provider choice and some out-of-pocket costs, or the HMO program with a specific provider list and no out-of-pocket costs. A true American program, this health care system might prove to be a model for the rest of the world.

Time Frame For Implementation

What about timing? How long would it take to put these benefit plans in place? Many of the estimates we hear about other health care solutions have significant time frames involved, as much as 5-7 years before full implementation.

How about 12 months from Congressional passage? With some cooperation, EqualCare USA could be up and running that quickly? Why? These PPO and HMO benefit plans already exist -- with Medicare. The HMO plan is available in a dozen or so states for Americans age 65 and over. The PPO program is the standard Medicare package. In other words, very little development is required, other than adapting them for use with the entire population instead of only seniors. In addition, Medicare is currently administered by private enterprise. The National Health Board could be appointed in a short period of time, and administrative bids could be solicited as soon as a Health Commissioner is selected.

As you will read in Chapter 11, our financing of EqualCare USA, the One Cent Solution, would also utilize existing collection facilities and procedures, making that aspect of our system one less hurdle to climb. Thus, the major components of EqualCare USA are already in place. We don't need to reinvent them. Many Americans are also familiar with Medicare and its benefits. EqualCare USA is a greatly simplified administrative version of it, with the one fee approach to provider charges and a series of cost containment procedures that I will detail later in this chapter.

If Congress acted on it immediately, and a non-partisan Commissioner then appointed at once for a short term (with elections for a non-partisan Commissioner to be held at the next regularly scheduled election), and a Board assembled shortly thereafter, EqualCare USA is a 12-15 month prospect that would begin saving all Americans money the day after it begins. I don't believe the American people want a new health care system that won't be fully in effect for several years before cost savings, if any, are realized. EqualCare USA would give access to all, offer essential and necessary health care for every American, and save all of us some significant dollars in the process within a short time frame. We the people can make this happen if we stand together and insist on EqualCare USA. Divided, we will fail.

Cost Containment

You now know who's covered: every American resident.

You now know what our specific benefit choices are: either a PPO or HMO program.

Details about how we will pay for it are in the next chapter.

What about cost controls? EqualCare USA would be, after all, our health care system, and we want to do everything within our capabilities to operate it effectively at the lowest possible cost. To do this, there would be several elements in our EqualCare USA system which would ensure that we spend only what we have to without any decline in the quality of health care provided. These ingredients are:

1. Managed care approach to our benefit structure.
2. One fee per service anywhere, pre-negotiated annually.
3. The Oregon method of identifying essential and necessary care.
4. Retrospective utilization review.
5. Tort relief for participating providers.

Each of these methods would help keep our health care expenditures at a reasonable level and, combined with our administrative savings, should make the financing of our EqualCare USA system even more cost effective.

1. Managed care approach to our benefit structure. Both the HMO and PPO coverage programs make use of a common method of controlling health care costs today. The services delivered under EqualCare USA would be based on rates already set by a National Board, a group of people who represent health care specialists best equipped to price medical care. This pre-negotiated fee structure would have been computed after some discussion to reach a fair rate nationwide. If we are able to control price and utilization, we would be able to provide essential health care at an equitable price.

2. One fee per service everywhere, pre-negotiated each year. Previously, I used an example of the going rates for an appendectomy, which varied by over 112% between New York City and Denver for the identical service. EqualCare USA would require providers to agree to the same pre-negotiated fee regardless of whre they practice, without exception. The participating providers would be precluded from exceeding these pre-negotiated fees, but could re-negotiate them at the next annual National Health Board meeting. This one pre-negotiated fee would be a vast difference from Medicare's current 233 different regional variations. The one fee method doesn't mean that the appendectomy rate would be Denver's $909. It certainly wouldn't be New York's $1,934. Perhaps $1,200 is the fair rate that would prevail. Whatever the final result, this is the charge all participating EqualCare USA providers would agree to accept. This reduction in the wide ranging price variations for medical services would produce dramatic administrative and overall medical cost savings. The one fee method would also assist the provider in avoiding the constant adjustment of fees based on who's paying the bill.

This one fee approach should also make it attractive for physicians to work in general and family practice specialties while desiring places to live and work other than large metropolitan areas. If providers moved to more rural areas to practice, greater choice among physicians would be accorded residents there.

The savings in administrative costs would free up more of our EqualCare USA funds to pay directly for health care services. This wouldn't happen in a government-run program like, as an example, public education, which is reported to take as much as 40 cents of every tax dollar allocated for the school program to pay for administration.

3. The Oregon method of identifying essential and necessary care. This year, the state of Oregon was granted federal permission to implement a program for their Medicaid beneficiaries which ranks over 700 medical procedures in order of their medical efficacy. They utilize a formula which involves the cost of health care, the number of people afflicted by a particular condition, an estimation of the effectiveness of treatment, when and if the condition is likely to recur, and the well-being of people after receiving treatment. The result is a list of medical procedures that would constitute the most effective and practical services with which to deliver essential, reasonable and necessary health care.

From Oregon's list, EqualCare USA would provide benefits for the first 587 conditions, among them, appendicitis, pneumonia, neonatal care, acute sinusitis, heart attack, tuberculosis, burns, and, number 587, a painful swelling of the esophagus. This ranking of conditions ensures that EqualCare USA would pay for essential health care delivery and not use taxpayer money to cover non-essential and often expensive forms of treatment.

This does not mean the services not covered under EqualCare USA wouldn't be available to the American health consumer. It simply means that tax dollars would not pay for the procedures. How Americans would secure this treatment will be detailed later in this chapter.

What EqualCare USA tries to accomplish through this method of cost containment is to control unnecessary health care spending that directly affects EqualCare USA taxpayer funds. Our system's goal is to responsibly use the money contributed by all Americans. As I see it, this Oregon plan would offer the most sensible way to begin capping treatments which, in essence, do not prolong life for any measureable length, or force the human body long past the original specifications, or only offer comfort for the individual. Where should EqualCare USA spend its money? Should $50,000 be used to prolong a 97 year old's life for 5 days, or use that same $50,000 to provide neonatal care procedures for 100 babies that have yet to live? You tell me.

Our method would also utilize a scale called QALY (Quality Adjusted Life Years) which would measure the value of treatment. In this calculation, the number of years the person could expect to live after treatment is multiplied by its quality. The result runs from -0- (death) to 1 (perfect) health with no disability), with all other results falling somewhere between these two extremes. Both the Oregon plan and this measurement are subjective to a certain extent, but based on extensive medical knowledge and research. It would provide all of us with an analytical answer to the question of whether to pay for a certain procedure once we understand what the quality of life is likely to be after the care is rendered.

The 435 Americans who will be appointed in their respective Congressional districts would have the opportunity annually to address the procedures on the list. If, as a result of overwhelming feedback, the American people want to add a procedure or two to the list, it would be done and the cost reflected in national assessment. If we agree as a country that we want additional treatments covered and are willing to pay an additional tax for it, if needed, EqualCare USA would react accordingly. This is our health care system.

4. Retrospective utilization review. Today, providers have been forced to increase clerical staff to comply with a mind-boggling amount of paperwork associated with up-front, prospective cost containment. The provider is watched through virtually every stage of the treatment process, having to solicit approval from some bureaucrat far removed from the doctor-patient relationship. The purpose of this prospective review is to ultimately contain costs; but, if it does, it's only for the third party payor. The provider has experienced increased costs as a result with an intrusive system that seriously impairs the ability to practice medicine.

EqualCare USA would change this complex, costly routine. As a true single buyer system, EqualCare USA administrators would be able to review utilization after the procedure has been performed. All of the nation's treatment information would be stored on one data base. EqualCare USA would measure outcomes and assemble data on each of our participating providers. It should be a simple task to review, retrospectively, any particular data we wish to analyze. If there are providers who tend to overutilize, they would be noticed quickly. Those who order more tests than others, perform more surgeries, see patients more for certain conditions, would be obvious to spot in the analysis of the information in the data bank. There may be perfectly valid reasons for these results. If not, the provider would have the opportunity to reduce utilization, and continue on as an EqualCare USA provider.

This outcome data would be extremely helpful in discerning trends or patterns in results nationwide and in interpreting this information for further use. We would assemble the most complete medical knowledge on earth, an exportable product to the rest of the world. This information could save lives, money, and research time. It would also be used to refine practice guidelines as consistency in treatment of conditions emerges from the mountain of data. Practice guidelines plot the most accepted method of treatment for a specific condition. Our EqualCare USA database would assist in keeping these parameters up to date.

The potential here is tremendous. For example, such an analysis was done at one hospital and involved monitoring the use of antibiotics for patients undergoing elective surgery. Results from the review of 3,000 patients revealed that the optimum time to administer this post-operative medicine was within two hours of surgery. Of 1,708 patients who received antibiotics within that time frame, only 10 developed surgical wound infections. This one study effectively decreased the post-operative wound infection rate by almost 80%. These infections added an average of $14,000 to the cost of each patient's care. By instituting this monitoring program, over $700,000 was saved in patient care costs. Think of the savings and results that could be achieved within EqualCare USA's central data bank!

Further, in establishing practice guidelines that are continually refined as a result of this type of retrospective utilization review, all EqualCare USA physicians would work with established protocol for the appropriateness of treatment given certain conditions. Practice guidelines are directed at the "how" of care. Medicine is not an exact science, yet the use of large samples of patient results can give strong indications of what works and what doesn't, reducing practice variation and making it easier to estimate costs per treatment in many health scenarios.

EqualCare USA would also put into practice the use of patient videos to help all of us better understand the treatment options available. This patient education program would reveal the many different courses of treatment that could be used for a single procedure. For example, treatment of low back pain can be handled by either surgery or a combination of non-surgical treatments which include exercise, medication, chiropractic and acupuncture. Benign prostate disease can be treated by a prostatectomy operation or by simply monitoring the symptoms. Mild hypertension can be remedied by drugs, or by changing one's diet and other personal habits. The suggestions obviously have a wide range of costs depending on which course you elect to take, with the assistance from your provider.

Kaiser Permanente, a HMO in California, began showing a video to patients with benign prostate disease. This tape explained the effects of surgery versus the use of medication and other therapeutic procedures. The incidence of surgery dropped by 44% in the first year. Many patients do not understand the circumstances surrounding possible treatments and alternatives, and videos are definitely an American way of offering enough information upon which to base a decision. Given this knowledge, a substantial number of people elected not to have the surgery. This empowerment of the consumer, the end-user of medical services would be reflected throughout our EqualCare USA system.

Retrospective utilization review would work because of EqualCare USA's central data bank. You've now seen the type of cost savings and critically important information it would generate. Today's cost containment procedures, which review and monitor the treatment from the beginning, were extremely successful early on in saving dollars. We have apparently maximized this savings and now the extra staffing requirements along with the necessity to explain each and every medical move, has driven provider costs and, ultimately, patient costs much higher. Utilization review is important and providers are willing participants if done to the advantage of all concerned. Our EqualCare USA method of measuring outcomes after the fact would save substantial time and money, while giving us even greater intelligence about medicine than we have ever secured before. The all important extra benefit that results would be a return to a stronger than ever doctor-patient relationship unencumbered by unnecessary requirements.

5. Tort relief. The final link in the EqualCare USA cost containment chain would be a change to our malpractice system. What we have today is a process which is, quite frankly, like a lottery, where a patient who experiences a bad result from medical treatment could get a settlement in an amount ranging from zero to five million dollars or more. It has created a legal scenario where the lawyer always gets paid, the injured party sometimes gets paid, the bad physician rarely gets penalized, and all Americans pay for it.

The fear of a malpractice lawsuit has forced many physicians to practice defensive medicine resulting in additional treatment ministered to protect the provider fiscally, more than the patient physically, and which adds billions more to the overall health care bill for the country. Examples of tests ordered in this manner include routine skull x-rays for head injury victims, continuous electronic fetal monitoring, and unwarranted lab exams.

Analysts of the legal system believe that, until 1970, there were a number of useful rules that discouraged people from filing lawsuits without a strong, definitive case. There were procedural controls and limits on the lawyers themselves. Judges' opinions were written in such a specific way as to indicate whether a strong case was present or not. Litigation was considered a last resort.

This is now a bygone era in legal practice. Attorneys today can advertise for lawsuits, expert witnesses are no longer well-screened, and unrealistic awards are a too common jury practice. The onus is almost always on the defendant to prove that the plaintiff didn't have $250,000 of emotional stress he or she claims to have. Lawyers typically receive one-third of a claimant's award, powerful incentive to keep the lawsuits flying and to seek the highest possible judgements since it can benefit them, too.

An example of defensive medicine might be found in the incidence of Caesarean Sections. This procedure is ordered most in areas where malpractice rates are the highest. Many of these procedures may have been unnecessary and could have potentially saved a substantial amount of health care dollars. Malpractice rates for OB/GYN physicians are extraordinarily high, making the option of a relatively safe procedure like a C-Section a more fiscally prudent course of treatment.

In our EqualCare USA system, participating providers would all operate under a medical malpractice program which would try and avoid litigation and attorney fees and provide a fair, equitable settlement for the injured party, while isolating the physicians who are truly bad practitioners. In doing so, this last element of our complete cost containment program would again save a huge amount of revenue which can be better spent on health care.

Today, if a patient goes in for an operation to correct a problem for an injured leg, and a bad result occurs whereby this person loses the use of the leg, the financial consequences could cover a wide range of possibilities. If it's determined to be no mistake on the physician's part, the claimant might well end up with no monetary compensation. If it was an honest mistake on the part of the practitioner, the injured party could collect, say, $1,000,000 as a result. If it's decided that this outcome was the result of criminal negligence on the part of the physician, the patient might receive $10,000,000.

What's wrong with this picture? The obvious answer is that, irrespective of the amount of money received, the physical end result for this person is the same: the loss of use of a leg which will have consequences extending through the remainder of one's life. Why should one person receive no financial award whatsoever, while someone else gets $10 million? It's still a bad result whether the physician was at fault or not. In the $10 million dollar settlement, the attorney may have walked away with one-third of it, malpractice premiums are immediately raised for every provider in the insurance program, provider fees are raised to cover the rate increases, and the physician most often would not be punished for negligence. Where is the justice in all of this?

EqualCare USA would establish, for participating providers, a Patient Casualty Compensation Fund. Each EqualCare USA provider would purchase base coverage of $1,000,000. Patients would not need to pursue legal recourse following a bad result from an encounter with a participating Equal Care USA provider. When a bad result occurred, the patient would automatically be eligible for reimbursement from the Fund, without regard to fault. If the individual died as a result of treatment, the family would receive the full $1,000,000. All other awards would be based on the percentage of disability that occurs as a consequence of the bad result, using the Workers' Compensation schedule to measure it. A 50% disability would generate a $500,000 payout; a 10% disability produces $100,000. The entire amount would be paid to the patient as there would be no need for an attorney.

Insurers of the Patient Casualty Compensation Fund would track claims and providers to see if there was an ongoing problem with specific practitioners. Premiums that providers paid for this coverage would be established based on their specialty experience, and claims made. Physicians whose work does not effect a bad result would subsequently have lower premiums than those who have bad results.

Most important, the patient would receive compensation for the bad result based on the seriousness of its effects without having to wait months or even years in court; without having to secure an attorney and give up a significant portion of any settlement paid; without regard to the fault involved in the mistake. The physical outcome of a bad result doesn't change with the settlement, and our EqualCare USA system would recognize this and compensate accordingly.

Physicians who are guilty of criminal negligence would face charges immediately. Physicians with excessive claims would watch their premiums skyrocket and perhaps lose eligibility to practice in our EqualCare USA system. Physicians with few, if any, claims would enjoy the practice of medicine without lawyers second guessing them.

Private insurance carriers would be able to provide supplements for the patient to purchase which would pay amounts above the $1,000,000 Patient Casualty Compensation Fund level. This idea will be detailed in Chapter Twelve, outlining the roles of various health care system personnel in our EqualCare USA system.

One last possibility for cost containment under EqualCare USA might come by use of living wills. We spend an inordinate amount of health care dollars watching loved ones die without dignity. Life support machines which prolong the essential functioning of the human body (not really life as we know it), carries an astronomical price tag. Most would not want to go through this themselves or subject their loved ones to it.

A woman whose grandmother came down with emphysema spent five agonizing weeks watching her fade away in the intensive care unit of the hospital. During one of her conscious states, the elderly woman informed her granddaughter, "next time, do nothing". Many patients remain comatose towards the end of life and, if they could speak, would likely ask to have the respirator turned off. Living wills allow that person's wishes to be honored.

Part of the EqualCare USA enrollment process might involve the signing of living wills. This should spare people the agony of pointless treatment and relieve physicians and family members from the anxiety associated with this situation. The standard document would give the patient, if medically competent, the option of continuing care or not. Most individuals would rather the money be spent for someone else with a chance at a normal life, instead of on someone who was losing ground, destined never to return to a normal state again. If the individual is incompetent and can't speak, the living will respects that person's wishes through transfer of power of attorney to someone who can convey one's feelings.

We are all aware of the high costs of health care associated with the last days of life. Aside from the cost, the emotional repercussions suffered by both patient and family members through this prolonging of the inevitable end is staggering. The utilization of living wills in our EqualCare USA system would allow individuals and family to make their own decisions. EqualCare USA is about individualism and empowering the end-user of medical services. Living wills would be an important part of this philosophy.

This is our EqualCare USA system. It is a single buyer program which would effectively use both government and private enterprise doing what they do best. Government would require all to participate and collect premium. Private enterprise would administer the system and deliver the care. A choice of two programs would be offered to every American resident; one a PPO, the other a HMO. The PPO plan offers complete freedom to select any EqualCare USA provider with some out-of-pocket costs, while the HMO program would require the selection of a primary care physician to coordinate your treatment, and for which little or no out-of-pocket costs would be incurred. Several specific methods of cost containment would be employed, including simplified administration, negotiated fees, use of a specific list of conditions which would be treated, lower cost and effective methods of treatment, retrospective utilization review and malpractice relief.

Our EqualCare USA system guarantees access for all to essential and necessary health care performed in the greatest health care system in the world. EqualCare USA addresses an important social need while managing the enterprise under the principles of capitalism that have made this country great. It would be the first venture into a partnership between government and private enterprise, and would create a model social program to be used as an example in rebuilding other similar bureaucracies.

EqualCare USA is the only proposed health care solution which can be up and running 12 months after passage. It is the only health care solution which truly empowers the end user. It is an American health plan, run by and controlled by all Americans. We would have the ultimate say in decisions made about any of the essential elements: benefits, premiums, administration, providers.

EqualCare USA would not, however, be our only medical system. It would be our tax-based system, and one we would all pay into and benefit from. But there would certainly be medical treatments not covered under our EqualCare USA program (as discussed earlier in the cost containment phase), and there might be providers who also wish to practice outside the scope of our EqualCare USA system.

The Private Health Care System

I have long been an advocate of letting Americans decide how much of their income they wish to spend on medical care. If Americans do want to spend their own money on health care, they should be allowed to do so without outside interference.

In our EqualCare USA system, there would be some procedures that wouldn't qualify as essential and necessary care. As you now know, our basic benefits package does not include treatments which might not necessarily extend life on a quality basis. However, if an individual desired this treatment anyway, and is willing to pay the out-of-pocket costs, we do not have the moral right to restrict this person's wishes. Thus, the care would be sought privately, and paid for with private funds, not our EqualCare USA tax dollars.

If a 75 year old American wishes to have disk surgery to relieve back pain and live the remainder of his or her life in greater comfort, the procedure would be performed and paid for privately. This medical service would have no effect on any of the rest of us. It would strictly be between patient and doctor, financially and medically. If an experimental organ transplant is desired and is not covered under our EqualCare USA plan, the individual desiring the treatment could work out a private payment arrangement with a provider, and the medical procedure then performed. EqualCare USA would never remove this type of private health care; instead, it would only exclude it from our tax-based system. Anyone with the means to afford treatment that is not included under our EqualCare USA system should certainly be allowed the right to obtain it.

Under a global budgeting type of system, that would not be permitted. That type of system limits total medical spending and would render some treatments as completely unavailable. Our cost containment parameters in our EqualCare USA system would be established to control medical spending within our tax-based system, but would impose no overall medical cap as global budgeting would. As Americans, we should protect the right of any one of us who wishes to spend money on any medical treatment, providing it does not impact the rest of us financially. Under our EqualCare USA system, this individual right to seek out treatment would be preserved.

This is how elective surgery is handled today. As one analyst summed it up, "Steroids, contraceptives, eyeglasses, gene therapy, growth hormones, breast implants, hair removal, nose jobs and surgeries to correct congenitally cleft palates are all human equivalents of stock car racing. The whole point is not to fix what got broken, but to improve the performance of what came off the dealer's lot." Today, individuals negotiate fees with providers and pay for these procedures outside third party payor lines.

As the population continues to age, there will be a greater demand for treatment and surgery that would likely be outside the boundaries of EqualCare USA treatment, such as artificial heart valves and plastic eye lenses. We must not deny this demand, but merely insist that each individual has the right to negotiate for the treatment if they wish. There may even be a demand by the American public to include some of these treatments under EqualCare USA and a willingness to pay for them. This public opinion would be brought before our National Health Board for the option of including it under our EqualCare USA system.

Providers, though having great incentive to practice under our EqualCare USA system, would not be required to do so. If you have a preference for a certain physician and the person has elected to practice outside EqualCare USA, you would still be able to utilize this provider for treatment. The practitioner would be required, as a prerequisite to licensure, to disclose up front what multiple of the EqualCare fee is being charged for any medical service. It might be 2 X EqualCare or 3 X EqualCare. Whatever the amount, you would know before any treatment is delivered.

After receiving the treatment, you would then submit a reimbursement request to your state EqualCare USA administrator to reimburse the fee which would have been paid for an eligible service delivered by an EqualCare USA provider. This claim payment would go directly to you since non-participating providers would not be eligible to take assignment. You could use this money as part of your payment obligation to the private practice provider. Our EqualCare USA administrators would not pay the provider directly if he or she operates outside the system. As a tax-paying American resident, you are entitled to reimbursement in the amount that would have been paid on your behalf within our EqualCare USA system.

The private system completes the full range of services under our EqualCare USA system. The next two chapters outline how we will pay for the plan and will also illustrate the roles to be assumed by various health care personnel, including physicians, hospitals, drug companies, nurses, insurance companies and agents, and their interaction with our EqualCare USA system. It is a solution destined to continue our health care program as the best in the modern world and set a new standard in health care for all countries.

This is truly health care reform, of the people, by the people, and for the people, a health care plan to free America. Divided, we fail.

CHAPTER ELEVEN

PAYING FOR EQUALCARE USA: THE ONE CENT SOLUTION

"I cannot save every undercapitalized business in America." - Hillary Rodham Clinton, as quoted in the Fayetteville (GA) Citizen

On September 21, 1993, it was my pleasure to be invited, along with other members of the National Association of Radio Talk Show Hosts, to the White House for a special briefing on what has become known as the Clinton Health Plan. While listening first to Mrs. Clinton and then to Ira Magaziner, the Administration's health care expert, I became suspicious that this plan was mostly an attempt to please political constituencies, and would in fact aggravate most of what is now wrong with our existing system and, if actually enacted, have its seeds of failure already firmly in place.

President Clinton's subsequent speeches did nothing at all other than to confirm these suspicions. Lawyers will tell you that if you have the facts, then you should present your case to the judge. If not, then make the jury cry. The President is a charismatic speaker and while his speeches are awash with tears, his health plan, unfortunately, will not relieve the pain and sorrow of those of whom he speaks so eloquently.

Setting up hundreds of government bureaucracies may promise to improve access to health care, but it won't lower its cost. A global budget would render health care, now a valuable and finite resource, even more scarce, unavailable and, ultimately, more costly. To blame 1500 claim forms for the paperwork that has overwhelmed our present system may make for good speeches, but as any doctor's office or hospital administrator will tell you, this is not the problem. The high cost of administration is caused by the three M's: Medicare, Medicaid and Managed Care. The variations and requirements within these structures is mind-boggling.

In Florida alone, come January 1, 1994, there will be eleven different buying alliances, each contracting with five (or more) provider groups or plans that will each have several coverage options. Can you imagine a hospital or doctor in Missoula, Montana trying to verify coverage on a patient from Naples, Florida during an emergency?

Can you imagine moving your family from Tallahassee to Tampa and then having to decide which of the Tampa alliance plans you should select and attempting to have the bureaucracy effect such change? Or can you imagine a family with the children of spouse one living in Seattle and the children of spouse two living in Tupelo, while Dad lives in Las Vegas? Can you imagine eleven different rate zones within Florida? Why wouldn't everyone and every business seek out the lowest rate zone? Daimler Benz just laid off 65,000 workers in Germany even as they are announcing their intention to open a new plant in Birmingham, Alabama. Birmingham, Alabama? Do you think employee benefit costs may have something to do with this decision? Why not open the plant in California or New York or Michigan or Massachusetts? President Clinton tells us that California has 12% of our nation's population and 25% of it's unemployed. Doesn't he know that every California business that can has relocated to Arizona, Nevada or Utah? Did employee benefit costs finally drive these companies away?

What the Clinton Health Plan shares with the other proposals on the table (other than EqualCare USA) is one common flaw that is basic to and has destroyed our existing system. Until we all understand and grasp this basic idea, there will be no real way to effect reform that will work. Here it is: the basic problem with our existing system and these other proposals is that there are too few people paying for the health care of too many. Think about it for a moment. Small businesses and their employees pay for the health care of the poor, senior citizens, government employees and big business employees.

How can that be? Small businesses, you say, are the ones that either don't have coverage or have to pay huge rates to get any coverage at all. Are they really paying for everyone else? Small businesses and their employees pay for the poor through inventory taxes, property taxes and the health care cost shift. Small businesses and their employees pay for senior citizens with payroll taxes and the health care cost shift. Small businesses and their employees pay for government employees with income taxes and the health care cost shift. Finally, small businesses and their employees pay for the health care of big business employees with 60 billion dollars a year in tax subsidy and the health care cost shift. All of this has made health care unaffordable, unavailable and too costly for small businesses and their employees, even as they pay for everyone else's health care.

Yet the reaction of our government has been to make them pay even more. We cannot fix our health care system by blaming those that are paying for it. We cannot fix the health care system by blaming those that are working in it. We can only fix the health care system by making the following decisions:

We must decide who will be covered, what will be covered, and how it will be paid for. I propose, with EqualCare USA, that the "who" should be every resident of the United States in the single buyer system detailed in Chapter 10. The "what" should be determined on the basis of efficacy and not on political clout. The "how" is that everyone, the poor, the rich, the young, the old, the small business employee, the big business employee, should all pay premium equally for health care. To pay for EqualCare USA on an equal basis will guarantee its success; any system that favors one group of us over another group is destined to fail. We must pay for our health care in a way that rewards productivity. Since only some of us earn, but all of us spend, then what we should assess to pay for health care is spending. In this chapter, I present to you, "The One Cent Solution for Health Care".

You now know the vehicle: a single buyer system. You also know the roles of both government and private enterprise and how they will contribute to the system. There are two comprehensive benefit choices available: a PPO and a HMO program. EqualCare USA would place a strong emphasis on controlling the amount of money spent on health care, but only within the single buyer system to which we would all pay premium. EqualCare USA would never attempt to control the amount of personal dollars one may wish to spend on health care.

As mentioned, financing a new health care system has been a glaring weakness with all of the proposals on the table, and is especially so with the Clinton Health Plan. These financing arrangements attempt to squeeze even more money from the very few people that are paying the health care tab for everyone else today. These proposals don't hold up because these payors cannot afford to pay any more into the system and continue to support those that now (and would continue to) receive political patronage.

What's happening today? The seniors have Medicare, largely financed by payroll taxes levied at small businesses and their employees. The poor have Medicaid, a government program which has forced providers to look to insured patients to make up their reimbursement shortfall. Federal employees have a great plan, funded by taxpayers. Big business has a great plan, funded by all of us who buy goods and services. Car companies have excellent coverage for their workers. They take a whopping tax deduction for providing benefits, then pass the net cost along to the consumer through higher car prices. The end result is that, when we buy a car, we are paying for health insurance for car company employees, and contributing to the company bottom line as well.

So who is on the wrong end of all this political favoritism? Small business and their employees are saddled with payroll taxes, inventory taxes, property taxes, sales taxes, state and federal income taxes, health care cost shifting and higher and higher prices for goods and services they require.

Yet today's solutions insist on hitting these small businesses and their employees up even more. Why? When we hear talk about "shared sacrifice", think more about the people who are doing the sacrificing. It's the same ones! Over and over again, these hard working individuals continue to carry the burden for the rest of us.

When health care costs go up, big business passes along the cost in the price of their products, to the rest of us. The employer mandate in the Clinton Health Plan has business paying for 80% of the health care premium costs for employees and their families. Those businesses that can pass along the cost, will do so, and all of us will pay, in higher product costs, less new hiring, employee wage freezes and lower pension earnings. The Clinton Administration would have us believe that small businesses will pass along their costs, too. This isn't true. Small businesses just cannot do it. Their customers have a limit to what they'll pay to have their cars washed, their hair cut, their lawns mowed. There will be a point where they'll simply perform these tasks themselves rather than pay the higher price. The car washes, hair salons and landscaping businesses are among the firms that make up our small business environment. Many of these folks will just go out of business as a result of the proposed Clinton Health Plan, leading to more unemployment and even fewer people paying the majority of the country's health care bill.

It is reported that when Marie Antoinette was informed that the French populace could not pay higher taxes, she replied, "Let them eat cake". When told that small business could not afford further taxes, Hillary Rodham Clinton answered, " I cannot save every undercapitalized business in America".

The cost of any health care plan must not punish productivity. Employers no longer have any business being in the health care financing process. Health care is an individual responsibility, and everyone in this country must participate equally.

Our health care is our own business, not that of our employer's. Today, an employer wants to know if you smoke, drink, ride a motorcycle, expect to start a family soon, or have any major medical history, primarily to see what hiring you might do to the costs of providing medical insurance for the entire firm. Random drug testing, smoke-free and drug-free workplaces have all been established to rein in company health care expenditures.

This must stop! Workers are penalized each day by opportunities lost due to job lock. If an employee wanted to change jobs or start up a business, he or she should not be forced to consider the loss of health care coverage as part of the decision.

Each day, America suffers because entrepreneurial talents are subverted. We have made it extremely difficult in this country for someone to break out on their own and start up a business. Yet, this is the very way in which we have reached the pinnacle of world-wide success. This is how Ford Motors, IBM and Apple Computers, among others, got their start. But the playing field is no longer level. The high costs of starting up one's own business, due to the continued financial burdens placed on the production side, make it highly unlikely that new corporate giants will rise from modest beginnings and present the always important challenge to the existing giants.

This is why we must liberate business once and for all from the task of providing health care. We must, once again, make it possible for the Bill Gates' and the Henry Fords to start in their garage with a dream and the desire to accomplish their goals.

Taking the employer out would also eliminate the $60 billion dollar tax break now allowed for corporations who provide coverage. Surely, a better use can be found for this money, such as reducing the national budget deficit. It would leave all working people, including the union worker and the federal employee, to negotiate a higher standard of living without interference of the subject of health care costs.

If all Americans are to pay for EqualCare USA, what equitable method of assessment could be used? What system of collection can be established whereby everyone contributes based on their ability to pay? How could we eliminate political favoritism and not overburden the people now paying the highest portion of the bill today? This is the key to the proper financing mechanism for any health care proposal.

Remember that EqualCare USA is a single buyer program. We are all the buyers and consumers of health care. If we are not going to take the money from the production side, then it must come from spending. It would be all Americans who would directly fund our EqualCare USA program. Everybody spends money. The individuals classified as "poor" today have more spending power than the middle class of the 1950's. Because they use health care, they, too, would want to pay their own way. Income taxes would not ensure the same equality. In EqualCare USA, all of us would provide the money with our pocket change. By utilizing a spending (often called transaction) tax, we would each pay in, pennies at a time, to the EqualCare USA program. EqualCare USA would not tax either income or productivity. Instead, every time money moved in this country, a small premium assessment would be taken for health care.

This concept of paying for a national program with our small change is not a revolutionary one, although the idea dates back to around the time of the American Revolution. Conceived by Alexander Hamilton, this country's first Secretary of the Treasury, the transaction (or spending) tax was the actual way we financed government until 1913, when the current income tax system was installed.

In arriving at the conclusion that the transaction tax was the proper method of revenue collection, Hamilton said, "The ability of a country to pay taxes must always be proportioned, in a great degree, to the quantity of money in circulation. One's personal estate, from the difficulties in tracing it, cannot be subjected to large contributions by any means other than taxes on consumption. Taxes on consumable articles have, upon the whole, better pretensions to equality than any others, equalizing the burden as far as it is attainable."

Every time money was spent, a small piece of it went into the national coffers. A few pennies here and there, spread out by the rate an individual consumed goods, was a relatively painless way to finance the government. As late as 1894, when an income tax law was passed, the Supreme Court struck it down as unconstitutional.

Will a few pennies taken here and there be enough to pay for EqualCare USA? Will it spread the burden equitably among the health care consumers in this country?

According to the Federal Reserve Board, over 300 trillion dollars is transacted each year in the United States. Every time money is moved, it is counted towards this 300 trillion dollar figure. When an employer pays you income, money is moved. When you take that money and buy a car, money is moved. When the car company takes that money and buys more inventory, money is moved. When the wholesaler invests their profit, money is moved. The same dollar may be spent hundreds of times over the course of the year, but the EqualCare USA tax is taken each time. In this example, the employer would pay when the paycheck was issued, the employee would pay when the car is purchased, the car company would pay when new inventory is obtained, and the wholesaler would pay when the invested funds earn money. In short, everyone pays.

Not just the few. Everyone. A small premium assessment on each transaction, whether it's the purchase of goods and services, stocks, bonds, imports, rents, investments, utilities or whatever, would raise sufficient funds in the most equal and least burdensome way for all Americans, and give us ample money with which to operate the individually-financed EqualCare USA.

If we set the original premium assessment as one cent for every three dollars transacted, annual revenue for EqualCare USA would total one trillion dollars, more than enough to provide essential health care for everyone. (1993 estimates are around $900 billion for total health care spending.)

ONE CENT for every three dollars. This is truly pocket change, which makes this ONE CENT SOLUTION so powerful. The better business is, the more money will be funneled into the system. Unemployment would drop. Income would increase. Spending would go up. Instead of the negative velocity cycle usually proposed, where business is taxed, leading to higher unemployment and lower wages, the One Cent Solution spins a positive velocity cycle for business and for all of us. As business does well, we all do well. As we do well, we spend more money, increasing premium payments to EqualCare USA.

ONE CENT for every three dollars. If your family ate dinner in a restaurant and paid $15.00, your bill would contain an additional five cent premium for health care. But the restaurant would also pay premium when they bought food to serve its guests. Everyone pays! If you purchase a car for $20,000, your EqualCare USA premium payment would be $66.67. It would be a financing system where health care is paid for with our small change. Everyone, without exception, would be responsible for the transaction tax. If we spread the premium payments around, the term "shared sacrifice" has a valid meaning. If we extend exemptions, that phrase is no longer viable.

The wealthy in this country earn only a third of their money each year from actual income. The balance is primarily from investments. The One-Cent Solution is the only system which would assess those earnings, too, making it more likely that the higher earners would pay the most into the system. The lower earner, consuming at a more reduced rate, would pay in a much smaller premium amount.

One cent for each three dollars spent would be the plan's starting point. Each year, a decision would be made to keep this premium assessment the same or alter it up or down, depending on our health care expenditures. Under no circumstances would we allow a surplus greater than 10% or any deficit. It would be a pay as you go plan, balanced at the end of each year. A large surplus would allow a reduced premium assessment the following year, or, perhaps, more benefits in the EqualCare USA plan. A deficit would necessitate raising the premium assessment, or reducing benefits.

The attraction of the plan is that all Americans would decide. We are the single buyers and the payors for the plan. EqualCare USA is about all Americans making choices, working together, deciding as one what their health care plan will look like and how it will be paid for. We all have a stake in health care, and we all should have input into and responsibility for our health care system. EqualCare USA is the only solution which actually empowers the end user of health care services.

One trillion dollars raised would, in light of the built-in cost containment parameters in EqualCare USA, likely be more than sufficient to pay for the nation's health care bill. The EqualCare USA Board, with consumer input, would make decisions regarding surpluses, deficits, funding, fees and benefits during annual meetings held to evaluate the system. We could even choose to utilize expected overages in revenue collection for other objectives.

We might even decide to prioritize EqualCare USA revenue distribution as:

1. Pay for EqualCare USA.
2. Eliminate corporate and business income taxes to encourage hiring.
3. Reduce national deficit and debt.
4. Eliminate personal income taxes.

Expanding the transaction tax from one penny on every three dollars transacted to every dollar transacted would raise three trillion dollars, more than enough to accomplish all four objectives. Not only is the One-Cent Solution the proper method to fund EqualCare USA, it is an opportunity to reduce our debt through everyone's payments, and change the way we currently pay revenue to the government.

The One-Cent Solution is the most equitable method proposed to finance health care. There is no political favoritism with this system. People who pay little in income tax currently would pay in with this type of financing mechanism. People paid off the books would pay premium. The wealthy would pay in based on all of their transactions, not simply by the amount of their actual income.

The income tax system in this country has made Congress a powerful entity, as it gives them the right to tax some and exempt others. Reducing this power would make it possible for Americans to take back their country. The transaction tax removes EqualCare USA's funding from Congress entirely. Government's responsibility, as previously outlined, would be to collect the money, not decide who gets an exemption from paying it.

The time has come for all Americans to demand that each one of us stands equal. We should no longer depend on business to provide and pay for our health care. We should no longer have to pay for big business' plans when we buy their goods or services. We should no longer have to pick up the majority of seniors' health care costs through Medicare. The need for Medicaid would be eliminated, since all Americans would be covered in the plan and paying for it in some fashion. All of us would know that everyone is paying for their own health care.

Paying our premium pennies at a time, through the transaction tax, would mean no more health insurance premiums, lower auto insurance premiums, lower property taxes, lower workers' compensation premiums, lower payroll taxes and lower inventory taxes. The One Cent Solution would liberate America by liberating our businesses.

We would also benefit, as mentioned, from business' relief, through more jobs, higher incomes, and lower costs for goods and services.

Americans making choices. That's what this country is about. Every American would also have access to supplemental insurance coverage to the EqualCare USA plans and the knowledge of a professional insurance advisor to help make sense of these various supplemental programs available. This would be paid for individually and would have no effect on the benefits EqualCare USA provides. Everyone would have the same basic coverage, regardless of their payment. An insurance supplement would be a choice for those who wished, to make.

Foreign visitors to our country would also pay into our health care system when they spend money here in America. There are no exceptions to this tax. If one pays, we all pay. People would subsidize EqualCare USA based on our spending; the less you have, the less you spend, the less you pay. However small your assessment, you will have access to the same program as every American. With EqualCare USA, everyone and everything is treated equally. We will all pay our equal share.

The One-Cent Solution is the heart of the EqualCare USA proposal. It gets down to the fundamentals of the American way of life, that we are all created with equal opportunity. EqualCare USA delivers the fundamental promise of America. A country where everyone shares to ensure benefits is the nation that will continue to rise above the rest of the world for decades to come. Divided, we fail.

CHAPTER TWELVE

THE IMPORTANCE OF THE PROVIDERS IN EQUALCARE USA

All of the individuals that currently work in our vibrant health care industry will continue to play vital roles in our EqualCare USA system. The best health care system in the world will become even greater under EqualCare USA. To accomplish this means an active effort on the part of our health care professionals to make our new and exciting health care program succeed. The key professions are:

- physicians
- nurses
- hospitals
- drug companies
- administrative companies
- insurance agents

The Role of Physicians

Chapter 10 detailed several aspects of the physician's part in EqualCare USA. Providers would charge one fee per procedure, regardless of location; malpractice relief would be available; they would get a 48 hour turnaround on claims processing; and a new retrospective utilization review program which would save them substantial money and strengthen the relationship between doctor and patient that has become so fractured under our present health care system. Also, each provider would have the choice to operate as a participating PPO provider, a participating HMO provider, or a non-participating private practice provider.

The advantages of being an EqualCare USA participating doctor would be many. In addition to having 270 million Americans holding the EqualCare USA ID card, the participating provider would have less extraneous detail to be concerned with under this system, and can instead concentrate on practicing medicine.

The one fee system would simplify administration for the participating physician. No longer would there be a concern, under EqualCare USA, about who the third party payor is, in order to determine what fee to charge.

The new one fee per procedure system would likely reduce what the physician in the high-cost metropolitan area receives, but this doctor still has the population advantage over providers in lesser populated areas. EqualCare USA would open up an entire new group of individual patients, who wouldn't have come to the office before as there was no assurance as to reimbursement. In the past, providers received little or no money to treat certain patients, and collection problems were extensive and expensive.

There would also be great incentive to locate in less populated areas where physician penetration is lacking. Today's present third party payment system hammers the small metropolitan or rural area physician twice. First, they are reimbursed at a lower dollar amount. Second, they live within a smaller population base, meaning fewer patients to treat. The result is an overloading of physicians in some parts of the country and underrepresentation in others.

Our EqualCare USA system would not have providers competing on the basis of price. Instead, practitioners would be measured by outcomes, service and efficiency.

The one fee system would also save administrative costs by reducing the amount spent currently chasing uncollectable bills. Since all Americans would be covered under our EqualCare USA program, participating providers would be assured of reimbursement directly from our EqualCare USA administrators.

Accounts receivable would no longer be a factor. The majority of providers today are computer-ready to be tied into EqualCare USA's electronic claims processing. This would allow the participating provider to treat any American, accept that person's I.D. card, run it through the computer system, deliver the necessary health care, register the procedure electronically, and receive reimbursement within 48 hours, a time frame virtually unknown to physicians today.

The other substantial administrative savings would result from the change in cost containment procedures. Doing utilization review after the treatment is rendered (retrospectively) will relieve the physician from the almost constant telephone communication and additional paperwork necessary to certify every medical move made during patient treatment. Under our EqualCare USA program, the participating physician could perform the necessary medical procedure without interference.

Monitoring utilization this way means that EqualCare USA administrators would only be identifying overutilization and contacting only those providers involved. Today's prospective system monitors all physicians and subjects them to a number of intrusive measures to try and hold utilization down for all. This method has driven provider costs up and forced them to increase fees, while feeling less in touch with their patients on a one-on-one basis.

This would not happen under our EqualCare USA system. We would only be interested in the small minority of the providers who are prone to overutilize and see no reason to subject every doctor to an intense management of their delivery of medicine. Under EqualCare USA, our participating doctors would be allowed to spend the majority of their time practicing medicine.

Finally, EqualCare USA would be of further interest to physicians due to the new Patient Casualty Compensation Fund that would replace the current malpractice system for these participating providers. Premium rates would be much more reasonable for the participating physicians, especially the ones with little or no bad expereince. The necessity to practice defensive medicine would be removed and the doctor can base treatment judgement on sound medical knowledge without the additional burden of trying to avoid a lawsuit.

With all of these new advantages under our EqualCare USA system, there would seem to be plenty of appeal in becoming an EqualCare USA practitioner. If so, there would be two opportunities to participate, the first as a PPO physician, the second as a doctor in a HMO program.

As a PPO physician, the doctor would enroll with the appropriate state administrator, be assigned a provider number, agree to the one fee schedule, and subscribe to the electronic claims processing system. This would allow them to treat any American, accept that person's ID card, run it through the system, deliver the necessary health care, register the procedure electronically, and receive reimbursement within 48 hours.

Time, effort and costs would be saved for both doctor and patient. There would be no balance billing. Treatment delivered, reimbursement received, record kept.

The other option is to be a part of a HMO program. Instead of the fee-for-service arrangement, pre-negotiated capitation rates could be agreed to and received. The electronic data system would only be used to identify a patient. The doctor would be either a primary care physician who would direct a patient's treatment, or a specialist who would receive patient referrals from the primary care doctor.

These are a tremendous number of powerful incentives for a physician to participate and be a part of our EqualCare USA system and we would expect that most doctors would enroll. However, if the physician does not want to participate in our exciting new health care system, the option to practice outside EqualCare USA's boundaries exists.

If a doctor chooses to be a non-participating physician, there would be no obligation to utilize the pre-negotiated fees that EqualCare USA had established. This doctor, as a pre-condition of licensure, would have to publish, in a prominent place, the multiple of EqualCare USA being charged. Medical procedures priced at 2,3,4 or some other multiple of our EqualCare USA fees, would have to be displayed in full view in the non-participating doctor's office to enable the patient to clearly see what the fee would be. If the charge is 2 X EqualCare, or 3 X EqualCare, the fee would be shown, and American consumers could decide if they wished to pay the fee or not.

Non-participating practitoners would also not be eligible to accept any kind of assignment. They would deliver the appropriate health care and make financial arrangements with the individual patient. It would then be up to that patient to file with the appropriate EqualCare USA state administrator to be reimbursed in the amount of the established EqualCare USA fee, and to determine if treatment is eligible for reimbursement. The administrator would not pay the physician directly, only the EqualCare USA patient.

Non-participating physicians would not be able to participate in the Patient Casualty Compensation Fund. They would arrange traditional malpractice coverage on their own.

The choice to practice as a non-participating physician would rest solely with each individual doctor. There would be obvious advantages to working within our new EqualCare USA system. But there are likely to be a number of individual patients not concerned with their out-of-pocket costs who'd seek treatment from a non-participating doctor. Americans who do not wish to give up their right to see a certain doctor might seek out a non-participating physician. Non-participating providers would attract a certain clientele, much as private schools do today. Our EqualCare USA system would never try to discourage this.

Finally, our EqualCare USA system would construct a series of incentives for new physicians to become general practitioners or family practice specialists. Today, barely 15% of our physicians are primary care doctors. With the HMO component of our EqualCare USA system set to utilize the primary care doctor as the individual controlling the flow of medical services, this type of practice should become more attractive to medical students.

In addition, our EqualCare USA system would form a scholarship-based program to encourage a student to pursue a primary care practice. Medical school expenses are a high initial overhead cost for the resident entering practice today. Our EqualCare USA's scholarship program would pay for a substantial portion of their tuition in exchange for selecting a primary care practice and agreeing to a 10 year plan to practice in any area of the country deemed understaffed by the National Health Board.

The primary care physician would be important to the success of our EqualCare USA program, which would have millions of patients seeking health care treatment who did not possess easy access before. Providing scholarship programs for primary and family practice specialities should increase the interest level in this type of medicine and help fill the geographical gaps where there is a scarcity of physicians.

EqualCare USA would also employ nurses in key roles designed to deliver primary health care in conjunction with a physician. The demand for primary care would likely rise under EqualCare USA's single buyer program, further increasing the importance of the primary care practice.

Whether it be as a participating or non-participating physician, life should be easier for the doctor in our new health care environment. These "front-liners" of medicine are the ones who deliver the highest quality health care in the world; a practice that would continue under EqualCare USA.

The Role of Nursing

As an occupation targeted for continued substantial growth this decade, the nursing industry has emerged as a key employer, a role that would expand even further under our EqualCare USA system. Our new single buyer approach ensures that all Americans would be covered for essential, necessary and reasonable medical services. Thus, demand for basic health care, or primary care services, would certainly increase.

Today, there aren't enough primary care type physicians to handle this demand. The role of the nurse practitioner, who can perform 60-80% of primary care services, would naturally expand to assist in delivering basic health care to all Americans. Currently, there are some 30,000 nurse practitioners in our country.

Our EqualCare USA program would establish a new type of primary practice where nurses would perform many of the basic services in association with the primary care physician. More nurses would be involved in this practice than physicians, and the key strengths of each utilized. Nurses would spend more time with the patient, while the physician would handle the more involved services which require higher medical training.

Registered Nurses and Physician's Assistants could all play a part in delivering basic health care, and could be trained to perform 70-80% of primary care. Together, they could perform exams, diagnose illnesses, and, possibly, if appropriate, prescribe medicine. Each would know their limit and the well-run primary care practice would have a structure whereby roles and authority would be clearly defined. Today, many Americans feel comfortable conversing and being examined by Registered Nurses, nurse practitioners and Physician's Assistants, setting the stage for efficient future delivery of basic health care services.

EqualCare USA's recuperative care benefits, whereby all Americans would become eligible for up to 100 days of nursing care would further raise demand for nurses, both in the hospital and at home. Clearly, the nursing industry will continue to be a place for Americans to work and continue to deliver the best health care in the world.

The Role of Hospitals

EqualCare USA participating hospitals would operate under the same structure as physicians. Those that choose to participate would be assigned a provider number by the state administrator, and have access to the same electronic filing system and the central patient information data bank.

Hospitals would accept the same type of Diagnostic Related Grouping (DRG) system that currently exists under Medicare, with some enhancements. DRGs dictate the length and cost of a hospital confinement. There would be one DRG for each condition just as there is one fee per procedure for doctors, without regard to geographic area or overhead expenses. The administrative savings inherent in a simplified DRG and electronic claims system should more than make up for any regional overhead differences. In addition, the same theory about higher population bases creating more patient opportunities would hold true with hospitals.

DRGs would be modified in two ways. First, hospital charges under our EqualCare USA system would be all inclusive. There would be no separate charges for the surgeon, anesthesiologist, radiologist, surgical assistant, emergency room specialist, or any other hospital-based specialty. The DRG fee would include all of the costs and paid in one fee to the hospital through the electronic claims filing system. The hospital would be responsible for financial arrangments with their specialists as these physicians would not be reimbursed directly by EqualCare USA.

Second, the DRG would have up to 100 days of short-term nursing care built in for recuperative care. Today, a number of patients are discharged early from the hospital which could be related to the number of days allowed under the DRG. The result has been a discharge to a nursing home as the individual is still in need of medical assistance.

Since hospitals are currently underoccupied (52% usage in Florida), there are a number of beds which can be set aside for recuperative care purposes. If a medically eligible patient wanted to have this nursing care at home, it can be arranged and reimbursement would be available to the provider through the usual EqualCare USA electronic claims processing.

Whether this recuperative health care is delivered in the hospital or at home, up to 100 days per incident is reimburseable under EqualCare USA. If further care is needed the patient should consider securing a private long term care insurance plan to assist in paying the additional costs. This automatic 100 days should provide ample time for most patients to recover and would avoid use of a nursing home for short stays. The hospital has the opportunity to utilize beds that are sitting vacant.

Hospitals not wishing to participate under our EqualCare USA system would not be required to do so. Here, the same guidelines for physicians in private practice would apply to hospitals: no use of the electronic claims filing, no assignment of benefits, and the prominent display of their fees as a multiple of EqualCare USA. If a patient received treatment in a non-participating hospital for a condition which would normally be reimbursed through EqualCare USA, this person would file a claim and be directly reimbursed for the appropriate EqualCare USA fee.

As a condition of licensure, all non-participating hospitals would still treat emergency EqualCare USA patients, stabilizing them before arranging transportation to a participating hospital. The non-participating facility would then be reimbursed, under these special circumstances, at our EqualCare USA rate for the services provided.

Again, the simplification of administrative procedures, the attraction of malpractice relief, and the ability to expect reimbursement for services rendered to any American within 48 hours would be compelling reasons for hospitals to participate in our EqualCare USA system.

The Role of Drug Companies

The pharmaceutical industry has taken a substantial amount of media and political abuse lately, but they will figure prominently in our

EqualCare USA program. Drug therapy and prescription drug treatments can save billions of dollars in medical treatment and EqualCare USA would maximize their effectiveness.

Under both HMO and PPO plans, prescription drugs, as noted earlier, are covered as an EqualCare USA basic benefit. Additionally, drug therapy would be utilized as an alternative to surgery. Studies have shown that individuals sometimes opt for this course of treatment rather than surgery, when made aware of all of their health care choices. As mentioned in the cost containment element of EqualCare USA, treatment options would be discussed as a matter of course between provider and patient.

An example of successful, less expensive treatment can be found in the treatment of ulcers today. It is much more cost and treatment effective to practice drug therapy rather than surgery. While drugs are viewed today strictly as a matter of pure cost, the reality is that this type of health care actually can save money.

Our drug companies would continue to play their current vital research role under our EqualCare USA system. The rest of the world has learned much about medicine as a result of these research efforts. EqualCare USA would continue to benefit from this research and encourage further development in an effort to reduce some frightening diseases into treatable medical conditions. Research results are another marketable export of our health care system and we would package this information for distribution around the world, further elevating our health care industry to be our economic leader into the future.

The Role of Insurers and Agents

There would be a number of market opportunities for our insurance industry to pursue and both insurers and insurance agents should benefit as a result. Both medical and malpractice supplements would likely be desired under our EqualCare USA system.

The basic benefits package of EqualCare USA would be clearly defined. The supplemental market that has been prospering by filling coverage gaps in the Medicare system should flourish under the new health care system, too.

Under the PPO plan, potential supplement buyers would be interested in deductible and coinsurance coverage to pay for their out-of-pocket costs. For both HMO and PPO plans, medical conditions not covered under EqualCare USA (determined utilizing the Oregon/QALY cost containment approach) would also be probable subjects for inclusion in a supplement.

Insurers would also be able to market "private practice" supplements for those individuals using providers not participating in our EqualCare USA system.

Since there would be an elimination of insurance premiums and Medicare taxes, Americans' discretionary income that could be used to purchase a supplement should be increased. In addition, employers, saving large sums of money previously spent on health care, might be interested in contributing to other employee benefit programs, or, at least, would establish a payroll deduction plan for the individual supplements.

All supplements would be individual. There would be no group plans or certificates of coverage. Every individual purchaser would own their own policy.

Thriving businesses can turn their employee benefit attention to pension plans, disability income plans, dental coverage, and similar programs which insurers would continue to promote and sell. The relief from the unknown and increasingly higher costs of health insurance should make employers interested potential buyers of these more stable product areas. Insurers would also be invited to bid on administration of our EqualCare USA system, as our National Health Board would be examining the most economical methods of processing claims and tracking patient data and outcomes.

Insurers are already experienced in these tasks, giving them an advantage over other potential bidders, if their price for handling the administration is competitive.

For insurance agents, the chance to sell supplemental policies would simplify marketing without having to change the current insurer distribution systems in place today. The number of potential customers would be substantial and interest in the supplemental plans high.

Additionally, agents could explain the benefits available under our EqualCare USA system much as they do today in clarifying Social Security benefits and identifying gaps which could be filled. This would be an opportune way to have experienced people explaining our new EqualCare USA program, rather than paid bureaucrats.

Agents would also benefit from the revived interest in other employee benefit programs. The opportunity to sell a number of funding vehicles for these plans should enhance the agent's livelihood, while increasing the financial security of many more millions of Americans.

Agents and insurers would also work with the new Patient Casualty Compensation Fund as well as supplements to that Fund over and above the $1,000,000 plan. Settlements would be simpler and easier to administer and court cases avoided. Tracking of malpractice data would be enhanced and it would be easier to assess premium rates while identifying providers with a significant number of bad results.

The role of insurers and agents would be preserved under our EqualCare USA system and, while the products they would market may be different, and the circumstances under which the plans are sold improved, the key role of handling catastrophic events for individual Americans would continue to be a noble cause for this important industry.

Conclusion

Providers form an integral part of any health care system. Under our EqualCare USA program, their roles would be no less important. However, the conditions under which they operate should be overwhelmingly improved to be able to maximize the individual strengths each brings to health care, enabling us to continue as the predominant health care country in the world. United as a people, we can bring health care for all Americans to new heights.

Our EqualCare USA System

Our new EqualCare USA program would make many positive changes for our economy, for our health care, and for us.

For our economy:

1. New job formation	INCREASE
2. New business formation	INCREASE
3. Take home pay	INCREASE
4. Local property taxes	DECREASE
5. Product prices	DECREASE
6. Welfare spending	DECREASE
7. National deficit	DECREASE
8. National debt	DECREASE

For our health care:

1. America would remain the leader in health care in the world.
2. Health care providers would compete on the basis of outcomes, efficiency and service rather than price.
3. Doctor-patient relationships would be restored.
4. The nursing industry's importance would be more emphasized.
5. Rural and other lower cost neighborhoods would become attractive to providers.
6. General, family and primary practice would become more

attractive to physicians.

7. Hospitals would handle more of the recuperative type of care than they do now.

8. Drug therapy and prescription drugs would be more widely used.

9. Private physicians and hospitals would thrive.

For all Americans:

1. Everyone would have access to worldwide, essential health care.

2. We would be empowered by being able to select the provider(s) or HMO we want.

3. We would be able to access non-essential care privately.

4. All Americans would be covered in a single buyer program.

5. Every American would pay equally by means of an assessment on spending.

6. Professional insurance advisors would be available to provide supplements and co-ordinating products.

This is the only solution that can happen now, and help all Americans immediately. If our voice is loud enough, together, we the people can make it happen. Divided, we fail.

CHAPTER THIRTEEN

BUYING HEALTH INSURANCE TODAY

Changes to the health care system, due to its complexity and the difficulty moving anything forward in Washington, may be some time before implementation. During this time, health insurance must still be purchased, decisions about coverage must still be made, options must still be evaluated and selected. The choices that an individual or employer must make are not easy today and mistakes can have far-reaching consequences.

One of the aspects of our real health care problem is fear. The fear of buying health insurance coverage that will not be there when you (or your employee) need it the most is a result of a third party payor system that's broken. But this is still the system we have from which to choose health coverage, and there are solid arrangements available that won't let you down at the most inopportune time.

When you review your plan on a regular basis each year, it is often done with the assistance of an insurance agent. Most agents provide excellent advice in considering which health plan can best serve the needs of you (and your employees). There are agents, however, that will not prove helpful and you should be careful that the advisor you've selected is the one whom you can rely on for constructive information and who understands your situation (and/or your company's) before imparting any guidance.

How do you choose an agent to instruct you in the area of health insurance? There are several methods you can apply to rating the agent that's best for you.

First, what kind of experience does the agent have? How long has he or she been in the insurance field? If experienced, what insurance companies is this person affiliated with? If relatively new, what insurance agency is this individual working with and what length of experience do they have? Ask for references of other clients, individual or business, for whom this agent has secured health insurance.

Second, does this person belong to any of the industry's professional associations? The Association of Health Insurance Agents (AHIA) and the National Association of Health Underwriters (NAHU) are the largest health insurance-specific organizations. The National Association of Life Underwriters (NALU), the Independent Insurance Agents of America, and the National Association of Professional Insurance Agents are other large industry groups to which the agent might belong and have access to current industry information.

Third, does the agent have any particular professional credentials? While the majority of states have some form of continuing education requirements, there are other industry designations an agent can be awarded after completing a set number of insurance courses, such as a Chartered Life Underwriter (CLU), a Chartered Financial Consultant (ChFC), a Registered Health Underwriter (RHU) or a Certified Financial Planner (CFP). These certifications indicate a willingness on the agent's part to put in some additional time to improve on their current level of knowledge; the additional education can often be put to use on the client's behalf.

What type of person is your agent? Does this individual explain benefits in a way you understand or confuse the issue further? Do you change insurance carriers each year at the agent's recommendation? Is the office in which this person works responsive to you and your needs?

This person will be giving you direction on the type and quality of health insurance coverage you select and will be available when you need claims assistance or other policyholder service. You must be comfortable with this person before committing your business.

The agent can play a significant role in explaining the complex language behind the health insurance plans today. Your understanding of the plan you buy will likely only be as good as the knowledge the agent possesses. The better the agent upon whom you rely, the more likely you'll be able to avoid the traps that are out there, disguised as viable health insurance plans. Errant suggestions can put you in an impossible position, as some of these individuals discovered:

- A firm of 50 employees received a 1988 premium notice indicating that monthly rates would increase from $9,000 to around $13,000. Not wishing to settle for that rise in cost, the firm's controller solicited health insurance bids, ending up with 37 different arrangements to sort through. 36 of the 37 were about the same in price, $13,000/month, while the other plan carried a $9,000 premium, virtually identical to their current rate. It was health insurance offered through a Third Party Administrator (TPA) but insured through a Florida insurance carrier rated an "A" company by A.M. Best, an insurer ratings company.

Things went smoothly for 18 months. At that time, a letter arrived announcing a change in the insurance company behind the plan. It was another "A" rated company and they were not going to change any of the plan details. In the weeks afterward, new forms were sent to the firm under a new TPA name from Georgia, but little else changed. However, not long after that, claims processing reached a standstill and no satisfactory answer was given as to the reasons for the delays. The next letter that arrived advised that the original TPA had not, in fact, found a replacement insurance company and had been self-insuring the plan for several months. In addition, coverage would cease as of the end of the month in which the letter was sent (only 2 weeks away).

The firm panicked and scrambled around to find replacement coverage. There were two employees with pending claims of significant amounts. Although new coverage was found at a higher price, there were a number of unpaid claims from earlier months that went unreimbursed.

- A three person firm had high, but manageable premiums until an employee's husband developed cancer and rates shot up by $5,000.00. The firm switched insurers, but the employee's husband was left uninsured because of the pre-existing condition clause in the new policy.

- A firm who had health insurance saw an owner's wife develop severe migraines. The health insurance plan was then sold by their current insurance company to another insurance company. The new company agreed to cover this pre-existing condition but at double the premium. The firm looked, but no other carrier wanted to insure the migraine problem. The other owners agreed to stay with the new company and pay the higher premium, figuring it could have easily been their spouse with the medical condition.

- A partnership in which its junior partner suffered a quadruple bypass, had its company health insurance premiums raised by nearly 50%. The senior partner decided against paying for the increase and instead informed the younger partner that the firm would no longer provide group insurance but would raise salaries to enable the employees (and the junior partner) to look for their own individual coverage.

These are not isolated occurrences. There are a substantial number of people that have been placed in difficult positions, either without coverage or paying a high price for it. A good agent can help you dodge these potential bullets; a poor agent can lead you right into the abyss. A 1990 article, citing an interview with a Florida state insurance official, revealed that the overwhelming number of consumer complaints involve a failure on the part of the agent to properly explain the health insurance benefits they had.

In evaluating health insurance coverage, there are a number of concepts to remember as you listen to the agent's recommendations.

1. Beware the lowest price. The lower premium is not usually the best deal, long-term, as the aforementioned firm who selected the lowest cost among 37 different plans finally discovered. There are some good buys out there, many of them involving some type of managed care arrangement where your rate and out-of-pocket costs remain low in exchange for using only the providers in the insurer's network.

If you have or see a low price, and it's not utilizing a managed care network, you will likely face one of two possibilities. First, you incur a claim that is not reimbursed at the level you expected. Citing higher than usual and customary charges, the carrier disallows some of the bill when they calculate what to pay the provider. The provider then often bills you for the balance. Second, when your first renewal premium comes due, the rates are increased dramatically. In either event, the low price you were getting is a trade-off for a later problem at another point in time such as policy renewal or submission of a claim. If you've been sick, you may be hit with an exorbitant rate increase; one you may be forced to pay since securing coverage elsewhere may not be possible.

When you shop for coverage obtain three or four quotes to evaluate. There should be some rating consistency. If one quote is significantly less than the others, be careful. Review the benefits closely as well as the company's rating methods.

2. What is the company's renewal rating practice? If you are quoted a low rate, you certainly should ask this question. Make it routine to ask the agent and/or company for it when you receive a quote. Rating is not a simple task for insurers and involves not only pricing competitively today, but having an adequate reserve for claims tomorrow.

Obviously, the coverage you choose will play a key role in the rate determination. Benefit-heavy plans with low deductibles will be costly. But it's this renewal rating philosophy you want to know, because it's not only the initial premium that's important, but how future premiums are calculated. A low price today that yields to an unaffordable rate when you renew gives you only short-term coverage.

Find out whether your insurance company bases their renewal

increases on the experience in a pool of groups or individuals within your region or are they based on your specific claims, which, if high, could lead to a substantial price increase. Pooling can help to stabilize the rate increases as low-risk and high-risk companies share experience.

There are three distinct strategies insurance companies use to calculate rate increases. The first is called "single" rating, meaning that all business the company has operates in one pool and new business (with little or no claims) subsidizes old business. This approach is no longer commonly practiced. The second method is "durational" rating, employing the philosophy that claims will generally increase over time and the longer the business has been with the company, the greater the anticipated claims. Business on the books three years will carry one factor; business that is four years old a higher factor, and so forth. This is a normal custom for health insurers. Finally, there is "tier" rating, which is how insurers practiced sick-sorting groups of individuals. In this instance, unhealthy people are separated and placed in one tier that experiences astronomical increases because the only people in this pool are sick. The healthy people go into a different pool with a lower rate to retain them for another year. At the end of the next year, the sorting continued with any new sick people placed into the sick pool while the healthy risks continued their stay in the healthy pool. An insurer that uses this philosophy will let you down when you need your coverage the most, and, therefore, is best avoided. Some company brochures indicate their rate renewal practice in their text and you should read the information carefully to understand it.

For example, the brochure might say:

"Fully pooled renewals -- cases cannot be singled out due to experience".

If an insurer is willing to publish this philosophy, it's a good sign that you might be able to avoid the large rate increase you can't afford to pay.

3. One of the myths you will encounter in purchasing health insurance is the notion that group insurance is less expensive than individual coverage. This is not true and never has been. If you are covered under your employer's group plan and you get sick and can't work, you may be relieved of your job duties. While you may be able to continue coverage in some fashion, through a conversion provision or COBRA extension, how are you going to afford paying the premium? Suddenly, when you need the coverage the most, you are forced to drop it because you can't pay for it.

If the government is going to mandate anything about health insurance, it should be that waiver of premium must be included in all health insurance plans to ensure continued benefits when we are sick and can't afford the premium payment. A waiver clause would postpone premium payments until we have recovered.

Group only appears cheaper, and it is designed from the onset to drop you when you're sick. Individual coverage is more expensive but, for that, you are given more control over your own destiny. Group also seems less expensive because the employer is often subsidizing it in some way.

Chasing low premiums by switching plans year after year is a deadly game of musical chairs. Sooner or later, there won't be a chair for you to sit on and you will find yourself insuring your own future (or current) claims.

4. Is the insurance contract between you and the insurance company? If it's an insurance policy, it is; if it's a certificate, it isn't. If you find the following wording on the face page of the contract, you should be concerned:

"This Certificate describes the principal provisions of, but does not constitute, the contract of insurance. The actual contract is available for inspection at the office of the Group Policyholder during regular business hours".

The more entities between you and the actual insurer, the more likely that, if you experience future problems, you will not be able to deal directly or have much opportunity for recourse with that insurance carrier. The contract is not really between you and the insurer, but between you and a go-between, often a third party administrator (TPA). The certificate is aptly described as a copy of someone else's contract.

5. Be wary of association medical plans. I have yet to see one of the medical plans stay the course for any reasonable length of time. These plans are often like a flimsy boat that appears sturdy when you first step in it, but the minute you hit heavy seas, guess what? No more boat.

Yet these association plans are often touted by popular magazines like Money and Consumer Reports, recommending that you join association groups to secure health coverage. They are obviously swayed by apparently lower costs, but it's hard to find one association medical policy that has endured without enormous rate increases for even one five year period. With association insurance, the insurers have been guilty too often of raising rates when you become sick, sorting you into an unhealthy pool, practicing post-claims underwriting, and doing whatever they could to drive off claimants.

When considering any medical association plan, know who the insurer is, how long they have guaranteed to insure the group in which you are a member, what their financial stability is (as well as the TPA's, if applicable), and what their renewal rating practices are. If your agent cannot or will not give you this information, find another agent.

Self-insured association plans are called MEWAs (Multiple Employer Welfare Arrangements). These are usually established to avoid federal and/or state regulation and have resulted in many employers losing millions in premiums paid when the MEWA goes out of business due to undercapitalization for claims or outright fraud. Between January of 1988 and June of 1991, failed MEWAs left nearly 400,000 individuals with almost $125 million in unpaid claims, according to the Government Accounting Office, with more than 600 MEWAs failing to comply with regulatory laws. If you become involved in a MEWA for any reason, ask to see their Form 5500, a financial disclosure statement that must be filed annually with the Internal Revenue Service. If they can't produce that, you know it's not anywhere near being a genuine operation. Don't take chances like that with your medical coverage and your own future.

6. Third Party Administrators: find out as much as you can before entering into any health insurance arrangement that involves the use of a TPA. You're usually better off if you purchase health insurance directly from the insurance carrier and have no in-between entity, because this system sometimes can be used as a way to circumvent stringent state regulation.

If you are using a TPA, there are certain questions you can ask to try and separate the reliable TPA from the unreliable one. Not asking questions beforehand is a poor business practice and certainly not one you'd use before making any other important purchase -- and health insurance is a critical buy.

Ask how long the TPA has been in business. Because the health insurance business has seen its share of good and bad claims periods, a lengthy track record indicates that the TPA has been through both ups and downs and has survived -- a positive sign.

Ask for a list of the carriers the TPA has represented and the length of the relationship. This will give you information about multiple short-term arrangements which may indicate an unhappiness on the part of the carrier with the TPA's performance. A number of long-term connections is more proof of a solid TPA. Ask for references at the same time.

Is the TPA registered and licensed? You can call your state Department of Insurance for this answer. If they're official, great; if not, the DOI would likely appreciate the information that an unregistered and/or unlicensed TPA is operating within their borders.

See if you can obtain a copy from the TPA of their formal administrative and/marketing agreement between the TPA and the insurance carrier with whom they are proposing to place your health insurance. Remember, you'll only receive a certificate, which is the copy of the TPA's agreement. If they won't give it to you, the items you specifically want information about are in the termination clause of this agreement. How long is the termination period? If it's only 30 days, you could be left without an insurer backing your coverage on short notice. This is totally unacceptable. You also should know if the TPA is directly linked to the insurance company or are they, too, a sub-contractor through another TPA. The more entities between you and the insurer, the more dangerous the arrangement.

Ask if the TPA is a member of the Society of Professional Benefit Administrators. This organization has over 400 TPAs registered with them and is another indication of a TPA that is more than just a fly-by-night operation. It shouldn't be your only source of hope, though, but merely one of a number of positive answers to these questions.

This type of detailed homework will pay off for you in the long run and help avoid the disaster of unpaid claims or cancellation when you least can afford it. There are many good TPAs out there, but there are many that could take your money and run.

7. Always find out what the market guarantee is of the contract you are purchasing. If the plan can be terminated with little or no notice, you could be in for significant trouble ahead. A company (or association or TPA) should be willing to give you a lengthy guarantee to enable you adequate time to find replacement coverage in the event your plan is cancelled.

Find out exactly what the cancellation practices are of the company with whom you're insuring and how they work. If your plan, for example, says that your policy cannot be cancelled unless the company cancels all policies of a similar classification, clarify what "classification" means. Does it represent "all balding, middle-aged men living in zip code 32808"? If so, and this describes you, one large claim could send a cancellation notice your way in a hurry. Once you determine how classification is defined, it will give you an idea of whether this description is broad enough to indicate a pool substantial in size or not. The more narrow the class, the more likely you will become subject to quick cancellation at some time in the future, if you become a claimant.

8. Buy into a PPO (Preferred Provider Organization) or HMO (Health Maintenance Organization) if you can. What this means is you will be obtaining discount prices on health services delivered to you. Hospitals and physicians have found the need to offer reduced price treatment and there is no reason you shouldn't have some of it. If you're not in a PPO/HMO arrangement, you are paying a higher price than is necessary for your health

insurance.

There may be a reason for not opting for these managed care arrangements. They require that you use one of their providers to maximize the cost savings in the plan. If you don't like the doctors and/or hospitals on the list, you may not want to join. Today, even veteran practitioners are signed up with a network, improving the odds that your favorite(s) will be on the roster.

It's an excellent way to keep your costs reasonable, both up front in premium, but especially at the claims end with lower out-of-pocket costs. These plans typically don't have the large deductible/coinsurance parameters, instead opting for a minimal co-payment ($5, $10, $15, for example) when you seek out a provider. It may be less freedom than you are accustomed to, but if your bottom line is out of pocket costs, and I suspect it is, selecting some type of managed care programs makes good sense. The majority of health plans today have a managed care feature and if you are not in one, you're paying retail instead of discount prices for medical services. Not being in some type of managed care program makes you a potential target for cost-shifting as providers try and cover their costs.

9. If you are between jobs and have no coverage, ask your agent about temporary medical insurance. This type of plan is designed as interim protection until you can latch onto another insurance plan. It is not very expensive and, while it doesn't cover pre-existing conditions, it will provide dollars for you if something else happens.

If you leave employment and are eligible for COBRA, your election of this right to continue health insurance for 18 months should not be viewed as a lengthy delaying practice to search for a new medical plan. The time to start hunting for a new health program is immediate. If you wait, buoyed by the presence of at least 18 months of coverage, you may find yourself in a situation where you sustain a heart attack in the 17th month and now can't obtain any other coverage due to your medical history. When the 18th month ends, so does your COBRA benefits and the inability to obtain a new policy could be a financial disaster for you.

The time to begin looking for new insurance is as soon after electing COBRA as possible to avoid being unable to purchase it at a later date. Don't take that chance!

If you find other coverage, don't stop paying for the COBRA plan or temporary coverage until the new policy has been issued and is in you hands. The conditional receipt from your new plan is exactly that - conditional; dropping your other program before issuance of a new one is an invitation to disaster. Even if it means double-paying a monthly premium up front, be sure the new policy is in your hands and in effect before cancelling the old contract.

In short, don't take the risk that you'll be uncovered at some point in time and don't delay your attempts to find a permanent replacement for your prior plan even if you elect COBRA. If you're going to wait out the full 18 months before trying to find another contract and take the chance that you won't have that heart attack in the 17th month, why buy COBRA at all?

10. If you are considering a plan which has a deductible, calculate the difference in cost between a higher deductible and a lower one. The higher deductible is always the better deal.

For example, a $250 deductible plan that costs $315/month for your family should be measured against the $1000 plan that costs $250/month, a difference of $65 each month, or $780 annually. That extra $780 month that you pay for the smaller deductible is more than the difference between the two deductibles (1000 - 250 = 750).

Granted, more than one person might satisfy the deductible, but this is not very common. If only one person is utilizing the plan benefits on a regular basis, the higher deductible is definitely a better buy. This also is more in line with how insurance is intended, to cover the more catastrophic-type financial problem. It's the $25,000 bill that you likely can't pay, not the $250 tab. In addition, the higher deductible plans are not usually as vulnerable to the volatile rate increases as the lower deductible programs. You can have affordable coverage that will be there when you really need it by adopting this approach.

Buying health insurance today can be frustrating, confusing and abundant with traps. These 10 points can help you with this purchase and assist in ensuring that the kind of plan you acquire will be there for you when you need it most. There are many quality agents and companies with whom you can do business.

Who knows what the future holds for health care? Waiting for our government to decide for us could be a delay of lengthy duration. For now, the methods expressed in this chapter form the best process to follow to secure medical insurance that can serve you capably in today's environment.

SOURCE LISTING

INTRODUCTION

1. AARP Bulletin, ''Americans Still Want It Both Ways''
2. Broker World, March, 1993, ''Cost or Spending'', pg. 96+
3. Business & Health, Mid-September, 1992, ''An Insider's View of the Politics of Health Care'', pgs 9-10
4. Canada News, February 12, 1993, ''Bourassa Begins Cancer Treatment in U.S.'', pg. 6
5. Executive Alert, National Center for Policy Analysis, ''Creating Jobs'', pg. 6
6. Florida Trend, January, 1993, ''Health Care is not a Right'', pg. 85
7. Forbes, October 26, 1992, ''Sick Solution'', pgs 25-26
8. Fort Lauderdale Sun-Sentinel, April 25, 1991, Joan Beck column, April 25, 1991, pg. 15A
9. Fortune, April 6, 1992, ''Is Health Care a Job Killer?'', pg. 30
10. Fortune, February 8, 1993, ''The Modular Corporation'', pg. 106+
11. Fortune, April 5, 1993, ''An Antidote to Health Care Costs'', pg. 24
12. Medical Benefits, December 30, 1990, ''Health Benefits and Small Business'', pg. 3
13. Medical Economics, February 22, 1993, ''Trends in Health Services'', pg. 8
14. Miami Herald, March 27, 1991, ''Study: 1 in 8 Children Underfed'', pg. 1A+
15. Miami Herald, January 1, 1992, ''Some Airline Workers Left Uninsured'', pg. 1A+
16. Palm Beach Post, April 17, 1991, ''Mulroney Mom Ill'', pg. 2A
17. Palm Beach Post, April 3, 1991, ''Should All Of Us Have The Right To Health Insurance''
18. Standard & Poor's, 1992 Report on the Health Industry
19. Statement of Senator Edward M. Kennedy on the Health Care Crisis in America, December 6, 1989
20. Time, June 18, 1990, ''A Nation of Hypochondriacs'', pg. 88
21. USA Today, March 1, 1993, ''Fear of Losing Aid Chains Some to Jobs'', pg. 1A+

22. USA Today, March 8, 1993, ''Employment Outlook: Report Surprises White House'', pg. 1B+
23. USA Today, March 24, 1993, ''Automakers Health Care Costs pg. 1B

CHAPTER ONE

1. Forbes, February 3, 1992, ''Health Care Costs Crossroad'', pg. 25-26
2. Fort Lauderdale Sun-Sentinel, July 7, 1991, ''Middle Class Feel Health Care Shock'', pg. 10A
3. Medical Benefits, March 15, 1993, ''How Our Health Care System Works''
4. Medical Economics, February 8, 1993, ''How Public Opinion Polling Really Works'', pg. 115+
5. Miami Herald, April 4, 1993, ''Advocates Fear Two-Tiered Health System'', pg. 7A
6. Miami Herald, May 16, 1993, ''The Tattered Insurance Net'' pg. 1A+
7. National Underwriter, February 1, 1993, ''Public's View Of Medical Costs Out of Whack'', pg. 31
8. Nation's Business, January, 1993, ''Views on Health Insurance'', pg. 77+
9. Time, Nov. 25, 1992, ''Ten Ways To Cure Health Care Mess''
10. USA Today, March 22, 1993, ''What Others Are Saying About Reform'', pg. 15A
11. USA Today, May 26, 1993, ''Lack of Health Insurance is Indeed a Real Crisis'', pg. 14A

CHAPTER TWO

1. 1991 Statistical Abstract of the United States, pgs 74-79
2. Canada News, April 24, 1992, ''Report Says Canada Best Place To Live Longer'', pg. 20
3. Census Bureau, 1990 Report
4. Conservative Chronicle, March, 1993, ''Myths About Infant Mortality'', by Mona Charen

5. Conservative Chronicle, April, 1993, ''Our Medical System Is Best In World'', pg. 17
6. Florida Trend, April, 1992, ''Our Healthiest Industry: Health Care'', pg. 126
7. Forbes, November 12, 1990, ''Salem, 1692, Revisited'', pg. 168
8. Forbes, April 1, 1991, ''Medical Opinion'', pg. 22
9. Forbes, June 22, 1992, ''Another Big Lie'', pg. 241
10. Forbes, October 26, 1992, ''Medicine That Kills'', pg. 228
11. Fort Lauderdale Sun-Sentinel, April 16, 1991, ''Health Coverage Lacking'', pg. 1A+
12. Fort Lauderdale Sun-Sentinel, November 24, 1991, ''Sickly Wheezing U.S. Health Care System Urgently Needs Radical Surgery'', pg. 5G
13. Fort Lauderdale Sun-Sentinel, April 8, 1993, ''Health Care Plan Focuses On Preventive Medicine'', pg. 4A
14. Fortune, July 13, 1992, ''The Upbeat Generation'', pg. 42+
15. Health Insurance Matters, August, 1992, ''Why We're Different'', pg. 1+
16. Health Insurance Underwriter, October, 1991, ''Tracing Medical Costs To Social Problems'', pg. 17
17. Health Insurance Underwriter, July/August, 1992, ''The Hazards of Corporate Disability'', pg. 19
18. Health Insurance Underwriter, December, 1992, ''Lies, Damn Lies and Statistics'', pg. 6
19. Medical Benefits, September 15, 1991, ''What Health Care Cost Crisis?'', pg. 4
20. Medical Benefits, October 30, 1991, ''Demographics and Health Spending'', pg. 3
21. National Underwriter, July 27, 1992, ''Some Disease and Health Goals Advance in '80's'', pg. 12
22. New Book of World Rankings, Third Edition, 1991, pg. 484+
23. Newsweek, April 28, 1975 and Newsweek, June 1, 1992
24. Palm Beach Post, February 7, 1992, ''U.S. Infant Mortality at Lowest Ever'', pg. 3A
25. Palm Beach Post, March, 1993, ''Universal Health or Science Fiction'', Jan Welder Versteeg column
26. Rolde, Neil, ''Your Money or Your Health'', Paragon House, New York, 1992
27. Time, June 11, 1990, ''Should Every Baby Be Saved?''

28. Time, September 16, 1991, ''Why Do Blacks Die Young?'', pg. 50+
29. United States Educational, Scientific and Cultural Organization, Statistical Yearbook, 1989
30. USA Today, April 6, 1993, ''USA Teen Birth Rate'', from Center for Study of Social Policy
31. USA Today, ''Did Journalists Tip Waco Cult?'', pg. 1A
32. U.S. Department of Education, National Center for Education Statistics, 1991

CHAPTER THREE

1. Best's Review, ''In Search of Health Care Access and Affordability''
2. Broker World, September, 1990, ''Health Benefit Plans: Is The Diagnosis Fatal?'', pg. 120+
3. Broker World, March, 1991, ''Small Group Health Reform'', pg. 58+
4. Florida Department of Insurance, December, 1992, ''Improving Individual Health Insurance in Florida''
5. Florida Trend, May, 1991, ''With Surgery Comes Post-Op Pain'', pg. 61+
6. Forbes, April 1, 1991, ''Unintended Consequences'', pg. 39
7. For Brokers Only, July 7, 1990, ''These Are The Best of Times'', pg. 2+
8. Kiplinger's Personal Finance Magazine, October, 1991, ''When Your Health Insurance Makes You Sick'', pg. 64+
9. Life Association News, April, 1990, ''Do Health Insurers Blacklist Some Groups?'', pg. 39
10. Medical Benefits, May 31, 1991, ''The Deteriorating Administrative Efficiency of U.S. Health Care'', pg. 4+
11. National Underwriter, September 3, 1990, ''Health Insurer Tactics Threaten Future'', pg. 54
12. New England Journal of Medicine, June 18, 1992, ''The American Health Care System: Private Insurance'', pg. 1915+
13. Newsweek, February 22, 1993, ''Insurance: The Death Spiral'', pg. 47
14. Palm Beach Post, February 4, 1990, ''Individual Insurance Hard To Get'', pg. 1D+
15. Profiles, 1992, Life and Health Companies, The National Underwriter

16. Reader's Digest, June, 1992, "Is Your Health Insurance Safe?", pg. 90+
17. South Florida Business Journal, August 10, 1992, "State Law to Put Brakes on Health Insurance Cherry-Picking", pg. 19
18. U.S. News & World Report, May 13, 1991, "A Paper Blizzard Costing Billions"
19. Wall Street Journal, September 8, 1992, "Ailing Insurers (Health Care Coverage For Small Firms Springs A Leak)"

CHAPTER FOUR

1. AARP Bulletin, Special Report: "Which Way Reform? AARP Offers Blended Proposal"
2. Best's Review, January, 1993, "The Changing Face of Health Care", pg. 35+
3. Broker World, May, 1990, "Broker Words", pg. 6+
4. Business & Health, December, 1990, "What's Ahead for Retiree Health", pg. 25+
5. Business & Health, Mid-March, 1993, "Small Group Spends Majority of Health Care Dollars", pg. 18
6. Consumer Research, July, 1992, "Denying Health Care To The Elderly", pg. 14+
7. Financial Planning, May, 1990, "Managing Medicaid"
8. For Brokers Only, July 31, 1992, "If You Sell Anything, You Should Read This", pg. 1+
9. Fort Lauderdale Sun-Sentinel, March 25, 1992, "Health Care Focus Lands on Florida", pg. 1A+
10. Fort Lauderdale Sun-Sentinel, Weekly Business, May 18, 1992, "Asset Comparison May Be Telling", pg. 29
11. Fortune, January 13, 1993, "The Tyranny of America's Old", pg. 67+
12. Insight, January, 1990, "Demographic Changes Signal Opportunity", pg. 5
13. Medical Benefits, March 30, 1991, "Long Awaited Capital Payment Plan Unveiled", pg. 7
14. Medical Benefits, April 15, 1991, "Entitlements and the Aging of America", pg. 5
15. Medical Benefits, September 15, 1992, "Retiree Health Care", pg. 1+

16. Medical Benefits, June 30, 1991, "How Elderly Fare In HMOs", pg. 5
17. Miami Herald, June 29, 1992, "HMOs: Is There One In Your Future?", pg. 20+
18. Miami Herald, "Secondary Policy Should Be A Safety Net", Adam Taft column
19. National Center for Policy Analysis, February, 1989, "The Elderly: People the Supply-Side Revolution Forgot"
20. National Center for Policy Analysis, June, 1989, "Health Care After Retirement: Who Will Pay the Cost?"
21. National Center for Policy Analysis, September, 1989, "Taxing the Savings of Elderly Americans"
22. National Center for Policy Analysis, Executive Alert, "Spending on Elderly Entitlements as Percentage of Payroll"
23. National Underwriter, December 24, 1990, "Coming Soon: A New Health Insurance Crisis", pg. 16
24. National Underwriter, March 25, 1991, "Grandparents or Grandchildren", pg. 18
25. National Underwriter, April 4, 1991, "Trickle Down Effects of Medicare Costs", pg. 58
26. National Taxpayers Union Foundation, 1991, "Public Per Capita Health Care Spending on Elderly as a Percentage of Public Per Capita Spending on Non-Elderly"
27. National Taxpayers Union, February, 1993, "Estate Tax Tornado Threatens Millions", pg. 3
28. New York Times, March 16, 1993, "Elderly Care: The Insurer's Role", pg. C-1+
29. Palm Beach Post, June 22, 1990, "Surgery Needed, Not Transplant"
30. Statistical Bulletin, Jan.-March, 1993, "Geographic Profile of the Aged", pg. 2+
31. Time, October 8, 1990, "Suffer the Little Children", pg. 40+
32. USA Today, April 6, 1993, "Health Care Costs Keep Skyrocketing", pg. 11A

CHAPTER FIVE

1. Forbes, December 10, 1990, ''For Budget Cuts, Read Tax Increases'', pg. 31
2. Forbes, October 28, 1991, ''How To Do In Democrats'', pg. 23
3. Forbes, July 20, 1992, ''Free To Choose What?'', pg. 31
4. Forbes, March 15, 1993, ''Why the Deficit is the Wrong Number'', pg. 79+
5. Forbes, April 12, 1993, ''Anti-freeze'', pg. 93
6. Fortune, April 5, 1993, ''Watch Out for those Backdoor State Tax Increases'', pg. 19+
7. Heritage Foundation, The Index of Leading Cultural Indicators, March, 1993
8. Health Insurance Underwriter, October, 1992, ''Informed Discretions ... Enlightened Decisions'', pg. 6
9. Medical Benefits, October 15, 1992, ''RAND Study Said to Dispute Military Managed Care Savings'', pg. 5
10. Medical Economics, March 22, 1993, ''If Medicare Ran Baseball''
11. Money, August, 1992, ''Congress: 2.8 billion per year'', pg. 129+
12. Orlando Sentinel, March 5, 1993, ''Retired General: We Don't Need VA Hospitals Here''
13. USA Today, February 17, 1993, ''It's Federal Spending, Sweetheart!'', pg. 13A
14. USA Today, March 19, 1993, ''Michigan district: No Cash, No School'', pg. 8A

CHAPTER SIX

1. American Health, November, 1991, ''Doctor Fun'', pg. 38+
2. American Hospital Association, National Hospital Panel Survey, ''Trends In Hospital Profits and Occupancy''
3. Business & Health, March, 1990, ''Unbundling Could Cost You A Bundle'', pg. 20+
4. Business & Health, May, 1990, ''Medicare Cost-Shifting: You Ain't Seen Nothing Yet'', pg. 46+
5. Business & Health, April, 1992, ''Hospitals Receive 39% Of Health Care Dollar'', pg. 22
6. Business & Health, January, 1993, ''Seeking the RX for Rising Drug Costs'', pg. 24+

7. Business Week, April 1, 1991, ''Medical Costs Are In Orbit, Right? Well, Maybe'', pg. 18
8. Chicago Sun-Times, March 16, 1990, ''AMA Kicks Out 31 Doctors''
9. Florida Times-Union, First Business, August 26, 1991, ''Bigger, Bitter Pill'', pg. 1+
10. Florida Trend, May, 1991, ''No Margin, No Mission'', pg. 65+
11. Florida Underwriter, September, 1992, ''Whistling In The Dark?'', pg. 4
12. Florida Underwriter, March, 1993, ''Laws, Lawyers and Lawsuits'', pg. 39+
13. Forbes, December 24, 1990, ''A Few Winners, Many Losers'' pg. 164
14. Forbes, May 27, 1991, ''Upgrades'', pg. 125+
15. Forbes, November 11, 1991, ''An Unproductive War Against Drugs'', pg. 41+
16. Forbes, September 24, 1992, ''The Lawsuit Industry'', pg. 30+
17. Fortune, August 26, 1991, ''Trial Lawyers Face A New Charge'', pg. 85+
18. Gainesville Sun, Business Monday, May 28, 1990, ''Hospital Bills Written In Mysterious Code'', pg. 12
19. Health Care Issues Update, Special Edition, January, '93
20. Health Care Price Index, September 15, 1992, Monthly Update
21. Health Care Price Index, February 26, 1993, Monthly Update
22. Health Insurance Underwriter, May, 1990, ''You Should Know...'', pg. 19+
23. Insurance Review, November, 1991, ''A Travesty of Justice'', pg. 53+
24. Medical Benefits, December 15, 1990, ''Hospitals Are Under Pressure To Justify Cost-Shifting'', pg. 6
25. Medcial Business, South Florida Edition, March 17, 1992, ''Attorneys: Cost Shifting A National Disgrace'', pg. 3
26. Medical Economics, December 10, 1990, ''The History of Medicare'', pg. 77+
27. Medical Economics, March 4, 1991, ''Patients Want Doctors Who'll Talk To Them'', pg. 13
28. Medical Economics, May 6, 1991, ''Let's Expose Medicine's Real Price-Gougers'', pg. 21+

29. Medical Economics, June 17, 1991, ''Doctors Make Too Much? No Way?'', pg. 136+
30. Medical Economics, November 18, 1991, ''The Simplest, Best Cure For Our Health Care Crisis'', pg. 135+
31. Medical Economics, February 17, 1992, ''How Four Health Care Gurus Would Change American Medicine'', pg. 64+
32. Medical Economics, August 3, 1992, ''There's No Quick Fix To Our Health Care System'', pg. 29+
33. Medical Economics, December 21, 1992, ''Wanted: 10,000 More Doctors For America's Heartland'', pg. 26
34. Med Tap, 1991, ''Future Potential For Pharmaceuticals''
35. Miami Herald, Tropic Magazine, June 24, 1990, ''The Bill'' pg. 9+
36. Miami Herald, May 13, 1992, ''C-Section Overused, Group Says'', pg. 1A+
37. Money Extra, 1990, ''A Cure Your MD Won't Like'', pg. 54+
38. National Underwriter, April 27, 1992, ''How Much Do Medical Malpractice Fears Contribute?''
39. Orlando Sentinel, Central Florida Business Section, March 23-29, 1992, ''Healing Hospital Profit Margins'', pg. 14+
40. Orlando Sentinel, Central Florida Business, December 21-27, 1992, ''Breakdown Shows Up In Emergency Rooms'', pg. 12+
41. Palm Beach Post, May 11, 1992, ''Hospital Billing Enough To Make Family Feel Sick''
42. South Florida Business Journal, August 27, 1990, ''More Physicians Lack Malpractice Coverage'', pg. 4
43. South Florida Business Journal, December 24, 1990, ''Uncompensated Charity Care At Selected South Florida Hospitals'', pg. 14
44. Standard & Poor's Industry Surveys, August 21, 1992, Health Care, H-21+
45. Studies on the Socio-Economic Environment of Medicare, ''Medical Professional Liability Claims and Premiums, 1985-1988''
46. Time, May 7, 1990, ''A Call For Radical Surgery'', pg. 50
47. Time, September 24, 1992, ''Is Health Care Too Specialized?'', pg. 56
48. USA Today, July 15, 1992, ''Runaway Medical Costs Hit A Wall'', pg. B-1

49. USA Today, March 2, 1993, ''Drugs Save Lives and Ease Suffering'', pg. 13A
50. USA Today, March 8, 1993, ''Lessening Drug Focus Risks Making Problem Worse'', pg. 9A
51. USA Today, March 15, 1993, ''Physicians Keeping the Family Practice Together'', pg. 4D
52. USA Today, March 15, 1993, ''Iowa to Hillary: Rural Hospitals Need Help'', pg. 13A
53. USA Today, March 16, 1993, ''Former Teacher Heeds The Call For A New Career In Medicine''
54. USA Today, March 17, 1993, ''A Shift Towards Family Care'' pg. 9D
55. USA Today, March 17, 1993, ''Retail Sales of Prescription Drugs Climb'', pg 1A
56. USA Today, May 5, 1993, ''Costs Hurt Patients, Doctors Alike'', pg. 15A
57. USA Today, May 26, 1993, ''Need for Doctors on Rise?''
58. USA Today, ''Defensive Medicine Adds $36 Billion to Bill''
59. USA Today, ''Clinton Tells AMA Task Force Is No Place For Special Interests''
60. Wall Street Journal, October 21, 1992, ''Studies Confirm Patients Pay More For Care When Doctors Own Facilities'', pg. B6
61. Wall Street Journal, November 27, 1992, ''Health Care Lobbies Are Mobilizing Their Forces'', pg. A10

CHAPTER SEVEN

1. AARP Bulletin, July-August, 1992, ''Dubious Deliveries'', pg. 2
2. Consumer Reports, July, 1992, ''Wasted Health Care Dollars'', pg. 435+
3. Fort Lauderdale Sun-Sentinel, November 24, 1991, ''Psychiatric Hospital Fraud Claimed'', pg. 3A
4. Leesburg (FL) Daily Commercial, January 10, 1993, ''Fraud Hits Health Care Costs''
5. Maturity News Service, ''The Language of Fraud'', compiled by Peter Vilbig
6. Medical Benefits, August 30, 1990, ''How Fast Will Private Insurers Adopt RBRVS?'', pg. 10

7. Medical Business, South Florida Edition, October 29, 1991, ''Surgeons Gaming Medicare/Medicaid Codes'', pg. 14
8. Miami Herald, December 31, 1987, ''Four Charged In Insurance Fraud Cases'', pg. 3BR
9. Modern Maturity, April-May, 1991, ''The $10 Billion Dollar Blank Check'', pg. 38+
10. U.S. News & World Report, February 24, 1992, Health Care Fraud, pg. 34+
11. West Side Gazette, Fort Lauderdale, February 12, 1991, ''Tips on Preventing Medicare Fraud and Abuse''

CHAPTER EIGHT

1. Broker World, October, 1991, ''Canadian Health Care'', pg. 44+
2. Business & Health, April, 1991, ''News Briefs'', pg. 10
3. Business & Health, November, 1991, ''Does U.S. Health Care Need A Dose of Canadian Medicine?'', pg. 34+
4. Business & Health, May, 1992, ''Is Dutch Health Care A Model For The U.S. Health Care System'', pg. 34+
5. Business & Health, Mid-September, 1992, ''Opinions on Health Care Reform'', pg. 18+
6. Calgary Herald, July 7, 1991, ''Credit May Be A Cure'', pg. C5
7. Canadian Business, February, 1993, ''What A Glorious Future We Never Had'', pg. 14+
8. Canada News, March 22, 1991, ''Less Health Care For Atlantic Canadians'', pg. 13A
9. Canada News, November 1, 1991, ''More Hospital Beds May Be Closed'', pg. 6
10. Canada News, January 15, 1993, ''Saskatchewan Puts Limits on Out of Country Care'', pg. 3
11. Canada News, January 29, 1993, ''Woman Battles With OHIP'' pg. 18
12. Canada News, April 2, 1993, ''Canadian's Tax Load Soared 25% Between 1990 and 1991'', pg. 30
13. Canada News, April 16, 1993, ''Ontario Hospitals Seeking Patients in U.S.''
14. Canada News, April 23, 1993, ''Waiting List Insurance Unveiled'', pg. 1

15. Daytona Beach News Journal, December 3, 1991, ''Insurance Worries Send Canadian Tourists Home''
16. Daytona Beach Sunday News Journal, February 28, 1993, ''Providing Health Care For All: How Other Nations Manage'' pg. 4B+
17. Employee Benefit Research Institute, Washington, D.C., 1990, ''Real Annual Growth in National Health Care Expenditures''
18. Financial Planning, June, 1990, ''Companies Oppose National Health Insurance'', pg. 17
19. Florida League of Hospitals, ''Does It Make Sense For Florida? The Canadian System of Universal Health Insurance''
20. Forbes, December 9, 1991, ''Dead But Fair''
21. Fort Lauderdale Sun Sentinel, July 26, 1990, ''National Health Insurance: Joan Beck column'', pg. 17A
22. Fort Lauderdale Sun Sentinel, October 20, 1991, ''Socialist Democrats Favored In Canadian Vote'', pg. 17A
23. Fort Lauderdale Sun Sentinel, December 8, 1991, ''Canada Examining Health Care System'', pg. 26A
24. Fortune, May 7, 1990, ''A Soviet Tragedy'', pg. 120
25. Fortune, Louis Harris Poll, ''Office Workers Rate Their Jobs: U.S., European Community, Japan''
26. Fulton, Jane, ''Canada's Health Care System: Bordering On The Possible'', Faulkner & Gray, February, 1993
27. General Accounting Office, ''Canadian Health Insurance: Lessons For the United States'', June, 1991
28. Health Underwriter, March, 1991, ''Can Americans Accept Social Medicine?'', pg. 14
29. Heritage Foundation, February 19, 1992, ''Problems In Paradise: Canadians Complain About Their Health Care System''
30. In Health, January/February, 1991, ''Health Assurance'', pg. 39+
31. Investor's Business Daily, October 2, 1991, ''Germany: Medical Care Model?'', pg. 1+
32. MacLeans, March 26, 1990, ''A Radical Proposal To Cure Health Care'', pg. 19
33. MacLeans, January 13, 1992, ''An Economic Warning'', pg. 31
34. MacLeans, January 13, 1992, ''Facing Radical Surgery'', pg. 38+
35. MacLeans, February 24, 1992, ''The Communist Threat in Ontario's NDP'', pg. 11

36. MacLeans, March 9, 1992, ''Time To Kiss Off Universality Myth'', pg. 37
37. MacLeans, April 20, 1992, ''Leftist Straws Blown Away In The Wind'', pg. 13
38. MacLeans, February 15, 1993, ''A Crisis In Medical Care'', pg. 29
39. Medical Benefits, February 15, 1991, ''Canadian Health Care Costs'', pg. 2
40. Medical Benefits, July 15, 1991, ''Health Care Costs: State Profiles, 1991'', pg. 7
41. Medical Benefits, August 15, 1992, ''Canada Takes Cue From U.S. Managed Care'', pg. 5 Sources Page 16.
42. Medical Benefits, November 30, 1992, ''U.S. Health Expenditure Performance'', pg. 7
43. Medical Economics, December 24, 1990, ''If America Were To Adopt Canada's System'', pg. 125+
44. Medical Economics, November 26, 1991, ''Here's How Rationing of Care Really Works'', pg. 79+
45. Medical Economics, January 6, 1992, ''Does Germany Hold The Key To U.S. Health Care Reform'', pg. 148+
46. Medical Economics, February 3, 1992, ''Families Face A Doubled Burden In Health Care Costs'', pg. 192
47. Medical Economics, March 12, 1992, ''Does Canada Really Contain Health Care Costs?'', pg. 11
48. Medical Tribune, January 7, 1993, ''Canada's Health Plan Exhausting Finances''
49. National Center for Policy Analysis, ''The 20 Myths of National Health Care'', 1990
50. National Review, April 16, 1990, ''An Expensive Way To Die'', pg. 30+
51. New York Times, September 16, 1992, ''Socialists Suffer Major Defeat in Swedish Vote'', pg. 1
52. New York Times, March 7, 1993, ''Now Patients Are Paying Amid Canadian Cutbacks'', pg. 1
53. Orlando Sentinel, December 13, 1989, ''Phooey on Free Medicine, 'average Canadian' says'', pg A-16
54. Palm Beach Post, January 19, 1993, ''Angry Canadian Doctors Move To U.S. For Money'', pg. 10A
55. Reader's Digest, September, 1992, ''How Not To Improve Health Care'', pg. 49+

56. Reader's Digest, October, 1992, ''Whatever Happened to Socialism?'', pg. 111+
57. Rising Health Care Costs For America, A Families USA Foundation Report, October, 1990
58. South Florida Business Journal, October 1, 1990, ''Role Of Public Health Insurance Programs'', pg. 13
59. Toronto Star, November 18, 1991, ''200,000 Health Care Workers Protest Budget Cuts In France'', pg. A13
60. Toronto Star, ''Clinics Offer Fast Food of Medicine: Quick Relief''
61. USA Today, March 18, 1993, ''Germany Draws Rein On Costs'' pg. 9A+
62. USA Today, March 18, 1993, ''Weighing Heart Treatment in U.S. Health Care'', pg. 1B
63. USA Today, March 25, 1993, ''Retirees Have Little Left After Communism'', pg. 6A
64. Wall Street Journal, December 11, 1991, ''Don't Look For Better Health Care From National Health Insurance''
65. Washington Inquirer, March 12, 1993, ''And The Dogs Get Better Medical'', pg. 4

CHAPTER NINE

1. AARP Bulletin, April, 1993, ''Coming: Price Controls'', pg. 1+
2. Agenda For American Renewal, President George Bush, 1992
3. Best's Review, April, 1992, ''Stating the Case For Health Care Reform'', pg. 36+
4. Best's Review, November, 1992, ''Fair Coverage For All'', pg. 57+
5. Business & Health, June, 1990, ''Health Insurance in Hawaii: Paradise Lost or Found?'', pg. 52+
6. Business & Health, January, 1992, ''Everyone Pays When Small Businesses Are Left In The Cold'', pg. 42+
7. Business & Health, April, 1992, ''Is Federal Health Plan Worth Imitating?'', pg. 82+
8. Business & Health, Mid-September, 1992, ''Funding Difficulties Predicted For Pay or Play'', pg. 22
9. Business & Health, Mid-March, 1993, ''Doubts Emerging On Managed Competition'', pg. 51
10. Business & Health, Special Report, ''Reforming Health Care''

11. Business Week, March 29, 1993, ''Health Care: Just Address The Bills To Corporate America'', pg. 66+
12. Consumer Reports, September, 1990, ''The Crisis In Health Insurance, Part 2'', pg. 608+
13. Consumer Reports, August, 1992, ''Are HMOs the Answer?'', pg. 519+
14. Conservative Chronicle, February, 1993, ''The Health of America is Threatened'', pg. 12
15. Council for Affordable Health Insurance, April, 1992, Position Paper
16. ECFC Innovations, Summer, 1990, ''High Anxiety'', pg 5+
17. Financial Planning, April, 1993, ''Health Care Reform Plans Create Uncertainty'', pg. 84+
18. Florida Agency for Health Care Administration, ''A Blueprint for Health Security'', December, 1992
19. Florida Trend, February, 1993, ''Market Based Health Care'', pg. 63+
20. Forbes, March 5, 1990, ''Someone Else Will Pay'', pg. 93
21. Forbes, February 3, 1992, ''Health Care For All: Without Government Control'', pg. 35+
22. Forbes, January 4, 1993, ''Designated Bad Guys'', pg. 43+
23. Fort Lauderdale Sun Sentinel, May 28, 1991, ''Health Costs Straining U.S. Competition'', pg. 7B
24. Fortune, May 21, 1990, ''How To Close The Health Care Gap'' pg. 123+
25. Fortune, March 23, 1992, ''Let's Really Cure The Health Care System'', pg. 46+
26. Fortune, May 17, 1993, ''The Coming Health Care Shakeout'' pg. 70+
27. Hawaii, State Health Insurance Program, State Department of Health
28. Health Insurance Underwriter, July/August, 1991, ''Senate Introduces Universal Health Insurance Bill'', pg. 7
29. Health Insurance Underwriter, January, 1993, ''Is The Health Care Rapture Near?'', pg. 6+
30. Heritage Foundation, 1989, ''A National Health System For America''
31. Investor's Business Daily, November 18, 1991, ''Are Health Reforms At Hand?'', pg. 2

32. Life Association News, February 15, 1993, ''Can We Survive Managed Competition?'', pg. 25+
33. Life Association News, March, 1993, ''Health Talk: Medical Savings Accounts'', pg. 30
34. Medical Benefits, November 3, 1991, ''Is It Cheaper To Pay Than It Is To Play?'', pg. 3
35. Medical Benefits, July 30, 1992, ''Rethinking the Delivery of Workers Compensation Benefits'', pg. 8
36. Medical Benefits, August 30, 1992, ''Actuarial Issues In Pay or Play'', pg. 4
37. Medical Economics, February 3, 1992, ''Health Care Reform: What Does Hawaii Have To Teach?'', pg. 158+
38. Medical Economics, December 21, 1992, ''The Health Plan Clinton Will Send To Congress'', pg. 37+
39. Modern Maturity, August-September, 1992, ''Prescription For Change'', pg. 22+
40. National Center for Policy Analysis, ''An Agenda For Solving America's Health Care Crisis?'', June, 1991
41. National Underwriter, April 20, 1992, ''Health Panel Debates Need For National Reform'', pg. 12+
42. National Underwriter, February 15, 1993, ''Anti-Trust Challenge to Managed Competition'', pg. 3+
43. National Underwriter, March 1, 1993, ''What's It All About?'', pg. 50
44. Nation's Business, April, 1992, ''States Take Lead In Health Care Reform'', pg. 18+
45. Nation's Business, May, 1992, ''Employer Health Plans Decline'', pg. 64
46. Nation's Business, February, 1993, ''Benefits Costs Surge Again'', pg. 38+
47. New York Times, February 16, 1993, ''The Xerox Health Care Model'', pg. 1 (Business)
48. Palm Beach Post, April 8, 1991, ''Most Want Change In Health Care But Don't Know How'', pg. 1A+
49. Palm Beach Post, February 6, 1992, ''Pay or Play Health Proposal Really Means Pay and Pay''
50. South Florida Business Journal, December 9, 1991, ''Cost Conscious Employers Turning To Managed Care''

51. Tampa Tribune, September 18, 1991, "Alliance Could Cut Health Care Costs", pg. E-1
52. Time, November 25, 1991, "Condition Critical", pg. 34+
53. Time, May 31, 1993, "What Price Mental Health?", pg. 59+
54. U.S. News & World Report, November 23, 1992, "Clinton's Big Test", pg. 26+
55. USA Today, January 27, 1993, "All Players Have Ideas To Overhaul Health Care", pg. 8A
56. USA Today, May 13, 1993, "Health Team Favors Premium", pg. 1A
57. Wall Street Journal, January 3, 1992, "Play or Pay Health Care Plan Bound to be a Loser", pg. A6
58. World Monitor, April, 1992, "A Cure For Health Costs", pg. 34+

CHAPTER TEN

1. All About Medicare, 1993 Edition, The National Underwriter, Cincinnati, Ohio, March, 1993
2. Business & Health, October, 1991, "Many Roads Lead To Health System Reform", pg. 38+
3. Business & Health, November, 1992, "Cash Incentives", pg. 23
4. Daytona Beach Sunday News Journal, April 11, 1993, "Rationing Health Care", pg. 1B+
5. Florida Underwriter, June, 1991, "Florida View", pg. 12+
6. Florida Underwriter, February, 1992, "Capitol Line", pg. 6+
7. Fort Lauderdale Sun-Sentinel, February 9, 1992, "The Health Care Pulse", pg. 1A+
8. Fort Lauderdale Sun-Sentinel, March 20, 1993, "Oregon Health Plan Gets U.S. Approval"
9. Insurance Review, October, 1992, "Life & Health", pg. 11
10. Journal of American Medical Association, May 15, 1991, "Expanding Medicare: Employer Plans To Achieve Universal Health Care", pg. 2525+
11. Journal of American Society of CLU and ChFC, September, 1991, "Planning Ahead for Incompetency", pg. 38+
12. National Underwriter, April 27, 1992, "HIAA: Outcomes Information is 'Hot Button' for Insurers"
13. National Underwriter, March 1, 1993, "WEDI Aims To Tame Health Care Paper Tiger", pg. 30+

14. National Underwriter, March 8, 1993, ''Altman: Include Workers Compensation in Reform'', pg. 17
15. Newsweek, May 14, 1990, ''Not Enough For All'', pg. 53
16. New York Times, June 9, 1991, ''For Oregon's Health Care System...''
17. Orlando Sentinel, October 8, 1992, ''500,000 to Delay Death...'', pg. 8-17
18. Pulse, January 4, 1993, ''The Value of Life'', American Medical Security
19. Time, January 19, 1993, ''Paging Dr. Clinton'', pg. 24+
20. Wall Street Journal, February 25, 1992, ''Videos Aim To Expand Role Of Patients In Treatment Decisions''
21. Washingtom Post, July 1, 1991, ''Oregon Plan Covers All Needy But Not All Ailments'', pg. 1+
22. Washington Post, January 15, 1993, ''Health Care Organizations Back National Data Base''
23. Wellness Today, September, 1991, ''Treatments That Are More Lethal'', pg. 10+

CHAPTER ELEVEN

1. Chommie, John B., ''The Law of Federal Income Taxation'', West Publishing Co., St. Paul, Minnesota, 1973.
2. Fayetteville, Georgia Citizen, Clinton speech reference, September 29, 1993
3. Financial Services Journal, November, 1991, ''Who Foots The Bill?''
4. Forbes, June 22, 1992, ''Who Says Americans Are Undertaxed?'', pg. 35
5. Forbes, November 23, 1992, ''Medical Budget Fantasies'', pg. 194
6. Marcus, Richard B., editor, ''Alexander Hamilton and the Founding of the Nation'', The Dial Press, New York, 1957
7. Medical Benefits, June 15, 1991, ''How To Pay Your Share Of Health Care'', pg. 4
8. Mitchell, B. ''Alexander Hamilton: The National Adventure 1788-1804'', The MacMillan Company, New York, 1962
9. National Underwriter, October 11, 1993, ''Stark Lambasts the Clinton Health Plan''

10. Newsweek, September 20, 1993, ''The Clinton Solution,'' pg. 30+
11. Orlando Sentinel, October 7, 1993, ''Rash of Questions Unanswered'', David Broder column, pg. A-19
12. Orlando Sentinel, October 7, 1993, ''Enough To Make You Sick'', Cal Thomas column, A-19
13. Taxpayers Association, Inc., Largo, Florida, ''The 1% Commerce Tax''
14. USA Today, September 24, 1993, ''Fit For Rocket Scientists'', pg. 2B
15. USA Today, October 25, 1993, ''Unhealthy Alliance For Business'', pg. 13A
16. USA Today, October 28, 1993, ''A Closer Look At The Security Act'', pg. 10A
17. Wall Street Journal, September 30, 1993, ''Health Plan's Devilish Details''

CHAPTER TWELVE

1. Business & Health, June, 1990, ''Strategies for Managing Prescription Drug Costs'', pg. 41+
2. Business & Health, April, 1992, ''Uncle Sam Tries To Spread the Managed Care Word'', pg. 58+
3. Business & Health, ''The State of Health Care In America'', 1993
4. Business & Health, ''Reforming Health Care: State and Local Action''
5. Forbes, February 18, 1991, ''The Doctors' New Allies'', pg. 85+
6. Forbes, March 18, 1991, ''Let the Loser Pay'', pg. 96+
7. Fort Lauderdale Sun-Sentinel, April 3, 1991, ''Low Medicaid Causes Doctor to Refuse Poor Patients'', pg. 5A
8. Fort Lauderdale Sun-Sentinel, March 31, 1993, ''Doctors Overpaid, Survey Says'', Pg. 1A+
9. Fortune, January 11, 1993, ''Nurses and the Doctor Shortage'', pg. 102
10. Medical Business, South Florida Edition, November 26, 1991, ''Insurance Credit Cards Seen By Year 2000''
11. Medical Economics, July 9, 1990, ''And Next: An FMG Data Bank?'', pg. 16
12. USA Today, March 10, 1993, ''Mining the Task of Health Care Reform'', pg. 11A

13. USA Today, March 15, 1993, ''AMA Exec Balks At Nurse Practitioners Who Play Doctor'', pg. 1D
14. USA Today, March 15, 1993, ''Family doctors: Reform's Missing Link''
15. USA Today, March 23, 1993, ''Beware the Lure of Price Controls on Health Care'', pg. 12A

CHAPTER THIRTEEN

1. AHIA Public Policy Position Statement, ''Regulation of Multiple Employer Welfare Arrangements''
2. Contingencies, July/August, 1992, ''Reforming Small Group Health Coverage'', pg. 30+
3. FALU News Bulletin, ''Beware the Wa-Wa's When Selling MEWAs''
4. For Brokers Only, October 25, 1991, ''Finding the Right TPA'', pg. 1+
5. Fort Lauderdale Sun Sentinel, Weekly Business, April 29, 1991, ''It's A Pain to Buy Your Own Health Insurance'', pg. 29
6. Life Association News, July, 1992, ''AHIA Urges State Regulation of MEWAs'', pg. 21
7. Medical Economics, August 3, 1992, ''Finding Affordable Health Insurance For Your Practice'', pg. 160+
8. National Underwriter, May 13, 1991, ''Smart Agents Act A Lot Like Sherlock Holmes'', pg. 7+
9. Nation's Business, October, 1992, ''How To Buy Health Insurance'', pg. 16+
10. Newsweek, April 23, 1990, ''A Buyer's Guide To Cheaper Rates'', pg. 50+

INDEX